David Lynch's American Dreamscape

David Lynch's American Dreamscape

Music, Literature, Cinema

Mike Miley

BLOOMSBURY ACADEMIC

NEW YORK · LONDON · OXFORD · NEW DELHI · SYDNEY

BLOOMSBURY ACADEMIC
Bloomsbury Publishing Inc
1385 Broadway, New York, NY 10018, USA
50 Bedford Square, London, WC1B 3DP, UK
29 Earlsfort Terrace, Dublin 2, Ireland

BLOOMSBURY, BLOOMSBURY ACADEMIC and the Diana logo are trademarks of
Bloomsbury Publishing Plc

First published in the United States of America 2025

Cover design by Eleanor Rose
Cover image: David Lynch supervising a fire scene while shooting *Straight Story* (1999).
Photograph, 01 October, 1998 © William Campbell / Sygma / Getty Images

Library of Congress Cataloging-in-Publication Data
Names: Miley, Mike, author.
Title: David Lynch's American dreamscape : music, literature, cinema / Mike Miley.
Description: New York : Bloomsbury Academic, 2025. |
Includes bibliographical references and index.
Identifiers: LCCN 2024028742 (print) | LCCN 2024028743 (ebook) |
ISBN 9798765102893 (paperback) | ISBN 9798765102930 (hardback) |
ISBN 9798765102909 (ebook) | ISBN 9798765102916 (pdf)
Subjects: LCSH: Lynch, David, 1946–Criticism and interpretation. |
Motion pictures and literature. | Motion pictures and music. |
United States–In motion pictures. | LCGFT: Film criticism.
Classification: LCC PN1998.3.L96 M55 2025 (print) | LCC PN1998.3.L96
(ebook) | DDC 791.43023/3092–dc23/eng/20240701
LC record available at https://lccn.loc.gov/2024028742
LC ebook record available at https://lccn.loc.gov/2024028743

ISBN: HB: 979-8-7651-0293-0
         PB: 979-8-7651-0289-3
       ePDF: 979-8-7651-0291-6
      eBook: 979-8-7651-0290-9

Typeset by Integra Software Services Pvt. Ltd.
Printed and bound in Great Britain

To find out more about our authors and books visit www.bloomsbury.com
and sign up for our newsletters.

You move me, Amelia.
You mark me the deepest.

CONTENTS

FIGURES

ACKNOWLEDGMENTS

There may be only one person's name on the cover of this book, but it took a lot of people to bring this book into print. I am fortunate to have received more support and assistance than I deserve, and this book would not be what it is without the contributions of the following talented individuals and groups.

Thanks to Katie Gallof Houck, Stephanie Grace-Petinos, and everyone at Bloomsbury Academic for their enthusiastic support from day one.

I owe a great deal to the organizations that allowed me to present earlier stages of this work over the years at their conferences: the Literature-Film Association and the Association of Adaptation Studies (Chapters 1, 3, 6, and Conclusion), the Society for Cinema and Media Studies (Chapter 4), and Music and the Moving Image (Chapters 5, 7, and 8). Versions of Chapters 5 and 7 were also published in the *Music and the Moving Image* journal, and I am grateful to Ronald Sadoff, Gillian Anderson, and Robynn J. Stilwell for their kindness and editorial expertise. A portion of the concluding chapter appeared in *Literature/Film Quarterly*, and my deep thanks go to Elsie Walker and David T. Johnson for taking a chance on a nontraditional approach.

Many institutions have encouraged my work materially and professionally. First among these is Metairie Park Country Day School, who funded my travel and research via the best professional development program there is. Carolyn Chandler, Rob Hereford, Augustine Whyte, and Kate Turnbull helped me find funding to present my research at conferences, the LeCorte-Marsiglia families gave me the time and resources to discover the overall scope and shape of the book through the Faculty Fellows Program, and Howard Hunter pulled every string he could find to give me room to grow and thrive.

Loyola University New Orleans also contributed to the creation of this book. My warm gratitude goes to Hillary Eklund for letting me teach a course on Lynch online during the Covid-19 pandemic. The enthusiasm of the twenty-five students in this class sustained me during that difficult time and helped me to see how vital and full of secrets these films remain. Thanks also to the Interlibrary Loan staff at the Monroe Library for finding books and articles from far and wide.

Thank you to Michael Pepin and Emily Wittenberg at the Louis B. Mayer Library at the American Film Institute. Material from David Lynch's Harold Lloyd Masters Seminar ©2001, courtesy of American Film Institute.

Thank you to Zach Atchley for research assistance on Chapter 7.

Maybe the horror stories about academia aren't true, or maybe I've been lucky to have met the best of the best who offered guidance, feedback, and encouragement along the way: David Bering-Porter, Vincent Bohlinger, Amanda DiPaolo, Liz Greene, Julie Grossman, Randolph Jordan, Amanda Konkle, Danijela Kulezic-Wilson, Alistair Mactaggart, Katherine Reed, Will Scheibel, Jeff Severs, Jessica Shine, Katherine Spring, Leah Toth, and Reba Wissner. I am better and happier because I know all of you. I also want to thank reviewer #2. Wherever and whoever you are, I accept you without revisions.

Several generous people offered crucial feedback on the chapters of this book: Eric Dienstfrey, Pete Kunze, Sheila Liming, Matt "ADNT" Luter, Alex Moran, Jay Shelat, Jon Sternfeld, and Peyton Thomas. Whatever sense this book makes, it's to your credit.

Then there are the wonderful friends and colleagues who showed up and cheered me on. Matt Bucher, Liam Campbell, Becka Curry, Sam Ferguson, Justin Gricus, Robin Heindselman, Dave Laird, Lucas Miller, Brendan Minihan, Betsy Petersen, Jen Sciortino, Rob Short, Pam Skehan, Erin Walker, and Chris Young: You all may not think you did anything, but trust me, it meant everything.

Thank you to my parents for their tireless support and encouragement and for the best high school graduation present ever: taking me to see *Lost Highway* the moment we arrived in New York City in May 1997.

Malcolm, Ezra, and Hawthorne, I am so grateful to you for giving up time with me so that I could write this book. I hope it makes you as proud of me as I am of each of you.

Finally, no support can equal and no words can express the unflagging love and support I've received from Amelia Chen Miley since 1998. Every time I felt down, you would grab my shoulders and tell me the same thing: "Mike Miley, you've been waiting your whole life to talk about David Lynch." I'm lucky to have someone who believes in me as much as you do. I share this, and everything, with you.

CONTENT ADVISORY

Although David Lynch is a popular American filmmaker whose work has aired on broadcast television and received numerous awards and nominations, he is not a filmmaker one should approach with their guard down. His films contain frequent—and frequently graphic—depictions of violence, sexual assault, incest, suicide, self-harm, drug abuse, mental illness, misogyny, and the psychological distress that attends surviving such experiences. While this book does not linger over descriptions of specific scenes of this nature in these films, it does make reference to them and the thematic purposes they serve in his filmography. Readers for whom this material may be disturbing or upsetting are encouraged to engage with the text at whatever level they are most comfortable and to prioritize their own care and well-being as they read.

Introduction

The Harmonics of the Tree

Charting the various influences on an artist is a tricky game, and in many ways a losing one. First, proving convincingly that one artist influenced another requires some kind of authorization or documentation: an admission in an interview, a note in an archive, some kind of direct and unambiguous allusion in the text itself, all of which still might not persuade hardened skeptics. Secondly, this thirst for authentication presents an additional problem for scholars in that it has the critic looking to the artist for confirmation of an interpretation, essentially limiting scholarship to boundaries drawn by the artist themselves.[1] The more open an artist is about their influences, the more critics tend to focus their efforts on investigating those influences, effectively closing off a discussion before it has an opportunity to open.

To make matters more frustrating, even if one succeeds at this difficult task of proving one artist's influence on another, the question of what difference the influence makes persists. Artist A influenced Artist B: so what? Does the influence offer deeper insight into the work, or does it remain merely an interesting observation? As such, discussions of influence can run the gamut from being little more than a parlor game of spot-the-reference to diminishing the work of the influenced artist to something wholly derivative of and subservient to the artist(s) who inspired it. And still the fact remains that artistic influence seldom traces a straight line that neatly and unambiguously links two artists or works directly without detours, blind corners, or unconnected dots. While artists certainly respond to specific groundbreaking works all the time, they also just as often work with themes and materials that permeate in the culture, never consciously tethering their work to another or bothering to name it explicitly.[2]

One artist whose relationship to his various influences has received sustained critical attention is the filmmaker David Lynch. When scholars are not discussing Lynch's films as the product of a wholly original talent, they frequently analyze it in terms of how it has been influenced by filmmakers such as Maya Deren, Alfred Hitchcock, and Billy Wilder, artists such as Francis Bacon and Salvador Dalí, or theorists such as Carl Jung, Jacques Lacan, and Laura Mulvey. As rich and varied as such conversations continue to be, perhaps they are not varied enough. Although plenty of undeniably valuable work has been done treating Lynch either as a sui generis artist with more imitators than predecessors or as an artist deeply engaged in film history, perhaps too much time has been spent following the same grouping of influential artists and theorists in the same art forms. The continued focus on previously explored and accepted approaches has limited our understanding and engagement with his work and, by extension, the work of other filmmakers. Perhaps Lynch's work is in a broader, more dynamic dialogue with other texts than previous studies of his work allow for.

The echoes of other art forms in Lynch's work merit more scrutiny. For example, because Lynch is such a strong visual and sonic stylist, he is not thought of as particularly literary. Books do not often come up in discussions of Lynch, even though Lynch has singled out Franz Kafka as "the one artist that I feel could be my brother."[3] Despite such an intense statement of connection, however, scholars seldom explore the ways that Lynch's work can be connected to literary sources beyond that of a convenient adjective ("Kafkaesque") or a brief comparison (such as Lynch's ripe quip describing *Blue Velvet* as "the Hardy Boys go to Hell").[4] But what if his engagement with literature runs deeper than these shorthand references? Hossein Eidizadeh begins to unpack the relationship between Kafka and Lynch in his 2018 article "When You See Me Again, It Won't Be Me: *The Metamorphosis*, Franz Kafka, and David Lynch's Life-Long Obsession," but other critics have yet to accept his invitation to explore more literary connections to Lynch.[5] What are we missing out on by ignoring the literary connections Lynch's films invite? In what ways are his films responses to literary traditions and concerns? How is his work less the work of a singular filmmaker but more part of an aesthetic continuum that extends beyond cinema?

Even though Lynch has a well-established musical career and is vocal about the music that he likes, most scholarly discussion about the way his films engage with music comes in the form of analyzing the skillful blend of previously recorded music, original scoring, and sound design on his soundtracks. There has not been enough discussion about how his films mimic, embody, or trade on the form, history, and iconography of popular American music. Two articles by Mark Mazullo and Nicholas Rombes have opened this line of inquiry. In "Remembering Pop: David Lynch and the Sound of the '60s," Mazullo argues that each of Lynch's films has "a unique expressive sound signature," with early 1960s pop "occupy[ing] a privileged position" in Lynch's sonic landscape because the recording techniques used, much like Lynch's films, capture the uncanny in a three-minute commercial product.[6] Rombes's article "Blue Velvet Underground: David Lynch's Post-Punk Poetics" compares "the gross disjunction between sincerity and irony" of Lynch's films to that of punk acts such as the Ramones and Blondie and proto-punks such as the Velvet Underground to show how all present "an alternative to the binary sincerity/irony reading paradigm" that Rombes calls "sincerity-in-irony" which punk gestures toward and Lynch's work actualizes.[7] Might Lynch's conception of music reverberate beyond the soundtrack to affect the entire film—the script, the décor, the cinematography, even scenes without any music in them? Eidizadeh's, Mazullo's, and Rombes's work invites more sustained inquiry into Lynch's *oeuvre* than can be contained in a journal article. I am interested in broadening the scope of their work to show how Lynch's films are in dialogue with art forms not often associated with him.

David Lynch's Affiliations

Answering such questions requires a different approach, one that mere influence cannot accommodate. Thankfully, over the last half-century, critics have expanded our understanding of how one artist's work can interact with another's. Julia Kristeva, building upon the work of Mikhail Bakhtin, introduced the concept of intertextuality in her 1966 essay "Word, Dialogue, and Novel." Kristeva argues that rather than possessing a fixed meaning and definitive sources and referents, a text can instead be treated as "*an intersection of textual surfaces*," "a mosaic of quotations" that "absor[bs]" or "transform[s]" another text.[8] Whether they be comprised of words, images, or sounds, texts are composed in languages that have "vast histories of meaning" inscribed into them; therefore, Kristeva asserts that the reader can regard every word in the text as "an intersection of word (texts) where at least one other word (text) can be read."[9] With that sentence, Kristeva opens up an entire world of interpretive possibility that makes discussions such as the ones offered in this book imaginable.

Roland Barthes builds upon Kristeva's definitions by emphasizing the distinction between a "work" with a singular form and finite physical and methodological boundaries and a "text" that is "a methodological field" or "process of demonstration" that is "held in language."[10] A text is "plural" and "irreducible," Barthes claims, a "network" that "answers not to an interpretation, even a liberal one, but to an explosion, a dissemination" of "citations, reference, echoes, [and] cultural languages."[11] Barthes compares this explosive text to a piece of music, except rather than being performed by a maestro on a stage before a silent and passive audience, this is "a score of [a] new kind: it asks of the reader a practical collaboration."[12] This collaboration between the reader and the text produces a "*jouissance*," a "pleasure without separation" as each is engaged in creating the text anew through their interpretation.[13]

If an intertext is, as Michael Riffaterre defines it, "the corpus of texts the reader may legitimately connect with the one before [their] eyes, that is, the texts brought to mind by what [they are] reading," then this corpus will naturally depend upon what texts each reader has encountered in the past.[14] Therefore, as the text and its writer (or, as Barthes and Kristeva would say it, "scriptor") is a collection of citations "constituted by the texts of its culture" that are themselves patchworks of the "*already read*," so too is the reader.[15] Like the writer, the reader can bring these already-read texts to bear on any new text they encounter. A reader with a wider awareness of texts will be able to bring more texts into their interpretation, making the potential interpretations of a text as broad or as narrow as a reader's cultural awareness.[16] In short, the reader makes a text intertextual, and the more texts they are aware of, the more intertextual potential a text they encounter has.

While there is little that is controversial about this conception of intertextuality, there are different types of intertextuality that have been proffered in the years since Julia Kristeva coined the term, so much so that some critics fear intertextuality has become a term with as many meanings as there are scholars using it.[17] So what kind of intertextual approach do I bring to the films of David Lynch? I believe when we look outside the world of literary criticism we can find a succinct and incredibly useful conception of intertextuality. In her book *Hearing Film: Tracking Identifications in Contemporary Hollywood Film Music*, Anahid Kassabian outlines the way that audiences interact with film scores, dividing film scores into two categories: those that offer what she calls "assimilating identifications" and those that foster what she terms "affiliating identifications." Scores encouraging assimilating identifications are generally made up of music composed specifically for the film and as such "try to maintain fairly rigid control" over how audiences receive or identify with this music and the scenes they accompany.[18] Affiliating identifications, on the other hand, frequently feature previously recorded and released music that audiences may have encountered prior to viewing the film, making their identification with the music and, by extension, the film in question, more variable because these identifications "depend on histories forged outside the film scene."[19] These histories can involve the viewer's knowledge about the performer and their career, their personal experiences with the song, or their awareness of the song's use in another text—it all, as Riffaterre puts it, "depends upon the [audience's] culture."[20] Where a score relying on assimilating identifications strives to "try to narrow the psychic field" of the audience and direct their interpretation, affiliating identifications use the familiar to "place [viewers] on their unconscious terrains," thus widely expanding that psychic field and granting the viewer more agency in how they interpret the film.[21]

Although Kassabian does not mention intertextuality in *Hearing Film*, her concept of affiliating identifications offers a clear understanding of how intertextuality works and what makes it distinct from influence. An audience member can interpret a needle drop in a film based on their familiarity with another film that uses the same needle drop. Even if the filmmaker is not directly referencing (or even aware of) the previous needle drop, the viewer's reading could be quite useful and transformative in understanding the film because these works coexist in the culture and are connected and made significant by the viewer. In Kassabian, we find an intertextual approach that connects Riffaterre's arguments about the role an audience's cultural literacy plays in one's engagement with a text to Kristeva's and Barthes's conception of a text as a networked mosaic of quotations from already-read texts composed by already-read scriptors. The assimilating identification operates more like Barthes's definition of a work, whereas an affiliating identification treats the song as a text with its own history that interacts with another text (the film in question) in a new context. These affiliations open a range of interpretive possibilities that will not apply to every viewer; however, those who can make such affiliations will arrive at a different and perhaps richer experience of both works as a result. When we expand these interpretive horizons in this manner, we can see in Lynch's work less the expression of a singular genius or work wholly immersed in one art form but rather a whole landscape of popular literary and musical cultures, one as in dialogue with culture as culture has been in dialogue with it.[22]

What I have just described are the notions of intertextuality that inform and guide the analysis undertaken in this book, and what follows in each chapter are different literary and musical affiliating identifications one can make with the films of David Lynch. Kassabian and other theorists will appear later in the book when necessary, but this discussion of intertextuality should provide readers with a sufficient understanding of how this book approaches Lynch's films. I do not wish to push any particular theoretical reading too forcefully because such work about Lynch has already been done many times before. Despite all the exciting work that heavily theoretical approaches to Lynch accomplishes (e.g., Lacanian psychoanalysis), there is something overdetermined about it, a fit that at times feels as constricting as it is illuminating. An intertextual approach loosens these theoretical constraints enough to permit the interaction between the reader and the text to guide the way these texts are read. Further, by exploring the myriad American literary and musical traditions Lynch's films participate in, we can begin to map the terrain of David Lynch's American Dreamscape to arrive at a fuller picture of his vision of the postwar United States: its reality, its fantasy, its destiny.

A Good Tree

It might seem odd to advocate for an intertextual approach in a single-author study. After all, the death of the author is a key feature of intertextuality because, as Barthes writes, the dialogism of intertextuality "destroy[s] man's epic and tragic unity as well as his belief in identity and causality," making "one who writes the same as the one who reads" because they are "no more than a text rereading itself as it rewrites itself."[23] Further, Barthes argues that "this 'I' which approaches the text is already itself a plurality of other texts"; therefore, to search for "the 'sources,' the 'influences' of a work, is to fall in with the myth of filiation."[24] An intertextual single-author study would appear to reconstruct the monument to the "epic or tragic unity" that is filiation. If intertextuality liberates criticism from fidelity to the author as creator and disseminator of meaning, why focus on one author?

Because David Lynch is a filmmaker who is best understood intertextually.

While Lynch certainly participates in and benefits from the legacy of auteurism, his relationship with authorship remains ambivalent and serves as an illuminating case study for how authorship functions in a postmodern media ecosystem. In her article "'It's No Longer Your Film': Fictions of Authorship in Lynch's *Mulholland Drive*," Elizabeth Alsop demonstrates how Lynch's 2001 film critiques both the image of the director as the author in control of a film and the insistence that the director is not the central figure in a film's making. Director figures litter *Mulholland Drive*'s landscape—the black-clad prima donna Adam Kesher, the "bumbling hack" Bob Brooker, or the omnipotent puppet masters such as Mr. Roque, Club Silencio's emcee, and the Cowboy—yet all fundamentally mock the notion of the controlling director by either lacking competence (Bob) or possessing so much power that their influence strains credulity (Mr. Roque).[25] However, Lynch's self-aware play with film noir and melodrama—the formulaic stuff classic auteurs were made of—creates a tension that makes it impossible to write off auteurism completely.[26] *Mulholland Drive* dramatizes this tension and demonstrates how "the process of meaning-making is far more complicated than traditional *auteur* theory would have us believe" without omitting the director from the process entirely, as some would have us do.[27] To resolve this tension, Alsop argues for a new image of the director as an "oneiric" figure, an "involuntary dreamer" who "generates the raw material for a film" but also edits it, acting as both "the purveyor of 'raw' content and the filtering apparatus."[28] Under this model, the director does not so much create out of nothing but rather functions as a "conduit" or channel that ideas from outside enter and are then shaped by before passing out as the finished work.[29]

I would like to extend Alsop's conception of the oneiric *auteur* to argue that such a figure is inherently intertextual and their work invites an intertextual approach. Lynch serves as an ideal subject for this model because his films, for all their originality and daring, are also comprised of what Barthes calls "tissue[s] of quotations drawn from the unnumerable centres of culture" that feature what Kristeva describes as central facets of intertextual discourse: "abrupt transitions and changes; high and low, rise and fall, and misalliances of all kinds. [...] put together as a pavement of citations."[30] Such qualities hardly support treating Lynch as a single-authorial consciousness operating in an aesthetic vacuum, especially when viewed alongside Lynch's numerous references to and quotations from films such as *The Wizard of Oz*, *Sunset Blvd.*, and *Vertigo*.[31] When asked in 2001 whether aspects of *Mulholland Drive* were influenced by *The Wizard of Oz*, Lynch answered, "There's not a day that goes by that I don't think about *The Wizard of Oz*."[32] This response may not be a direct answer to the question, but that is because it goes somewhere over the affirmative. Pinpointing every exact point where an influence this pervasive appears would be impossible but undeniable; *Oz* is simply something in the air for Lynch, a signal he is tuned into. Even though one can find enough *Oz* references and echoes to fill a feature-length video essay, it is not the only text that occupies this kind of space in Lynch's work. In fact, the way that he uses *Oz*, *Sunset Blvd.*, and *Vertigo* illustrates his approach to any intertext: rather than making mere direct allusions to particular aspects of a work, he "us[es] the cultural real estate [the work] occupies in our public consciousness," giving the audience ample space to roam their "unconscious terrains" as they experience his film.[33] Lynch's intertextual approach to cinema shows the degree to which all filmmakers working in the oneiric auteurist mold are conduits for a larger "tissue of quotations" that they tap into and trade upon as much as they do some autonomous "personal vision."

Further, Lynch himself seems to invite such an approach in his quasi-Barthesian view of ideas and their origins. To Lynch, "Ideas are the strangest things, because they suddenly enter into your conscious mind and you don't know really where they came from—where they existed before they were introduced to you. They could mean something, or they could just be there for you to work with. I don't know."[34] Lynch's stance, while clearly influenced by his practice of Transcendental Meditation and a more general, mystical view of the artistic process, also presents ideas themselves as Barthesian texts, open-ended patchworks of the already read that one appropriates and combines. "I think people are like radios," he told an interviewer in 2019. "They pick up signals."[35] This notion of the radio perfectly captures Alsop's conception of the oneiric *auteur*: these texts, these ideas, are "in the air." People receive them, and some process those signals and then broadcast their own to be received anew by others. How much of that signal comes from a previous transmission cannot always be easily quantified, but a sense remains that without those other signals, this new one would not exist.

Lynch also remains unusually open to the diverse interpretations that have been applied to his work, denying that he possesses any unique or special insight or that one approach is more valid than another. In interview after interview, Lynch frequently dissuades his audience from viewing him as the central consciousness of his work, the locus of its meaning, "the final signified" that "close[s] the writing."[36] Instead, Lynch places his "faith in the audience's own eyes and ears" and chooses to "speak directly" to them cinematically, leaving them to make of the film what they choose.[37] At times, of course, these responses can be playfully cagey, as though Lynch delights in "offering remarks that are intentionally obfuscatory, rather than revealing, of directorial intent."[38] Ironically (or perhaps purposefully), such deferments have only solidified his *auteur* status. Although it may be tempting to view such behavior as part of a cynical strategy to bolster his brand, much more can be gained from treating him and his work as a discursive channel through which postwar American culture courses.

Lynch offers a marvelous metaphor of the symbiotic relationship between creative and critical processes in his response to a screenwriting fellow in a 2001 Harold Lloyd Masters Seminar at the American Film Institute. The fellow asked Lynch about his awareness of theory and the varied theoretical interpretations that have been applied to *Blue Velvet* by various fields in the academy. Lynch responded by saying:

> I'm not aware of theory, and I'll tell you how I'm aware of theory if I'm aware of theory at all. It's staying true to the ideas, and if you are in love with the ideas and stay true to them … it's weird. Say the idea is like a seed, and so you really know the seed and it's talking to you, and you don't really know about the oak tree. You just know about the acorn sort of. But it's growing out. And if you're really true to it, you'll get this, you know, tree. And then the tree … many people study trees from, you know, various angles and they paint them and they study the bugs that go on them, and stuff like this. But you've done a good tree. And it may have harmonics that you don't even understand. I know that people see these things from different angles and write many things. But I think it all kind of holds together if you're true to the idea.[39]

In advocating for his own absence and his appreciation for the "harmonics" others detect in his work, Lynch presents himself as a conduit for a culture that "already knows [its] narratives are *already* deconstructed."[40] Like Riffaterre and Kassabian, Lynch's cinema is an open one allowing for a media-saturated culture to arrive at the work with their own experiences and affiliations in order to participate in the construction of the text. As such, Lynch's intertextual cinema becomes yet another discursive site through which these texts (or texts that interact with those texts) can interact with other texts, a medium or a channel through which the subconscious of American life finds its way into full view. In this respect Lynch is less an ironic postmodern gamesman and more akin to Rombes's claim that Lynch is "exploring [American myths] in a cinematic language that has a history."[41] In mapping out these identifications, the goal of *David Lynch's American Dreamscape* is to create space for a richer and more interpretively open discussion by sharing potential identifications, not to arrive at any definitive interpretation but rather just another among many that hopefully generates even more.

Such an approach may raise questions about boundaries. As Jay Clayton and Eric Rothstein ask, when one takes an intertextual approach, "where does one draw the line between relevant and irrelevant references?"[42] This is certainly a fair question. After all, if we do not know whether David Lynch has read McCarthy's *The Crossing* or West's *The Dream Life of Balso Snell* or has listened closely to "Tell Laura I Love Her," why spend time discussing how these works interact with his films? Locating a copy of a book on his nightstand in a photo from 1996 or finding a Shangri-Las CD in his car might have an authority that would make one more comfortable with endorsing the kind of readings offered in this book, but such evidence is not the kind of proof I seek, the kind that is definitive, reductive, or "correct." Such confirmation can certainly act as an insurance policy or receipt, but it also presents a different problem in that it puts the interpretive emphasis back on the author rather than the works and the role that they play in the culture, as both cultural products and products of that culture. More importantly, it makes the reader's agency secondary. The way the work interacts with other work through the eyes and cultural experience of other viewers is the interest here, one in which the roads don't lead back to Lynch in some kind of closed loop but rather radiate outward in an ever-expanding web that expands further with each reader. While a less bounded intertextual analysis does run the risk of creating a *mise-en-abyme* of textual associations and interpretations, the benefits of such an approach are far greater because they create space for more of the readerly pleasures Barthes speaks of in "From Work to Text," the kind in which the interpretive play never ends.

Chapter Summaries

David Lynch's American Dreamscape is divided into two parts, "Words" and "Music." Each chapter will explore a different film of Lynch's, moving more or less chronologically within each section. (I have omitted *The Elephant Man* and *Dune* from this analysis because both films have distinct textual or historical references, and, more importantly, neither film is set in America.) "Words" will focus on how Lynch's films resonate with and participate in several strong literary traditions overlooked in his work due to a focus on him as a visual and sonic stylist. Chapter 1 compares *Eraserhead* with works of hysterical literature such as Charlotte Perkins Gilman's "The Yellow Wallpaper" and Sylvia Plath's *The Bell Jar* to show how Lynch's male protagonist defamiliarizes narrative tropes of domesticity and psychosis. Although it is not a literary work, *Eraserhead* functions as a hysterical text, and its apparently singular impact and resonance benefit heavily from the viewer's affiliating identifications with this literary tradition. Viewing *Eraserhead* as a hysterical text in dialogue with Gilman and Plath reveals these works to be battles for identity and autonomy waged in space and through language. These pursuits, while irrational and mad on the surface, transcend the oppressive binaries of the patriarchal order and access a plane of existence beyond rationality, one defined by multiplicity and possibility. Reading *Eraserhead* as part of this discourse opens new ways of understanding its singular artistic successes as well as its singular aesthetic and political shortcomings. By applying the characteristics of hysterical literature toward a protagonist who embodies and benefits from the very order hysterical literature typically opposes, *Eraserhead* reveals a reactionary core that works against its potent political critique and establishes a template regarding gender politics that lingers through Lynch's 1980s work. However, this chapter also examines how Lynch's spiritual remake of *Eraserhead*, the 1992 *Twin Peaks* prequel *Fire Walk with Me*, performs important recuperative work, realigning Lynch's treatment of hysterical literature more closely with its literary antecedents and sparking a new phase in his career as a filmmaker.

Chapter 2 turns its attention to *Blue Velvet* and its kinship with children's literature. While one would never mistake David Lynch as a creator of work suitable for children, several of his films follow a template similar to that offered in children's literature in that they track a youthful protagonist's traumatic journey from innocence to experience. Tracking the affiliating identifications between *Blue Velvet* and children's literature such as *Where the Wild Things Are* illuminates how each uses fantasy to similar, equally troubling ends. Sendak and Lynch appear to align with the literary and social conventions of children's literature only to call these binaries into question and demonstrate the ways in which these binaries are themselves fantasy creations of the society that uses them to impose its imagined sense of order. *Where the Wild Things Are* and *Blue Velvet* remain wild texts in the sense that they utilize the tools of social instruction—children's literature—to subvert the very structures these tools intend to erect, arguing that wildness cannot in the end be tamed.

Reviewers and critics alike frequently mention Nathanael West's 1939 novel *Day of the Locust* in discussions of Lynch's 2001 film *Mulholland Drive*; however, almost none explores the similarities between these two authors, instead referring to West's novel as a kind of shorthand descriptor for any work offering a dark take on Hollywood. But West's work resonates with Lynch's film beyond tonal similarity and geographical overlap. Chapter 3 shows that, when discussed in relation to the rest of West's work, *Mulholland Drive* presents the most complex and thorough rendering of West's fictional project in cinema. Further, West's fiction—the Dadaist *The Dream Life of Balso Snell*, the expressionistic satires *Miss Lonelyhearts* and *A Cool Million*, as well as the Hollywood novel *Day of the Locust*—grants viewers a more useful mapping of *Mulholland Drive*'s uncertain terrain that straddles the border between utopia and apocalypse in the city of dreams. Rather than peel back the sunny veneer to reveal the darkness lurking underneath the infinity pools (as Lynch does in the opening sequence to *Blue Velvet*), these works show how both the fantasy and the reality pursue the same cataclysmic end: annihilation and oblivion.

Episode eight of *Twin Peaks* (2017) is already on its way to becoming one of the most-discussed hours of television, and Chapter 4 explores how Lynch's representation of the atomic bomb in *Twin Peaks* (2017) resonates with Cormac McCarthy's abstracted representation of the same event in his 1994 novel *The Crossing*. Read together, these two works and their treatment of the relationship among atomic bomb, broadcast media, and violence reveal each conceives of the Bomb and the fallout from its creation as one of Timothy Morton's hyperobjects, an entity so immense and widespread as to elude not only time and space but understanding. Lynch's depiction of the Bomb and the abundance of media on display and in use throughout *Twin Peaks* (2017) extends McCarthy's ideas to suggest the Bomb finds its ultimate potency in media, both through the content media disseminates and the apparatuses that transmit them. Media becomes a viscous hyperobject through which the Bomb (and the creative energies and destructive evils that attend it) penetrates and permeates the world. McCarthy and Lynch argue that consuming media ushers us into the nuclear age and exposes us to its horrors, which we absorb unconsciously and which manifest as intimate personal trauma.

Part Two, "Music," argues that examinations of Lynch's use of music must go beyond the traditional understandings of a Lynchian soundtrack by investigating how musical forms and themes inform not only his soundtrack, but his visual and narrative filmmaking practices. In films like *Blue Velvet*, *Lost Highway*, and *Mulholland Drive*, Lynch uses popular rock material to expose what Mazullo calls "the darker psychosocial functions of mid-century American popular music culture" in a manner that does not confirm its traditional status but rather serves to alienate the viewer from what has become familiar and comfortable.[43] This method, according to Louise O'Riordan, "constructs new meaning around the music [...] that creates a foundation for the added value that the continued use of the song will build on throughout the film."[44] As a result of Lynch's subversive style, the meaning of these songs becomes "conflicted": not only can the song "never be heard the same again," but the song will "consistently undermine any pure or 'clean' readings of sentimentality that could be constructed around the piece again" through its reuse.[45] It is in this way that a pop song in a Lynch film becomes what O'Riordan calls "performative."[46]

This part challenges and broadens this conception by asking the reader to view each Lynch film as a performative text that is shaped by musical affiliating identifications. Chapter 5 shows that, contrary to the predominant attitudes toward *Wild at Heart*, Lynch's 1990 film is not a nostalgic pastiche of rock iconography, nor is it a cynical barrage of postmodern superficiality; rather, the film self-consciously deconstructs rock aesthetics and tropes to test the limits of music (and, by extension, art) as a means of warding off the chaos of the world. Formal analysis of music's function in the film and an explication of the mythic power of rock in America show how rock 'n' roll in Lynch's film is more than a stylistic reference point for a pop-nostalgic lovers-on-the-run romance: it is the subject and essence of the film itself. The form and content of rock (and its ancestors blues and country) suffuse the content of the film as Lynch, through music, searches for an affirmative answer to the most vital question a work of art could ask: Can the power of art contain and defeat the darkness of existence in a world that is "wild at heart and weird on top"?

In addition to its participation in the often-explored cinematic and televisual genres such as film noir, soap operas, and police procedurals, *Twin Peaks* also participates in the musical genre known as the "teenage tragedy song." Chapter 6 looks at how all three iterations of *Twin Peaks* act as extended teenage tragedy songs, ballads of loss and lament that mourn the horrific loss of not only a love interest, but also the ideals of beauty and excellence that she has been made to embody. As a teenage tragedy song, the *Twin Peaks* universe offers a panoramic view of Lynch's vision of America: a seemingly innocent lover mourning the tragic loss of their ideal beloved and the innocence that attended that love.

Chapter 7 discusses how closer attention to how cover songs are used in *Lost Highway* reveals a more intricate strategy in the film beyond a kitchen-sink assemblage of mid-1990s alternative acts attempting to open additional revenue streams for Lynch's uncommercial twenty-first-century noir nightmare. Indeed, scholarship regarding cover songs echoes and extends scholarship on postmodern identity in *Lost Highway* and on the compilation soundtrack itself. Each cover song appears at a crucial moment in the film's narrative, and each exemplifies what Michael Rings calls a "generic reset," a transformative recording that shifts genre and style to create a new song complete with the ability to alter the meaning of the song and, in the case of *Lost Highway*, the film as well.[47] *Lost Highway*'s covers ensnare the audience in a sonic *déjà vu* in which the comfort of recognition collapses into disorientation, not pleasure. By subverting audience identification with the soundtrack, *Lost Highway* broadens noir conventions musically and opens new lanes to understanding the compilation soundtrack as a vehicle for subverting and resisting control and pleasure, *chansons fatales* whose identities are as fluid and beyond the audience's control as the femme fatale is from the male noir protagonist.

In one way or another, all of Lynch's films are explorations of trauma, but none plumbs the depths of trauma as poignantly and thoroughly as *The Straight Story*. Lynch's G-rated Disney pastoral may not look traumatic on the surface, but nor does the musical art form that it most resembles: American roots music. Chapter 8 looks at *The Straight Story* as a cinematic report from the world of Harry Smith's *Anthology of American Folk Music* and Bob Dylan's *The Basement Tapes*, both of which address trauma in ways so unassuming as to be completely disarming: it is nothing less than the central fact of life. In sharing their trauma with an audience, Alvin's, Smith's, and Dylan's folk singers open space and time for others in the audience to reveal their trauma to others and to themselves. Each confession demonstrates the dual nature of their trauma and Alvin's: it is both the thing fueling their stubborn refusal to move on and the engine for transcending their past. In this way, the folk revival catalyzed by Smith's *Anthology* and Alvin's tractor perform the same function: both cling to anachronistic methods to sow tales of redemption and liberation that heal the old wounds preventing them from engaging fully in the present. These old forms are less about nostalgia for the past as they are a way of confronting it, of making sense of it, so that they can see the stars again and locate their place within the cosmos.

Assembled from a handful of previously produced projects for DavidLynch.com (e.g., *Rabbits*) and new material produced without a larger project in mind, *Inland Empire* seems the ultimate compilation film for a new era of digital filmmaking. Although one cannot deny *Inland Empire*'s status as a digital film, Lynch's digital turn differs from most filmmakers in that his use of digital technology, both in the film's look and its production style, enlists affiliating identifications with a distinctly analog practice: mixtape creation. Lynch's affiliating identifications with the aesthetics and ethos of mixtapes not only imbue *Inland Empire* with a warmth and a presence many early digital films lack, but these affiliating identifications also enhance, clarify, and shape the film's scattered narrative to deliver Lynch's most intimate and personal testament on art's ability to establish an ethical way of being in an increasingly chaotic, fragmented, and digital century.

Finally, if this book is going to look at how Lynch's films interact with literature and music, it seems only fitting to explore how other literary and musical texts interact with his films in the same manner. While there is certainly no shortage of writers and musicians whose work has been influenced by Lynch either through direct collaboration or allusion, there are some for whom "influence" is too light a term for the degree to which they absorb Lynch's work into theirs. *David Lynch's American Dreamscape* concludes by examining how David Foster Wallace and Lana Del Rey have grafted Lynch's cinematic sensibility onto their own artistic projects. Each of them produces work that is autonomous while simultaneously participating in and engaging with Lynch's work on a dialogic, genetic level that runs deeper than mere inspiration toward something that more closely resembles liberation. Engaging with Lynch's work is not derivative but *generative* for them: it transforms their careers and proves critical to the development of their signature aesthetic. Such a reading *broadens* the scope of their artistry and Lynch's because it allows one to appreciate the fluidity in their work both in form and content with greater depth than a more limited focus on their textual or musical influences would allow. Further, acknowledging and investigating the depth of the impact a filmmaker has on creators on other media illuminates the extent to which contemporary artists attend to and are influenced by modern image culture.

Intertextual Weather

In the daily weather reports that he resumed posting to his YouTube channel after the onset of the Covid-19 pandemic, Lynch has taken to telling subscribers what song he is thinking of that day.[48] Some of these songs are familiar and expected because Lynch has either used them explicitly in his films (e.g., Gene Vincent's "Be-Bop-a-Lula") or has used other songs in the same style (e.g., the music of 1960s girl groups). In addition to serving as amusing recommendations in a rather adorable daily ritual, these songs also invite an intertextual reading of Lynch's work. By introducing the song with "today I'm thinking about" rather than "today I am listening to," Lynch demonstrates how songs (and, by extension, other texts such as books or films) operate in our lives. They are not simply things we read or listen to but rather things that we *think about*, even when we are not reading or listening to them. The products of that thinking can take many forms or none at all: thinking about a song can lead to a poem, even if the two bear little obvious resemblance to each other. Such is simply the way that we live in a mediated world. We are radios surrounded by signals. We cannot help but pick them up and find them incorporated into our own output. Lynch does not articulate how the things he is thinking about make their way into his work because, as he says "if things get too specific, the dream stops."[49] This book is not an attempt to stop that dream; rather, to borrow a phrase of Lynch's, it is my hope that the intertextual approaches to his films taken up in *David Lynch's American Dreamscape* give readers more "room to dream" within and around the films.

Each piece of media does not exist in a cultural vacuum: they coexist alongside other texts in other media. Not looking at how other media might impact or inform an understanding of a particular film—not asking ourselves what we are thinking about as we encounter a work—can serve as a great loss to us as receivers and appreciators of culture. It closes off the ways works talk to each other, but it also closes off how we talk to each other, how we talk to ourselves. An intertextual approach that crosses media boundaries can inject a much-needed vitality and sense of play into the act of interpreting a text and sharing that interpretation with others. As potentially tenuous or indeterminate as this play may sound, this play need not be frivolous or wasteful—rather, it illuminates the varied and dynamic ways cultural objects interact through their creators and their viewers. The work is always talking to other work, sometimes with an intermediary, the reader, who introduces them to each other and tells them that they have a lot in common.

PART ONE

"Read? Read What?": Words

1

"Out In" the Liminal Interiors of Gilman, Plath, and Lynch

Even after repeated viewings and copious amounts of secondary reading, David Lynch's debut feature *Eraserhead* perpetually eludes ironclad interpretations. Further, Lynch's unwillingness to elaborate on the themes and ideas of this film—perhaps most succinctly captured in the exchange below with Jason Barlow at Lynch's BAFTA David Lean Lecture—offers the viewer little assistance in getting their bearings within this film.

> Lynch: "Believe it or not, *Eraserhead* is my most spiritual film."
> Barlow: "Elaborate on that."
> Lynch: "No, I won't."[1]

Truly, there are as many approaches to *Eraserhead* as there are critics to approach it; however, most affirm one sentiment: the absolute singularity of the work. *Eraserhead* is "the work of an American visionary"[2] that "open[s] a vast new dimension"[3] and "remold[s] the cinematic conventions"[4] with a "nightmare clarity"[5] that "define[s] a direction of film in our times"[6] and "perfectly expresses both the sources and consequences of our humanity."[7] Critics do take care to note some of Lynch's antecedents—Méliès, the German Expressionists, Buñuel, Cocteau, and Deren—but often do so to note how much Lynch's first film transcends their influence to be "completely immersed in [its] own hermetic world"[8] in way that both liberates its maker from that influence and catapults him to "the first echelon of avant-garde filmmakers"[9] whose indisputably "*sui generis* masterpiece"[10] can only be admired or (badly) imitated. However, insisting on *Eraserhead*'s singularity across the arts overlooks a major literary tradition that it is a key, if unrecognized, entry in: hysterical literature.

Hysterical literature is a late Victorian/early Modernist literary tradition depicting the fraying mental states of women diagnosed as "hysterical" by their "rational" patriarchal authorities. In works such as Charlotte Perkins Gilman's story The Yellow Paper, Susan Glaspell's 1916 play *Trifles*, or Mary Jane Ward's 1946 novel *The Snake Pit*, women who are dissatisfied with the confines of domesticity or who display any kind of creative or individualist impulse are treated as deviant and subjected to further oppressive male control. This tightened patriarchal grip causes them to advocate for themselves more fervently, leading to them being pronounced hysterical and confined to a carceral space where their assertions of sanity and autonomy are taken as further proof of their absolute, incurable madness. While the late nineteenth and early twentieth centuries represent the peak of this literary tradition, its influence has persisted in literary works such as Sylvia Plath's early 1960s poems and 1963 novel *The Bell Jar* and other media such as Susanna Kaysen's 1993 memoir *Girl, Interrupted* and Olivia Wilde's 2022 film *Don't Worry Darling*. These more recent works showcase how this tradition remains a useful template for the effects of patriarchal authority on the women who continue to live under its domineering thumb.

According to Elaine Showalter, the so-called hysteric's inability to narrate her experience in a manner deemed sensible was not a symptom of hysteria for these male physicians but rather was hysteria itself. This predicament demonstrates how the diagnosis of hysteria renders the woman's situation more of a narrative condition than a medical one because it operates as a counternarrative to women's personal stories that men wished to dismiss.[11] Similarly, Paula A. Treichler reads "The Yellow Wallpaper" as fundamentally "a confrontation with language" in which the illegible, shape-shifting wallpaper acts as a "metaphor for women's discourse" that reveals the patterns of women's thought and expression that patriarchy "ignores, suppresses, fears as grotesque, or fails to perceive at all."[12] Literary symbols and devices in works of hysterical literature such as the titular wallpaper and bell jars make visible the "slight hysterical tendenc[ies]" that are papered over elsewhere, illustrating how, as Diane Price Herndl writes, hysteria represents a response to "a system in which [a woman's] subjectivity is continually denied, kept invisible."[13] The works often experiment with fragmentation in their form to dramatize the woman's deteriorating mental state; however, these formal breakdowns also can signal the arrival of a new kind of liberated consciousness that suggests these protagonists are not hysterical at all but rather possess a perception which extends beyond the patriarchal conception of rational reality. An approach to the world and one's place within it that welcomes ambiguities and resists resolution releases the confined subject from the oppressive physical, spatial, and linguistic binaries that impose the diagnosis of hysteria on them.

Although it is not a literary work containing direct allusions to this literary tradition, *Eraserhead* functions as a hysterical text, and its apparently singular impact and resonance benefit heavily from the viewer's affiliating identifications with this literary tradition. Viewing *Eraserhead* as a hysterical text in dialogue with hysterical literature such as "The Yellow Wallpaper" and the work of Sylvia Plath reveals these works to be battles for identity and autonomy waged in space and through language. The spaces these protagonists are forced to occupy reveal "the invisible forces that create a hostile social reality" that are normally obscured by the boundaries of the social order.[14] In these works, the "new" and "visionary" discourse of the so-called hysteric squares off against the dominant discourse of the patriarchal order in not only physical space, but also emotional, psychological, and artistic space, as the protagonists pursue a space separate from these "hostile social realit[ies]" that will acknowledge their autonomy over their bodies, minds, and art. These pursuits, while irrational and mad on the surface, transcend the oppressive binaries of the patriarchal order and access a plane of existence beyond rationality, one defined by multiplicity and possibility.

Because the experimental and avant-garde style of these works often conflicts with the expectations and discourse of traditional narrative storytelling, these works, like their protagonists, are often viewed—at least initially—as incoherent and in need of "explaining"; however, the scholarship on hysterical literature shows how this demand for rational explanation functions as an oppressive construct of its own, one that these works openly defy. Reading *Eraserhead* as part of this discourse opens new ways of understanding its singular artistic successes as well as its singular aesthetic and political shortcomings. By applying the characteristics of hysterical literature toward a protagonist who embodies and benefits from the very order hysterical literature typically opposes, *Eraserhead* reveals a reactionary core that works against its potent political critique and establishes a template regarding gender politics that lingers through Lynch's 1980s work. However, Lynch's spiritual remake of *Eraserhead*, the 1992 *Twin Peaks* prequel *Fire Walk with Me*, performs important recuperative work, realigning Lynch's treatment of hysterical literature more closely with its literary antecedents and sparking a new phase in his career as a filmmaker.

Although this analysis may appear to place works other than *Eraserhead* at the forefront of the conversation, such a move is necessary in understanding *Eraserhead*'s place in a tradition larger than Lynch's filmography. There are indeed many things which make *Eraserhead* a singular, visionary work; however, this long-standing practice of placing Lynch's debut feature in a class by itself has run its course. It may appear counterintuitive, but *Eraserhead* can accrue greater meaning when it is not at the center of a discussion but is instead put in dialogue with the work that it relies on and responds to.

The "Sour Air" of Domestic Space

Notions of hysteria and hysterical fiction appear concurrently with the very conception of interiority within physical space, which held that "spatial and psychic insides might swaddle the individual in shared protections against a traumatic exterior" brought on by industrial and political revolution.[15] In their landmark work *The Madwoman in the Attic: The Woman Writer and the Nineteenth Century Literary Imagination*, Sandra M. Gilbert and Susan Gubar describe confinement in domestic space as: "to become literally a house [...] to be denied the hope of that spiritual transcendence of the body [...] which makes humanity distinctly human."[16] Hysterical texts such as "The Yellow Wallpaper," *The Bell Jar*, and *Eraserhead* depict characters resisting this transformation into a domestic space in pursuit of that spiritual transcendence.

Gilman, Plath, and Lynch all interrogate definitions of gender and artistic autonomy by setting their work in liminal, heterotopic spaces. Carmen Bonasera claims that such spaces are simultaneously hostile and enriching toward the construction of a female artistic identity.[17] Following Foucault, Bonasera defines heterotopia as a space that exists outside of and apart from other so-called normal or ordinary spaces. Hospitals, prisons, nursing homes, or asylums are designed to be at a remove from established society, generally for the purpose of instructing (or correcting) "individuals whose behavior deviates from the required social norms" so that they can either re-enter normal social space rehabilitated or, if rehabilitation is impossible, be kept apart from the social in order to protect its allegedly normal inhabitants from psychological contamination or physical harm.[18] In this respect, heterotopic and liminal spaces are inextricably linked: liminality by its very definition is a space in between other, more established spaces which "entails ambiguity and otherness," and heterotopic spaces are designated as sites of otherness, in-between places for nonconforming individuals to go for either rehabilitation or isolation.[19]

Gilman, Plath, and Lynch conceive of space more broadly as both physical and spiritual, making the search for space about more than merely finding a room of one's own in which to exist and think but rather to find space outside of and apart from existing spaces, an alternative space beyond the available conceptions of space. Showalter argues that "The Yellow Wallpaper" reclaims the so-called hysterics from hysteria. Instances of insanity and hysteria in the narrator—hallucinations, paranoia, etc.—

appear not because her attempts to create a narrative are disordered and irrational but because she is *not allowed* to write.[20] Likewise in *The Bell Jar*, Esther Greenwood's condition appears when her desires to write grind against the social pressures she faces to become a mother and domestic, after which time she "would feel differently [and] wouldn't want to write poems anymore," or so she is told.[21] Henry Spencer may not voice any creative aspirations in *Eraserhead*—all we know about his work is that Mary believes he is "very clever at printing"—but he spends much of his alone time gazing longingly into the middle distance and imagining the desolate world around him coming to life. His visions of animated worms, ladies in radiators, and factories in his mind suggest an active imagination with artistic potential. These flights of fancy, however, remain imprisoned in his mind, never escaping into the exterior world due to limitations imposed upon him by his domestic life. While we cannot know for certain what would come of these daydreams, we can infer that Henry could develop an artistic life if he were given more, to borrow Lynch's phrase, "room to dream." The fact that Lynch conceives of daydreaming in interior, spatial terms—a room—is of great importance here, especially when one considers that Henry's dream space—his one-room apartment—is invaded by others, sending him deeper into psychological space in the hope of regaining this lost space.

In these works, the protagonists face confinement in a series of oppressive heterotopic spaces by coercive or carceral means, making these spaces battlegrounds for autonomy. The speaker of "The Yellow Wallpaper" is forced into the world of the rational and the physical, a world that, like her husband, is "practical in the extreme," exhibiting "no patience with faith," "an intense horror of superstition," and open hostility for anything that cannot "be felt and seen and put down in figures."[22] Despite the fact that "he does not believe [she] is sick," her physician husband prescribes a rest cure for her allegedly nonexistent illness.[23] The cure matches her husband's mindset in that it is almost wholly concerned with the physical in the sense that he recommends moving through space—"journeys, and air, and exercise"—according to "a schedule prescription for each hour in the day" that demands she not "stir without special direction."[24] The space outside exhibits equally policed boundaries as well: there are "hedges and walls and gates that lock," "box-ordered paths" that are "lined" with trees and "lots of separate little houses."[25] (The greenhouse windows, spaces that would blur the lines between inside and outside, are all broken.) Ironically, though, these plans and prescriptions have little bearing on her treatment because it appears that the narrator seldom leaves the nursery. The space she is confined to may feature "windows that look all ways, and air and sunshine galore," but the real goal of her treatment is to restrict her access to space as a means of controlling her mind and body.[26] The most telling detail that demonstrates this desired level of control is the fact her husband strictly prohibits writing, even though the speaker feels that writing provides "a great relief to [her] mind."[27]

The titular wallpaper demonstrates how the spatial and psychological restrictions for the narrator are one and the same. The narrator's first description of the wallpaper characterizes its main offense as being spatial in nature: It is "one of those sprawling flamboyant patterns committing every artistic sin [...] dull enough to confuse the eye in following, pronounced enough to constantly irritate and provoke study, and when you follow the lame uncertain curves for a little distance they suddenly commit suicide—plunge off at outrageous angles, destroy themselves in unheard of contradictions."[28] The wallpaper is continually depicted as irrational, but its irrationality presents itself spatially: it is "sprawling" with "lame uncertain curves" that "plunge" when the eye attempts to "follow" them. From this description, the speaker clearly seeks a path "to some sort of a conclusion," a pattern that will guide her out of this heterotopic space to a kind of personal and aesthetic freedom in which she can "think straight."[29] Unfortunately, this wallpaper "commit[s] every artistic sin," and its aesthetic failures stymy the narrator's mental improvement and artistic ambitions.

Although it might seem like a retreat into private space would be exactly what one would need in order to establish a stable identity as an artist and person, Gilman, Plath, and Lynch demonstrate that private space does not exist for the so-called hysteric. Their private spaces seldom remain so, and the continued intrusion upon their solitude represents what Elizabeth Boa calls a "subjectivity vulnerable to social penetration."[30] In fact, these works are populated with heterotopic spaces masquerading as private spaces of autonomy and freedom. Esther's arrival at the psychiatric facility in *The Bell Jar* illustrates how heterotopic spaces are less separate from the so-called normal world than they are tools that reinforce the order of the world and police those who cannot mold themselves into whatever shape it dictates. Esther's first impression of the facility and its grounds is that it seems like a "replica" of "down-at-heel seaside resorts" she has visited in the past.[31] However, the strange motionlessness of the people unnerves her, and Plath's language abruptly shifts to the language of mass-production and commerce to describe the uncanniness of the facility/resort. The "uniformity" of these motionless patients resembles "shop dummies" that "had lain for a long time on a shelf" of "an enormous department store."[32] The horror of the scene appears to come from its surreality: here the insane unsuccessfully pantomime sane human behavior, what Esther calls "counterfeiting life"; however, the comparison of the facility to a resort and a department store and the patients to mannequins creates another, more terrifying idea: this space is no different from the overly commercial, materialistic spaces in Manhattan that drove Esther to attempt suicide.[33] Outside the facility grounds, in the so-called real and normal world, fearful, conforming people strive to mimic movements and reproduce desires dictated to them by the forces of advertising and Cold War logic. The facility lays bare "the invisible forces that create [the] hostile social reality" in the "real" world. This heterotopic space coerces Esther back in line immediately: upon her entry, she and her mother become mannequins too when they sit "without speaking" and await the doctor's instructions.[34] In the following paragraph, Esther is being led to her first electro-convulsive therapy treatment.

While Henry Spencer may appear to have more freedom of movement in *Eraserhead*, all his movements outward result in his being further confined into interior space. Richard Martin argues that Henry's fundamental problem is spatial in the sense that he has "an inability to occupy space successfully: he is perennially displaced and terrified by his surroundings."[35] The "hostile public spaces" of Lynch's Philadelphia of the mind—with its constantly erupting phallic smokestacks and ceaseless industrial hisses, clatters, and clangs—drive Henry indoors toward the domestic to face "an invasion of random pipes," or what Justus Nieland calls "the uncanny infrastructure of the violated interior."[36] Lynch wastes little time in depicting Henry's spatial situation as hopeless. After a long trek through a series of obstacles—dirt mounds, toxic puddles, and vast stretches of dirt and concrete—Henry arrives at his one-room apartment that should provide a respite from the oppressions of the public sphere. Instead, it only confirms the impossibility of his escape. In an attempt to unwind from the day, Henry stares at his radiator as its hiss grows louder on the soundtrack. Lynch cuts to a shot looking at Henry's window, revealing the only view it offers him is a brick wall. Before the plot even gets underway, we can see that the walls have already closed in on Henry—literally. By the day's end, Henry will return home from a dinner with his estranged girlfriend's family committed to a wife and child, his personal space shrunk even further.

Henry's dinner with the X family features the kind of ersatz normality Plath displays at the psychiatric facility in *The Bell Jar*. For all its horrifyingly surreal touches—the nursing puppies, the man-made chickens that move on their own and spurt blood, the catatonic grandmother, Mary and her mother's inexplicable fits, Bill X's numb arm, permanently bent knees and rictus—the scene runs through all the beats and tensions of any standard meet-the-parents scene. Lynch holds a funhouse mirror up to this commonplace domestic scene to, like Plath, portray such an existence as a grotesque, nightmarish, and coercive trap that strips an individual of their creative autonomy. The film uses this sequence to depict Henry's confinement into family life as the result of coercion, most obviously illustrated by Mary's mother's aggressive intimidation of Henry in which she backs him into an actual corner to get him to accept the responsibility of caring for Mary and their child. This coercion on top of the painfully awkward and stilted dinner renders the domestic space in *Eraserhead* as hostile and heterotopic. Once confined to this state, the film shows how Henry's avenues for escape grow narrower just as the need for them grows.

FIGURE 1.1 Mrs. X backs Henry into a corner. *Eraserhead* directed by David Lynch © Libra Films 1977. All rights reserved.

Lynch again turns to the radiator to depict the increased pressure that results from Henry's diminished options. The first time Henry comes home after Mary and the baby have moved in, he enters the room, lays on the bed, and stares into the radiator. The hiss of the radiator rises on the soundtrack again, and this time a light comes on inside the radiator; however, before any revelation can take place, the sound of a crying baby takes over. The light and the hissing sound disappear, drowned out by the baby's whines. The message could not be any clearer: whatever chances of escape Henry once had, the baby makes them impossible. Like the narrator of "The Yellow Wallpaper," external demands of whom and what Henry should be have hampered his ability to move freely through space, both physically and mentally. As we will soon see, when Henry finds that he cannot create—or when his creations turn out to be monstrous—he chooses erasure.

Both Plath and Lynch choose babies as the strongest symbols of these traps. Besides their monstrous features, the babies in these works share immobility as a defining factor, thus adding a spatial dimension to their role in the text. Being infants, babies are of course immobile, but they are also immobilizing because their literal lack of mobility renders their caregivers figuratively immobile and fixed in their proximity. Either Henry or Mary must remain in their apartment at all times in order to care for their gauze-swaddled mutant child, perhaps indefinitely. If Esther were to enter domestic

FIGURE 1.2 The liminal radiator. *Eraserhead* directed by David Lynch © Libra Films 1977. All rights reserved.

life with Buddy, she believes she would become like one of the jarred fetuses she sees with "gills just like fish," immobile, "sitting under the same glass bell jar, stewing in [her] own sour air."[37] A baby also figures in the protagonist's confinement in "The Yellow Wallpaper" because she has recently given birth and her husband will not permit her to be around her baby until she overcomes the "false and foolish fanc[ies]" that occupy her thoughts (likely postpartum depression).[38] Fittingly, the room the narrator is confined to "The Yellow Wallpaper" is defined by child-rearing: its previous uses were as a nursery, playroom, and gymnasium. Thus, the space lays out not only each stage in a child's development but also the narrator's entire future as a parent. The bars on the windows and the furniture nailed into place indicate that she will remain incarcerated and immobile, "stewing in [her] own sour air," until she stops "let[ting] any silly fancies *run away*" with her.[39] The previous uses of the room make the Kafkaesque irony of her predicament clear: she will not be let out of the room until she accepts that she will not be let out of the room. Each of the heterotopic spaces in these works poses the same paradox to the protagonists. They must conform to the dream version of reality or else face eternal imprisonment in the punishing nightmare version of that same reality. For Gilman, Plath, and Lynch, the patriarchal American notion of family is not the path to domestic freedom and contentment but a prison that smothers the creative imagination of its citizens until they are so "brainwashed" that they become as "blank and stopped as a dead baby," living in "the bad dream" that is patriarchal America.[40]

Liminal Liberty

As much as these writers depict many of these heterotopic spaces as places of horror and trauma, these spaces also become liminal sites of transformation and transcendence. Within each heterotopic space lies a liminal space— the yellow wallpaper, Henry's radiator, Plath's psychiatric facilities, Laura Palmer's picture frame—that externalizes the protagonist's internal struggle, making each "blurred boundar[y]" into "the spatial equivalent of the subject's transition between conflicting versions of the self, as well as between contrasting domains of reality and illusion, of death and rebirth."[41] Through these liminal spaces, the protagonists imagine and explore alternate ways of being that destabilize patriarchal conceptions of order, harmony, and reason to create "new and subversive configurations of identity" that continually resist confinement and finality.[42] Simply put, in these works, the only way out is in.

In "The Yellow Wallpaper," the ever-shifting pattern of the titular wallpaper signals the existence of new ways of seeing that are visions beyond the apparent unbound by the existing frameworks.[43] Although the narrator initially views the "absurd," incongruous, and illogical wallpaper as part and parcel of her husband's oppression and control, her fixation on the "optic horror" of its "pointless pattern" that defies "any laws of radiation, or alternation, or repetition, or symmetry" reveals those "interminable grotesques" of the wallpaper are not as disorganized and chaotic as they first appear but rather "form around a common centre."[44] That "common centre"? A woman whose form the narrator detects "stooping down and creeping about behind that pattern."[45] The most important thing about this woman, or at least the first thing the narrator notices, is that she moves. As the narrator tracks her movements, she discovers what they have in common: the woman, like her, wants to get out.

The narrator's discovery of the woman in the wallpaper turns the language she uses to describe it in the first half of the story on its head, revealing that the standards of spatial logic and order that she demanded the wallpaper conform to are the same standards of rationality her husband imposes on her and uses to confine her to the room. The wallpaper contains "a lack of sequence, a defiance of law, that is a constant irritant to a *normal mind*" because the moment when one "think[s] [they] have mastered it, [...] it turns a back-somersault and [...] slaps [them] in the face, knocks [them] down, and tramples [them]."[46] Any effort to discern or impose a rational order on the wallpaper ends in frustration and defeat, and prolonged attempts to do so may even drive one mad.

While this description sounds like more of the same, it can also be read in a subversive context, thanks to Gilman's addition of the phrase "to a normal mind." This phrase places the pattern of the wallpaper firmly outside the clear boundaries of reason and order that define that normality exhibited by the carefully arranged foliage outside the narrator's window and performed by the patients at the psychiatric facility in *The Bell Jar*. A simple reading of this observation is that the wallpaper's chaotic pattern is a failure of design. A more complex reading, however, could view this defiance of an accepted order to represent freedom from the kinds of oppressive constructs that lead to the narrator's confinement. Rather than existing *outside* of the law of the rational, perhaps the wallpaper exists *beyond* it. The narrator's new assessment of the wallpaper after she discovers the woman could just as easily apply to her newfound understanding of herself: her irrationality, her "defiance of law" that irritates the "normal mind" of her husband simultaneously oppresses her and liberates her. It confines her to a heterotopic space and transforms that space into a liminal one ripe with discovery and possibility.

This both/and reading of the wallpaper's irrationality allows the wallpaper, the narrator, and the story to exist in the space between this binary, conferring upon it a level of liminality that, for all its indeterminacy and ambiguity, ultimately comes to be liberating in the story. Because she does not "think straight," she must be fixed into place until she does; however, because she does not "think straight," she is free to move, shift, and elude according to the "uncertain curves" of an ever-changing pattern of her own design. Instead of yearning to get out of the room, the narrator seeks ways to descend deeper into it, locking herself in the room "until [she] ha[s] found it out."[47] Her goal in this is simple but profound: she wishes to "astonish" her husband.[48] Her choice of words indicates that she desires to show him something that he cannot explain, something beyond language. Gilman expresses this astonishment that is beyond the capabilities of the rational in one of the narrator's exclamations after she enters the wallpaper: "It is so pleasant to be out in this great room and creep around as I please."[49] While "creep around" or "as I please" may stand out as the defining phrases in this statement because they highlight movement and autonomy, the phrase "out in" captures the liberating irrationality of the moment and the story as a whole. Something cannot be both "out" and "in" and yet, by stepping into the vast expanse of the wallpaper, the narrator achieves both.

To the rational mind, this paradoxical statement serves as conclusive evidence that the narrator has let those "flights of fancy" carry her past the edge of sanity. However, the coexistence of the clashing "out/in" binary represents an escape from such rigid diagnoses, a world in which opposing binaries can coexist without punishment. As Esther remarks to Buddy in *The Bell Jar*, "If neurotic is wanting two mutually exclusive things at one and the same time, then I'm neurotic as hell. I'll be flying back and forth between one mutually exclusive thing and another for the rest of my days."[50] Like the narrator of "The Yellow Wallpaper," Esther's statement reads as agreeing with the rational male diagnosis initially; however, a word such as "flying" performs a double role that characterizes Esther as both neurotic and visionary. "Flying," an image Plath frequently employs in her poems, echoes those "flights of fancy" that the narrator's husband warns her against in "The Yellow Wallpaper," but "flying" also connotes transcendence, an escape from limited binaries represented by "two mutually exclusive things" such as out/in or sane/insane. Like Plath's choice of "flying," Gilman's paradoxical "out in" makes the autonomy of "as I please" and the movement of "creep around" possible. What first appears as a firm and impenetrable boundary, a wall, a diagnosis, becomes a pathway into another realm of understanding, one defined by movement and possibility, which is both the opposite of what it initially presents and made necessary by the imposition of that boundary. Most importantly, its existence outside the bounds of rational conception places it outside of male apprehension and control, making it a liberated space.

Esther's confinement leads her, like the narrator of "The Yellow Wallpaper," to view her treatments as forces to be transcended on par with her experiences in society. She arrives at her first appointment with Dr. Gordon in a state of complete despair that she characterizes as follows: "I saw the days of the year stretching ahead like a series of bright, white boxes [...] day after day glaring ahead of me like a white, broad, infinitely desolate avenue."[51] The prescribed treatment for this condition—electroconvulsive therapy— only yanks her into closer contact with this feeling. The shock "shook [her] like the end of the world" and "shrilled, through an air crackling with blue light, and with each flash a great jolt drubbed [her] till [she] thought [her] bones would break and the sap fly out of [her] like a split plant."[52] Electricity comes upon her as an existentially cataclysmic force seeking to turn the deepest parts of her inside out, to empty her until nothing remains inside and render her as inert and non-threatening as the Rosenbergs, whose execution is mentioned in the novel's famous opening line. These passages resemble the ending of *Eraserhead* when Henry embraces the Lady in the Radiator, only here they are not presented as peaceful, transcendent mergers with the infinite. What Esther views as the ultimate in hopelessness, Henry welcomes as bliss.

Although *The Bell Jar* does not finish with the violent climaxes of "The Yellow Wallpaper" and *Eraserhead*, its ending is more hopeful; transcendence seems more imminent, more lasting as Esther slowly constructs a new self. Instead of the oblivion of death or living as "blank and stopped as a dead baby" in a bell jar, Esther chooses to accept this pain as her "landscape."[53] Plath punctuates Esther's entrance into her new life by describing it spatially. Esther returns to college with the belief that "the usual order of the world had shifted slightly, and entered a new phase."[54] Movement through space defines her new self, one shaped by agency and autonomy. The final clause of the novel signals her arrival at a new and healing self: "I stepped into the room."[55] Like Gilman and Lynch, Plath asserts there is something more than continued oppression on the other side of liminality.

FIGURE 1.3 The Lady in the Radiator appears to Henry. *Eraserhead* directed by David Lynch © Libra Films 1977. All rights reserved.

The radiator in Henry's apartment functions as the liminal space most on par with Gilman's permeable wallpaper and Plath's electroconvulsive therapy. With its exposed interior pipes and piles of dirt and straw indoors, the environment of *Eraserhead* blurs the boundaries between inside and outside to make porous, liminal spaces out of every interior. Like Gilman's protagonist, Henry's endless staring into his radiator yields a vision that begins as indeterminate and unfulfilled but "get[s] clearer every day" as Henry's desperation drives him to look more deeply inward for a way out.[56] The first time the Lady in the Radiator (Laurel Near) appears, the hissing of the radiator grows louder and changes in pitch as light emanates from it. Lynch cuts to an extreme close-up on the radiator that tracks right and forward before cutting to another close-up of metal panels inside the radiator opening like elevator doors as the camera tracks deeper into the darkness until it reveals lights at the foot of a stage. The camera tracks right as each of these lights come on, stopping on a woman's feet before pulling back to reveal the iconic Lady smiling alone and dancing an awkward two-step on the stage as strange embryos fall from the rafters. Although her purpose is not entirely clear at first, her warm smile and wide eyes staring directly into the camera position her as a positive, nurturing figure. Her function in Henry's fantasy becomes clearer when she begins to squish these embryonic creatures that fall from the rafters. Although it remains uncertain what these creatures are exactly, they closely resemble the creature from the conception and birth sequence that opens the film. Based on these details, it appears that she offers

Henry a vision of an existence where the horrors of creation can be undone, where he can erase the results of his actions and escape the limitations and confinements of domesticity. This abortive fantasy does not grant Henry liberation in the real world, at least not initially. In fact, it backfires. When he returns to reality, his nightmare appears to be bleeding into his waking life when he begins pulling more of these embryonic creatures from Mary's body as she sleeps. This sequence shows that, unlike the narrator of "The Yellow Wallpaper," Henry's imaginative excursions into liminal space do not grant him the liberation he desires, but rather further imprison him in the nightmare existence from which he is trying to escape.

However, Lynch suggests, like Gilman, Henry's nightmare persists because liberation cannot be achieved through passive observation; it requires action. The sequence that follows Henry's unfulfilled first vision of the Lady in the Radiator has him waking to find Mary gone and his neighbor, the Beautiful Girl across the Hall (Judith Anna Roberts), locked out of her apartment. Perhaps emboldened by his vision of the Lady in the Radiator, Henry embarks upon a grander vision of escape and imagines the Beautiful Girl seducing him and the two of them descending into a tub of white liquid as they make love. The Lady in the Radiator emerges from somewhere in the darkness, repeatedly singing "In Heaven, everything is fine." Despite the simplicity of the lyrics, its two lines communicate Henry's vision of utopia. A line such as "in heaven, everything is fine" does not require much in the way of explication. The next line, however, proves incredibly illuminating because it provides a definition of what "fine" means for Henry. "You've got your good things and I've got mine" promises more than mere equal fulfillment. If Henry has his good things and the other person has theirs, then Henry does not have to go out and get those good things for himself or anyone else. This heavenly dream releases him from the need to provide for himself and others, freeing him from the expectation of being a male provider in a patriarchal culture and leaving him free to dream for as long as he pleases.

Lynch provides a visual representation of what existence looks like when "everything is fine." At the conclusion of the Lady in the Radiator's song, Henry enters her space and steps onto the stage. He is no longer on the outside looking in on this liminal vision. Like the narrator of "The Yellow Wallpaper," he has crossed over to fully inhabit his vision of an existence that offers him greater freedom of movement in more open space. As he approaches the Lady, she stretches out her hands to him. When he touches her, a blinding white light floods the screen and a loud whirring dominates the soundtrack. In a film as relentlessly dark as *Eraserhead*, both tonally and visually, this light represents a complete break from the ghastly order of the world he lives in. By touching the Lady in the Radiator, Henry escapes "the factory in his brain" and enters a place beyond the confines of his own head and the oppression of the industrial world around him.[57] It may shock

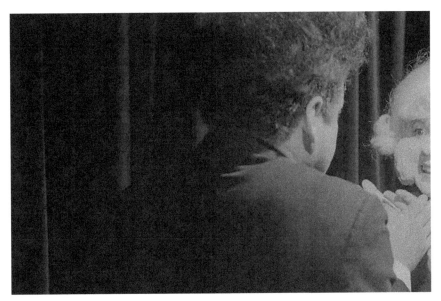

FIGURE 1.4 Henry touches another realm. *Eraserhead* directed by David Lynch ©
Libra Films 1977. All rights reserved.

Henry initially and drive him to retract his hand in fear, but he reaches out
again, eager to come into contact with something outside of his oppressive
world. Tellingly, this world outside of production is one devoid of shadows,
details, and textures. *Eraserhead* conceives of paradise as a complete blank,
with erasure as the ultimate escape. There is no need to create because all
has been revealed.

Even though Henry appears to wind up in a heaven in which all spatial
borders, boundaries, or limits have been completely erased, *Eraserhead*
offers the least hopeful view of this kind of transcendence. Unlike the
women of Gilman's and Plath's works, each of Henry's brushes with
the world beyond the rational ends in violent defeat. In his first return to
reality, embryonic creatures invade his bed. In his second, the domineering
Man in the Planet (Jack Fisk) and the grotesque baby infiltrate the fantasy
space of the radiator. His final trip into the radiator may be a permanent
escape from his world, but it is one thoroughly characterized and made
possible by violence, first in the murder of his child, and finally in his self-
annihilation. Todd McGowan reads all achievement of fantasy as violent.
Fantasy by its nature exists beyond the boundaries of the possible or the real,
so achieving fantasy requires destroying a boundary between fantasy and
reality.[58] McGowan reads the ending of *Eraserhead* somewhat optimistically
as Henry's subversive retaliation against the logic of capital: Henry succeeds

FIGURE 1.5 In heaven, everything is fine. *Eraserhead* directed by David Lynch ©
Libra Films 1977. All rights reserved.

by conquering his "investment in the very structure that [his] acts would
contest."[59] These violent acts may grant him entry into heaven, but they
are wholly apocalyptic acts that do not so much envision or create a new
order as destroy all existing ones. True, Henry may get what he wants in
Eraserhead, however, it costs him the world. With such an ending, *Eraserhead*
does not imagine a new or better world on the other side of liminality: there
is this world or there is nothing, and nothing is the more preferable of the
two because that is also what it demands of Henry, nothing. His act is a
solipsistic one, and the peace it brings is the peace of erasure, a nothingness
where he can shut his eyes forever.

Hysterical Erasure

The difference between *Eraserhead*'s ending and the endings imagined by
Gilman and Plath can best be explained by the gender of the protagonists.
As a hysterical text, *Eraserhead* is a fairly by-the-numbers entry in the
genre in content and, yes, even in style. A simple synopsis of the film
demonstrates how closely *Eraserhead* hews to hysterical literature's mold:
After an unplanned pregnancy forces them into domestic confinement, the
protagonist slowly loses their grip on reality until they lash out against their
oppressors in a spectacular act of violence that culminates in self-harm.
All the tropes are present in *Eraserhead*: pregnancy, confinement, madness,
violence, and self-harm. The conversation about *Eraserhead* should include

its relationship to this literary tradition, and our understanding of hysterical texts would be bolstered by including *Eraserhead* in the hysterical tradition, yet it is not, despite its obvious similarity. It may appear at first that this experimental style of Lynch's film is responsible for its ability to elude this kind of discussion; however, Showalter's analysis of hysterical literature demonstrates that Lynch's style, which is hardly more fragmented, surreal, or experimental than Gilman's eighty years earlier, is less responsible for *Eraserhead*'s omission from the discourse than gender. Put simply, *Eraserhead*'s hysterical approach gets praised as daring and innovative because it is made by and about a man.

This is not to suggest that gender is absent from discussions of *Eraserhead*, rather that gender has framed the conversation in such a way as to obscure (and perhaps excuse) certain dynamics at play in Lynch's film. When gender does arise in discussions of *Eraserhead*, most take the film's portrayal of gender at face value, overlooking how its presentation of Henry's conflict relies upon a firm patriarchal order. *Eraserhead* can be bluntly described in the words Boa uses to describe Kafka's *The Metamorphosis*: "the sufferings of a man who fails to be manly."[60] Like Gregor Samsa, Henry "seeks relief from the burdens of petty-bourgeois masculinity" in the form of an imagined return to a maternal womb represented by his visions of the Lady in the Radiator.[61] What the film offers in this fantasy and the destructive achievement of it is what Martin calls "a vision of reproductive failure, dysfunctional labor, and manufacturing stasis."[62] Some, such as Aaron Taylor, have even suggested that the opening sequence of the film and certain lines of dialogue during Henry's disastrous dinner at the X's indicate that Henry is the baby's father *and* mother, which certainly helps explain the abject nature of the child but also thoroughly characterizes Henry as a feminized male with a solipsism so total he can reproduce asexually.[63] And perhaps these observations are what makes Henry's plight harder to swallow: the film asserts—more or less uncritically—that Henry should not be emasculated, have his movement restricted, and give up his room to dream because that is simply not the way things are supposed to be; there is no room for finding happiness in his new domestic situation, there is only an earth-shattering horror show. The film presents Henry's reality as less sustainable than his fantasy, and something he must rebel against by any means necessary, even if it costs him his life.

Showalter observes that hysterical narratives about women often play out like Victorian novels in the sense that they are resolved through "marriage, madness, or death," while male narratives of hysteria more closely resemble modernist texts whose irrationality becomes described as fragmented, surreal, or experimental, daring rather than deviant.[64] Gilman and Plath employ Victorian plots designed to "cure" hysterical women—the marriage plot, the rest cure, etc.—to *subvert* the resolutions of those Victorian plots. *Eraserhead*, however, leans on the fragmented, surreal, experimental, and daring techniques of modernism to *endorse* Victorian ideals. As grotesque and traumatizing as the events of the film may be, the film lacks awareness of the degree to which the world it presents, even in such nightmarish form, is a patriarchal world designed to satisfy Henry's fantasy of being unburdened by the demands to produce or seduce. Where the female protagonists of Gilman and Plath attempt to write over the narratives imposed upon them, Henry's hysterical condition seeks to literally and figuratively erase all traces of his existence. If Henry cannot be given the space he deserves, if he cannot be the man in charge, he would rather not exist. Whether it comes in the form of killing his child, killing himself, or descending into an endlessly regressive and solipsistic *mise-en-abyme* of erasure and negation, *Eraserhead*'s main response to threats to masculine power is to implode.

In using the techniques and tropes of hysterical literature, *Eraserhead* attempts to have it both ways. Like his predecessors Gilman and Plath did, Lynch turns to this tradition for his first feature to declare his artistic independence. However, this declaration overlooks the degree to which the kind of power *Eraserhead* wishes to reinstate is the exact same power hysterical literature wishes to depose. Or, to offer a more charitable reading, the dominance of patriarchy is so total that *Eraserhead* can simultaneously see the oppression of its domestic structure and be unable to conceive of a world without it. And so *Eraserhead* emerges as a paradoxical work battling an internal contradiction. It is a major creative work about the terror of creation, a "self-portrait" of David Lynch and "a parable of reproductive dread" that has difficulty acknowledging a world outside the self which can view the portrait.[65] Singling it out as an example of cinematic creativity and independence without relating it to other works which it strongly resembles and owes a great deal of its creativity to reinforce the tropes that praise behavior in men that would be questioned or condemned in women. As writers frequently confined to the margins, Gilman and Plath can imagine alternatives to these contradictions. When Lynch adopts a woman's point of view in *Fire Walk with Me*, so can he.

Laura Is the One

Understanding *Eraserhead*'s shortcomings allows us further appreciation of the redemptive and recuperative work on display in *Fire Walk with Me*. Lynch's attachment to Laura Palmer (Sheryl Lee) and desire to see her escape the tormented life he had designed for her enables him to make an imaginative leap that affects not only the story of Laura Palmer but the trajectory of his career.[66] While the film is a prequel to *Twin Peaks*, it is also a spiritual remake of *Eraserhead*. If that seems farfetched, consider their similarity in style and structure. Both films concern themselves with protagonists besieged by "dark and troubling things" in their dream life that stem from a harrowing domestic life. In both cases, confinement in a heterotopic space apart from society is not necessary because the home is the carceral space and site of their oppression. There is no escape from this oppressive space for them; the punishment is unrelenting. As these attacks become more physically and emotionally violent, the protagonists search for an escape in liminal spaces within their walls. These spaces illuminate for them alternate ways of being and embolden them to reject the forces oppressing them. While both protagonists die at the end of each film, each ending suggests that they have accessed "a beyond which is clearly designated [...] as a place where one never dies," a place where everything is fine.[67]

These turning points not only make *Eraserhead* and *Fire Walk with Me* resemble each other; they also make them superlative cinematic exemplars of hysterical texts. In returning to the tropes of hysterical literature in *Fire Walk with Me*, Lynch displays a deeper, more empathetic understanding of trauma and, more importantly, critiques the oppressive societal forces that inflict this trauma. The film's uncompromising depiction of violence, trauma, and hysteria not only brings the film more in line with the political and historical roots of hysterical literature but it also rejuvenates Lynch's career. Where *Eraserhead* adopts the style of hysterical literature to largely affirm the patriarchal order, *Fire Walk with Me* inaugurates a new phase in his career as a filmmaker that rejects the sexist elements of his earlier films in favor of dissecting the physical and psychological effects of American patriarchy.

FIGURE 1.6 The static opening to *Fire Walk with Me. Twin Peaks: Fire Walk with Me* directed by David Lynch © CIBY Pictures 1992. All rights reserved.

The opening shot of *Fire Walk with Me* illustrates the dynamic of the film and of "The Yellow Wallpaper" in miniature. A chaotic pattern floods the screen, so blurry, abstracted, and unstable that viewers cannot discern what they are looking at. No amount of scrutiny or analysis will resolve the lack of meaning into a coherent signal. Then, slowly, the camera tracks backward to translate the abstract pattern into something recognizable and concrete: television static, "snow." This reveal may not be as revelatory as one might hope: it provides an "answer," but one that only confirms an absence in which meaning remains deferred. Gilman links the chaos of the wallpaper pattern with the patriarchy's fear of the "hysterical" woman by having a woman appear within the wallpaper. Lynch pairs the senseless pattern of the static with the male revulsion toward the feminine at the end of the shot when a hammer smashes this television, silencing the maddening and incoherent static just before the same instrument is used to silence Teresa Banks. The violence in the shot then represents both a strike against disorder and against a woman, which the film, like Gilman, reveals to be one and the same in the predatory eyes of patriarchy.

To look at the opening shot of *Fire Walk with Me* and see only static is a rational interpretation of this apparent lack of order, but it ignores the film's treatment of static and electrical signals, as well as its approach to the allegedly irrational. As the rest of the film demonstrates, this static, like the yellow wallpaper, is a liminal space that serves as a portal to another realm beyond what logic can account for. Television static or electrical glitches accompany nearly every fissure in reality in *Fire Walk*

FIGURE 1.7 Silencing Teresa Banks, silencing static. *Twin Peaks: Fire Walk with Me* directed by David Lynch © CIBY Pictures 1992. All rights reserved.

with Me. Static next appears in the Philadelphia FBI office when Phillip Jeffries (David Bowie) returns from his mysterious absence. As he recounts his experiences to Agents Cole, Cooper, and Rosenfield (Lynch, Kyle MacLachlan, and Miguel Ferrer), the same slow-motion distorted closeup of static from the first shot fades in, as do images of beings from the Black Lodge. Dissolves of television static fade in and out sporadically throughout the sequence as Jeffries shuttles between these two planes of existence. The static becomes more prevalent as Jeffries descends deeper into a psychotic episode, filling the screen as he breaks down and suddenly vanishes. This sequence alerts the audience to associate all static and other sounds of electrical signals with the Black Lodge and the Red Room, a reading which the rest of the film and *Twin Peaks* (2017) reinforces. More importantly, though, it alerts the viewer that material appearing to contain nothing actually contains the mysteries of everything. Static functions as a conduit to a place beyond rational perception that can lead to one's damnation, as with Jeffries, or, as with Laura, salvation.

The next time static appears in the film is when Mrs. Chalfont (Frances Bay) and her grandson (Jonathan J. Leppell) appear to Laura outside the RR Diner. In the scene, they give Laura a picture of an open door and ask her to hang it on her wall. Prior to receiving this picture, the liminality of Laura's room was one-way: BOB and other malevolent forces from the Black Lodge would enter her space through her bedroom window, but she could never access their space. The picture, however, allows her to, like the narrator of "The Yellow Wallpaper" and Henry in *Eraserhead*, enter this other realm and, in doing so, eventually discover a path out of her torment. Lynch shoots the sequence where Laura enters the picture from her point of view as she passes through a series of empty rooms marked only by floral wallpaper and open doors until the grandson snaps his fingers, filling the room with light as the screen dissolves to the familiar red curtains and black and white zig-zag floor pattern of the Red Room. The camera glides along the floor and tilts up to land on a pedestal holding the green signet ring. The Man from Another Place (Michael Anderson) and Agent Cooper appear. The Man offers her the ring, and Cooper, staring directly into camera, warns Laura not to take it. Laura wakes as if from a dream; however, a bloodied Annie Blackburn (Heather Graham) lays in her bed, and she tells Laura to write in her diary before she also disappears. With the dream apparently over, Laura looks in her hand to discover, to her horror, that she has taken the ring. The borders between these two worlds have become so porous that Laura can bring something back from her dream. However, the dream or vision has not concluded. Laura opens the door to leave her room and looks back at the picture to see herself in the image, standing in a doorway just like she is in her room, looking back at her sleeping body in bed. She wakes again, this time without a ring in her hand.

FIGURE 1.8 Laura enters the frame. *Twin Peaks: Fire Walk with Me* directed by David Lynch © CIBY Pictures 1992. All rights reserved.

FIGURE 1.9 Laura looks back at Laura. *Twin Peaks: Fire Walk with Me* directed by David Lynch © CIBY Pictures 1992. All rights reserved.

In addition to making liminality available to Laura, this sequence captures the duality of Laura Palmer in a way that other elements of *Twin Peaks* can only do obliquely. The series fixates on Laura Palmer's double life, treating her life, not her murder, as the real mystery in need of solving; however, viewers get to see two Laura Palmers in this sequence when, in a moment that feels straight out of Gilman's story, Laura looks back at the picture and sees herself in it. As McGowan has noted, the "dual nature" of Laura Palmer forms *Fire Walk with Me*'s potent critique of American patriarchy. As both the woman in the wallpaper and the woman outside discovering the woman in the wallpaper, Laura is herself a liminal figure defined by the coexistence of opposites, a both/and in a world that demands either/or.[68] Laura "embodies in one person all the contradictory male fantasies about women": she is the patriarchal ideal of the venerated virgin and the cautionary conception of the depraved whore wrapped into one.[69] Other early Lynch films split these categories across their female characters. *Eraserhead* pairs the dowdy blonde Mary X opposite the sultry brunette the Beautiful Girl across the Hall, *Blue Velvet* has the wholesome blonde Sandy and the tormented brunette Dorothy. These characterizations of women can come off as overly simplistic and archetypal, and, in the case of *Eraserhead*, work against its societal critique by reinforcing aspects of the ideology it is trying to subvert. In *Fire Walk with Me*, however, Lynch merges these equal and opposite cultural constructions of femininity into one person, Laura Palmer, and her both/and status shatters the boundary between the two to reveal the emptiness at the heart of the male fantasy that imagines itself as the upstanding and righteous patriarch preserving American innocence when it is in fact a ravenous monster bent on ruination.[70] Laura's alleged madness and depravity which are brought on by this fantasy therefore only highlights the depravity of an American culture driven mad by the potential autonomy of a young woman.

Laura's quest in *Fire Walk with Me* is a quest for knowledge equivalent to the quest of the protagonist of "The Yellow Wallpaper": she wishes to discover the source of her suffering and then liberate herself from it and, like Esther, construct an authentic autonomous identity. Although Lynch may not code Laura as an artist as explicitly as Gilman and Plath do their protagonists, it is important that her quest be read as a creative act. No one in the film grants her the space to complete this quest because the dream world they live in—the kitsch-perfect Americana that is Twin Peaks—depends upon the constructed feminine ideal that has been imposed upon her. Laura may ultimately pay for her autonomous identity with her life, but the final scenes of the film in the Red Room suggest that Laura attains a kind of redemption and peace. Her deliverance may derive from her taking the ring at the moment of her death, a thing that the controlling men around her, father and law figures such as Leland Palmer (Ray Wise) and Agent Cooper, warn her not to do. In defying them, she subverts a symbol of control into a symbol of power.[71] *Fire Walk with Me*'s last image freezes on Laura smiling her first genuine smile in the film, her face awash in bright, bluish-white light. This final frame has echoes of the last shot of *Eraserhead*, in which Henry achieves a similar transcendence in a bath of white light, but it also harkens back to the first shot of *Fire Walk with Me*. This time, however, instead of the dim, chaotic, and destructive bluish-white light of the television static, this light is calm and clear—all signal, no noise. This ending revises the despair of Laura's "falling in space" monologue earlier in the film to show that something comes after suffering if one embraces liminality. Laura may "burst into fire" at the film's end, but "this kind of fire" burning Laura only appears to be "death and disorientation" from within the boundaries of the oppressive reality Laura lives in.[72] The events of the film, however, assert that another space exists in which the burning stops.

Like the protagonists of Gilman and Plath, Laura discovers her power to transcend the *garmonbozia* of her life through her embrace of liminality and irrationality. Another character in *Fire Walk with Me*, Phillip Jeffries, takes a similar journey into liminality, only his experience causes him to unravel. Jeffries is a character marked by invisibility and silence, more absent than present. When he is visible to the eye, he goes undetected by cameras, and when he is on camera, he is not in space. His speech, defined by his first line, "Well now, I'm not going to talk about Judy. In fact, we're not going to talk about Judy at all. We're gonna keep her out of it," uses language as a blunt instrument that silences the hysteric he fears becoming. Upon his return from the world of the Black Lodge, Jeffries's entire world becomes porous as he passes maddeningly between two worlds. His language expresses his desire to blot it out of existence, to erase it before it destroys him. In this respect, Phillip Jeffries is Lynch's updated version of Henry Spencer, another man whose discovery of a world beyond the rational and the patriarchal drives him toward oblivion and negation. To look at him is to see a person truly falling in space. As the woman visible in the picture and visible in her

FIGURE 1.10 Laura's transcendent release. *Twin Peaks: Fire Walk with Me* directed by David Lynch © CIBY Pictures 1992. All rights reserved.

room, Laura Palmer can occupy two spaces at once. This experience does not push her past the brink of sanity as it does Jeffries; it liberates her from a so-called ordinary life that has been slowly grinding her down to nothing. Martha Nochimson and McGowan also read Laura's journey in *Fire Walk with Me* in these terms: Laura travels "through the multiple planes of the real" to discover "the boundlessness of reality," and this realization of reality's boundlessness opens the door for transcendence, for a discovery of "the outside within the inside, the infinite within the finite."[73]

By aligning *Fire Walk with Me* more closely with the tropes of hysterical literature, Lynch upends the patriarchal logic that has governed his earlier films to create a work that, unlike *Eraserhead*, successfully imagines a world outside the oppressive dominance of that logic. Where previous work cannot fully imagine a place outside and apart from suffering, *Fire Walk with Me*'s engagement with a female point of view makes room for a redemptive experience of liminality, not a catastrophic one. The shift in the Red Room from phallic signifiers in *Twin Peaks* to yonic ones in *Fire Walk with Me* noted by Nochimson signals the major transformation in Lynch's career toward a more explicit repudiation of masculine discourse and control toward a centering of the experience of being an object within masculine discourse.[74] Of Lynch's remaining features, only two, *Lost Highway* and *The Straight Story*, feature male protagonists, both of whom are broken by an adherence to masculinity, and Lynch's portrayal of their brokenness is far less exculpatory than *Eraserhead*.

Disruptive Multiplicity

Because all but one of Gilman, Plath, and Lynch's protagonists dies at the end of their stories, one can conclude, as Boa does, that these narratives do not offer liberation from patriarchy.[75] Indeed, a successful overthrow of the male power structure is noticeably absent from these works. However, even though most of these works end in death, they do not necessarily end in defeat. Rather, their endings point toward alternate definitions of resolution that exist outside the boundaries created by the power structure they seek to subvert.

These stories endure for the same reasons their hysterical characters do: they resist fixed interpretive conclusions by always existing somewhere just beyond such enclosures. One must keep in mind that Gilman's wallpaper never transcends its ugliness or resolves into an aesthetically pleasing pattern. It retains its contradictory nature and continues to be "indeterminate, complex, unresolved, [and] disturbing."[76] Likewise, these stories never conform to tidy resolutions: every approach to "solving" them fails to connect every loose end or answer every question. As short stories, novels, and films presented to a mass audience in America, these works exist within a set of expectations for narrative closure that, in the cases of Gilman and Lynch, conflict with their experimental and avant-garde style. Vivian Delchamps notes that these kinds of stories are "infectious" not only in the sense that they capture an audience's imagination but also in the way that this fascination stirs the desire to "doctor" or cure the narrative through finding a clear, rational resolution to the "unruly form" of the text.[77] In this way, the doctor's desire to perform a diagnosis mirrors the reader's desire to impose a stable interpretation on the narrative. Scholarship on hysterical literature shows this demand for explanation to be an oppressive construct, claiming that the notions of diagnosis and cure are equally destructive in these texts because they act as tidy resolutions imposed from without upon a narrative unwilling to conform to the expectations of the dominant power structure.[78] There is a desire for order and resolution that these situations present but that these works actively resist because that resolution brings on the very oppression that leads one to dream.

As such, these works are what Treichler calls "disruptive center[s]" that resist and splinter efforts to confine it to univocal meaning.[79] One could read such indeterminacy as entropic in the sense that every attempt to impose order simply increases the disorder; however, something much more exciting and affirming is true: the texts satisfy a yearning for what Nochimson identifies as "multiplicity."[80] It is multiplicity, not a binary, that represents transcendence. In embracing multiplicity, these narratives forge a new consciousness, one that is perhaps "unfamiliar" and "spontaneous" but also "coherent and normal."[81] Lynch's work in *Fire Walk with Me* fulfills this journey most completely because, unlike Gilman and Plath, he has more than words to work with—the image allows him to show fully a multiplicity that Gilman and Plath can only suggest or gesture toward.

This kind of multiplicity is also what this book aims for: not for fixing the meaning of Lynch's films in place but rather to stir up more affiliating identifications to reveal how vast and inexhaustible this work truly is. These works, like the wallpaper, continually shift under our observation and elude our scrutiny, allowing us to become more lost in their mysteries the more we try to explore them. While that might bring out "a slight hysterical tendency" in those of us who seek to inhabit these disturbing complexities, the energy of such pursuits brings us closer to a place where everything is fine.

2

"Let the Wild Rumpus Return!"

Blue Velvet and
Children's Literature

Critical positions on David Lynch's landmark film *Blue Velvet* have varied wildly since its release in 1986; however, one position remains so fixed that it is almost too obvious to state: *Blue Velvet* is not a film for children. From Slavoj Zizek to the MPAA, Laura Mulvey to Roger Ebert, the long-sought, ever-elusive critical consensus has been found at long last. Joking aside, it is hard to deny that the film's unflinching, graphic depictions of physical and sexual violence easily exclude it from even the most lenient viewing list for young people, as does its complex treatment of voyeuristic pleasure, sadomasochistic behavior, and the class distinctions surrounding beer. Even though the film's content would certainly alienate and traumatize a young viewer, that does not necessarily suggest that *Blue Velvet* does not have aspects that would feel familiar to a youngster. In fact, this familiarity would go a long way toward explaining why much of the film would be so upsetting: because so much of it would feel so close to home. This closeness comes from the fact that, for all of the film's graphic, hard-R-rated material, its narrative cues and organizing structures come from a place as G-rated as *The Straight Story*: children's literature.

Like many generic labels, children's literature exists as a genre both seemingly easy to recognize and nearly impossible to define. A definition as circular and literal as "literature made for children" may encompass the term, but only in a way that renders the definition functionally useless. The difficulty of defining children's literature has led some scholars to pursue definition more stridently and others to dismiss the need for definition entirely.[1] Marah Gubar provides an overview of this very debate in her article

"On Not Defining Children's Literature," arguing that, although a definition for children's literature may be possible, it would be "so long, complicated, and qualified" that it not only "would be of no value" but would itself fail to capture "the glorious messiness and multiplicity" of the genre.[2] Such an observation need not be an argument against definition. Rather, Gubar advocates for defining children's literature according to Wittgenstein's family resemblance model. By adopting a family resemblance model instead of a rigid definition, scholars amass "a constellation of criteria" that would account for the genre's "complex and capacious" nature with flexible boundaries and shifting meanings.[3] One loses precision under the family resemblance model, but one stands to gain a much greater understanding of how the genre adapts, as well as a fuller picture of the varied works it encompasses.

Blue Velvet indeed shares a family resemblance with children's texts: it is a maturation plot set in a storybook world in which a youthful, inexperienced protagonist embarks on a disturbing journey that ushers them from innocence to experience. After an accident incapacitates his father, the young hero makes a curious discovery while wandering on the outskirts of his village. This discovery introduces him to a dark and disturbing wilderness previously hidden from him that he simultaneously fears and desires. In this world, he finds himself enchanted by a woman held captive by an erratic and evil monster. This attraction draws the ire of the monster who seeks either to destroy the young hero or to seduce him to evil. The young hero resists these calls toward the dark side at first but gradually realizes the wicked forces he confronts also reside within himself. If he wishes to conquer these dark forces, rescue the captive woman, and restore order to his town, the young hero must defeat the evil monster or be destroyed in the process. Discussion of *Blue Velvet*'s relationship to children's literature goes beyond noting some shared tropes. Tracing the affiliating identifications between *Blue Velvet* and children's literature reveals how Lynch works with the archetypes and logic of children's stories to subvert the structuring assumptions not only of the genre but also of the society that uses these tales to mold its most impressionable citizens.

Typically, scholars apply psychoanalytic readings to *Blue Velvet*, reading the film as a portrait of a "world threatened by a catastrophic conflict between mother and child, burdened by the phallic power of the absent father, and soaking in the child's inevitable encounter with rejection and departure."[4] Although these approaches yield insightful readings of the film, I agree with Paul Coughlin that the sameness among these approaches suggests that the film is ripe for alternative points of entry.[5] Coughlin and other scholars have elected to chart how Lynch interrogates frameworks of representation through parody; however, in limiting their analysis to other cinematic works, they too have reached a point of similarity. In looking for literary entry points into *Blue Velvet*, scholars have an opportunity to discover more and deeper ways that Lynch's film is in dialogue with the American imagination.[6]

While *The Wizard of Oz* may present itself as the obvious reference point, the children's work *Blue Velvet* speaks back to best is Maurice Sendak's 1963 classic *Where the Wild Things Are*. Tracking the affiliating identifications between *Blue Velvet* and *Where the Wild Things Are* illuminates how each uses fantasy to similarly troubling ends. On the surface, both offer psychoanalytic dramatizations of an innocent-seeming protagonist using fantasy to confront and ultimately tame the wild elements of their psyche through encountering and subduing their *doppelgänger*. But this reading overlooks the ambivalence with which each work approaches the tropes of children's literature. While Sendak and Lynch's maturation plots may appear to instruct and tame, both espouse a more Romantic temperament that views humans more "as primal vessels of nature" instead of "pliable citizens-in-the-making."[7] This sentiment becomes most apparent in the resolution to these works, what Sarah Gilead refers to as "return-to-reality" where "the adventurers return home, the dreamer awakens, or the magical beings depart."[8] These returns purport to resolve the internal conflicts of the protagonist through the triumph of reality over fantasy and the fears and desires it was employed to confront.

Both Sendak and Lynch appear to align with the literary and social conventions of children's literature in the sense that the resolutions to *Where the Wild Things Are* and *Blue Velvet* depict characters returning to normal life tamed by their experiences and with a newfound commitment to the established order. Yet the formal construction of their final moments reveals there is little genuine indication that such a transformation has taken place. A different project has been at work all along, one that subtly reveals the ways that fantasy and wildness persist and how the so-called real world may be just another fantasy. With this tactic, Sendak and Lynch undermine the binaries that fantasy-based maturation plots depend on and demonstrate how these binaries are themselves fantasy creations of a society that uses them to impose its imagined sense of order. In this way, *Where the Wild Things Are* and *Blue Velvet* utilize the tools of social instruction and citizen-making—children's literature—to subvert the very structures these tools intend to erect, making them wild texts that argue that wildness cannot in the end be tamed. It is always present. And it will always return.

Framing Fantasies

Although not every children's story uses it, fantasy is a hallmark of the genre due to its ability to disguise the instructional or therapeutic functions of children's literature. As Philip Nell explains, children's literature proffers fantasy as "the best means [people] have for taming wild things."[9] Through fantasy, children's literature defamiliarizes the difficult emotions and situations young people frequently encounter and offers guidance on how to navigate these challenges, or at least provides them with a cathartic release from the pent-up anxiety and stress these conditions produce. Sendak himself saw his stories as offering children a way to grapple with the horrific and inexplicable in their lives, especially the confounding nature of the adult world.[10] For him, fantasy is not a distraction from the difficult emotions of childhood but rather a profound way to "resolv[e] universal psychic challenges."[11] These challenges often manifest for children in the form of clashing binaries that appear as they encounter the contradictions of life: right and wrong, wild and tame, child and adult. The world of fantasy and the world of reality stand as the most distinct of the two, but such obvious distinctions stand in for the more subtle reality-bound, repressive order of the social world that children must navigate to adjust to the demands of social life. Fantasy allows for these divisions not only to coexist, but for a character to pass fluidly between them so that the young audience may better understand how these opposing concepts function in real life. Through the "empowering dream-journey" in and out of fantasy in children's literature, the main character and the audience work through their negative emotions and emerge from the text better equipped to tackle the challenges of the real world.[12]

Both *Where the Wild Things Are* and *Blue Velvet* engage with fantasy by having their protagonists encounter two wildly contrasting worlds: one bright, placid world governed by harmony and authority, and one dark, hidden realm where law and reason do not dwell. However, the firm lines of demarcation separating the two worlds prove to be illusory. In *Where the Wild Things Are*, Sendak uses the layout of the book to illustrate the conflict between strict order and unrestrained desire. A sense of balance and order dominates the reality-based land of his mother: text and image are clearly set apart from each other, with all the words appearing on the left pages and all the images on the right, suggesting a world in which everything has its designated place. These images too are rigidly ordered, bounded by not only the clean lines of furniture and walls in the house but a method of composing that furthers a sense of entrapment: vertical and horizontal pen strokes form tight squares within the early images in the house, and white space frames the images over the first five pages. Collectively, these techniques give the world of Max's mother a sense of control but also confinement, suggesting that constraint maintains order. Max's actions upend this carefully curated sense of reason as he repurposes tools and home furnishings for his own rowdy designs: linens become ropes and tents, books become stools, and pets become prey for a boy who, if his wolf suit is to suggest anything at all, has become an animal. Max's rambunctiousness threatens to replace the world of reality with the world of wild fantasy, presumably with disastrous and potentially harmful results.

Sendak links language to authority and images to wildness in the opening pages of the book. Shortly after Max's "mischief" gets underway, his mother rapidly restores order by declaring him a "WILD THING" and sending him to his room without dinner.[13] This exclamation, the first spoken line of dialogue in the book, makes the layout of the book clear: there is the world of language, the world of order and reason, and then there is the world of images, the world of chaos. They must remain separate. And they do remain separate in the sense that text never appears on an image; however, to suggest that the order of Max's mother's world prevails would be incorrect.[14] As Max's room begins to transform into a forest, the fantasy world represented by the images on the right-hand pages grows in size with each successive page until it fills the page completely while the text remains the same size throughout the book. The images continue to grow as Max "sail[s] off through night and day" in "a private boat," spilling onto the left-hand side of the book until it occupies the upper two-thirds of both pages and shoves the text lower and lower on the page.[15] Once Max declares that the time has come to "let the wild rumpus start," text disappears from the next six pages entirely as readers take in three two-page spreads of unhinged revelry.[16] Here Max's fantasies enjoy ultimate fulfillment: the images are big, loud, and unrestrained. Instead of being confined and diminished, he is unleashed and exalted. The rigid lines created by items in the images and Sendak's crosshatch technique largely disappear as boundaries become rounder and smoother. Even some trees bend and curve as though relaxed in a world that knows no restriction. However, this fantasy is as short-lived as the order imposed by Max's mother. Max's journey back to "where someone loved him best of all" reins in the gains made by the fantasy world as more and more text creeps back in and the images retreat from the left page of the book.[17] By the book's end, image and text are separated again, so much so that the final page of the book has no images at all, just a few words of text confirming that Max's dinner "was still hot" after his sojourn among the wild things.[18] This ending serves as a bit of a reversal, suggesting that, for all of Max's anarchic cavorting, his rebellion did not make so much as a dent in the orderly power of the word.

Lynch creates a bifurcated environment in *Blue Velvet* reminiscent of Sendak's. Many critics note the feeling that "two very separate worlds" comprise the film: a "public social reality" that is the brightly colored, kitschy city of Lumberton and a "dark and violent" world of the subconscious residing across Lincoln Ave., a sinister world of violence, sex, and drug trafficking that "must remain hidden" from both that public social reality and private consciousness.[19] *Blue Velvet*'s two worlds are more subtle than *Where the Wild Things Are*'s in that they appear to exist in the same reality; however, they are no less fantastic in their conception and starkly different in their depiction. For all of its R-rated content, these two worlds feel like something straight out of a children's book in its presentation of a "storybook picture of glowing nuclear families and abiding values" moving about in "a shared trance of innocence."[20] As Dennis Lim describes it, the small-town idyll of Lumberton is a "picture-book" town populated with "overbright colors," "outsize monsters," and characters bearing names no adult would use to describe people, such as the Yellow Man and the Blue Lady, giving viewers the sense that the reality of the film is not being presented from the point of view of a fully developed adult but rather that it is "filtered through the still-forming psyche of a child."[21]

Lynch establishes the storybook quality of the film most strongly in *Blue Velvet*'s much-discussed opening sequence. The imagery walks a fine line between childhood wonder and adult nostalgia. The blindingly saturated colors and soft-focus images of iconic small-town American figures such as firemen and crossing guards gliding past carefully manicured lawns in graceful slow motion enchant viewers with an idealized vision of small-town life almost too wholesome to be taken seriously, a reactionary "Morning in America" fever dream. Lynch presents all the clichés about America as fact here: it is truly a shining city on a hill, a new Eden. The red roses and white picket fence juxtaposed against a blue sky in the first shot of this sequence encourage viewers to read the sequence as a celebration of "a privileged, prosperous nation [...] blessed by God."[22] However, as Irena Makarushka notes, the final moments of the sequence demonstrate that this Eden mirrors the old one all too well: a serpent lurks in the shadows. Beneath the shimmering surface of the world, wild things are poised to wreak havoc in the garden.[23]

If the sun seldom sets on the sunny side of Lumberton, the malevolent world across Lincoln Ave. knows only darkness. With looming factories, rundown apartments, crusty dive bars, and scores of shady characters, this part of Lumberton is no place for children. The creatures that prowl this terrain exist only to create "mischief of one kind and another," and Frank Booth (Dennis Hopper) is "the most wild thing of all."[24] The wild

FIGURE 2.1 The radiant storybook world of Lumberton. *Blue Velvet* directed by David Lynch © De Laurentiis Entertainment Group 1986. All rights reserved.

FIGURE 2.2 Red, white, and *Blue Velvet*. *Blue Velvet* directed by David Lynch ©
De Laurentiis Entertainment Group 1986. All rights reserved.

rumpus on display in *Blue Velvet*, however, is truly horrifying, a perversion
of joy. This is Lumberton through the looking glass, where light is dark,
affection is violence, and mirth is menace.

As coherent as these readings may be, these worlds are not as starkly
simple as these readings suggest. The difference Lynch and Sendak create
between the two worlds certainly motivates mistaking one world as more
"real" than the other; however, it is a misunderstanding nonetheless. Todd
McGowan convincingly argues that talking about *Blue Velvet*'s two worlds
in a real/imaginary binary makes a critical—and revealing—error. The
bright world of Lumberton is no more "the real world" than the depraved
Lumberton across Lincoln Ave. In fact, the utopic Lumberton of the opening
sequence of the film is the most intense fantasy on display in the film, one that
requires the dystopic fantasy of seedy Lumberton to reinforce it.[25] In fact,
these fantasies are mutually dependent. Just as Kansas functions to make Oz
a necessity, each fantasy in these works summons the other into existence.[26]
Lumberton promises a stability that it cannot deliver, which leaves one
dissatisfied and frustrated. Enter the nightmare of Dark Lumberton, which
explains the failure of the utopic fantasy by insisting the reason we do not
live in a utopia is not because the vision the utopia promises is impossible
but because evil forces are preventing our dreams from coming true.[27]

Likewise, the "real" world of Max's mother in *Where the Wild Things Are*
contains about as much reality as the land of the wild things. The artificial
qualities of the mother's world stand out most notably in the white frames
around the images. Sendak's choice to include varying amounts of white
space around the images calls attention to their status as compositions as
much as it bestows a sense of balance or order around them. It is interesting
to look at how this device, along with Max's white wolf suit, is racialized.
Scholars such as John Clement Ball see a colonizing logic at work in the
book's portrayal of an authority established by limiting and confining a

"wild" and less-than-human other.[28] The white space of the "real" world, combined with the jungle setting of the wild things, certainly lends validity to Ball's reading and gestures toward the extent to which this kind of order has been imposed on others throughout history. Lynch's Lumberton too is an almost exclusively white community in which all indicators of racial inequality—or even the existence of non-white people (note how one of the two characters of color in the film is also visually impaired)—have been placed outside its idealized, privileged 1950s frame. In fact, these framing devices work together to characterize the order on display as a limited perspective, a deliberate construction of a fantasy world that omits as much as it includes to achieve its utopic vision through violent exclusion and repression.

One cannot underestimate the influence the American sense of identity wields upon white American viewers of *Blue Velvet*. The key reason so many accept the bright world of Lumberton as "the real world" and not a fantasy is because its sense of reality overlaps exactly with mythical images of the American way of life, right down to the red roses, white fence, and blue sky.[29] The idealized moments in Lynch's film continually emphasize their unreality through the slow-motion photography of the opening, corny dialogue, or the bizarre mixture of the fashion and cars of different time periods.[30] The strife of American life has not disappeared: the American imaginary has simply relocated it on the other side of Lincoln Ave., where all the white fears of urban America fester and threaten to escape. However, as much as audiences may desire to separate the two worlds of *Where the Wild Things Are* and *Blue Velvet* in their minds, they cannot be separated; they not only depend on each other to function—they share a narrative structure.[31] We cannot detect this in reality, McGowan argues, because the way that they interact emphasizes their opposing qualities.[32] The project of *Blue Velvet* and *Where the Wild Things Are* is to make these worlds distinct so that the audience may discover their similarities to such an extent that separating them no longer becomes possible. Even though both stories end with the restoration of the order established at the beginning, it becomes clear to the audience that these opposing forces reside on the same street, in the same home.[33] They are, in effect, the same story.

Wild Nation

In the same way that dream and reality function as mutually reinforcing fantasies in *Blue Velvet* and *Where the Wild Things Are*, wild and tame are concepts that cannot exist independently. Jack Halberstam defines wildness in his book *Wild Things: The Disorder of Desire* as "a chaotic force of nature, the outside of categorization, unrestrained forms of embodiment, the refusal to submit to social regulation, loss of control, the unpredictable."[34]

The chaotic threat of the wild, its essential wildness, lies in the way that it "lays waste to oppositions that structure modern life."[35] Wildness, in effect, dissolves the binaries required for social organization, which explains why Halberstam's definition, with its resistance to fixed boundaries, is itself wild: this dissolution of borders constitutes an insurrection against the prevailing order, a grave threat which must be put down violently and with extreme prejudice.

Despite its reputation as a frontier paradise, America is no country for wild children. One need look no further for proof than children's literature, whose fantasy-based maturation plots perform a vital socializing function. The values expressed in these stories generally align with the society the child inhabits so that, through entertaining fantasy, the child receives social-emotional instruction necessary for a smooth entry into society. According to Golan Moskowitz, the notion of molding an innocent child to suit a country's values appears toward the end of the nineteenth century and can be roughly tracked in tandem with the rise of children's literature. This notion, fueled in large part by the desire among Americans for a "typical" and secure middle-class existence, only accelerates in twentieth-century America to become a tool of conformity normalizing the American way of life. The "normal" and socially well-adjusted American child becomes the symbol of the physical, emotional, and financial health of the family and nation that produced it. As a result, the culture comes to conceive of healthy American children as free individuals "suited to the public sphere and emotionally receptive to the nation's future goals."[36]

As Halberstam explains, wildness in *Where the Wild Things Are* (and in the greater social order) is characterized by violence. Not the violence of the wild thing, but the violence that excludes the wild thing from allegedly civilized society. Any discussion of wildness, therefore, doubles as a conversation about violence and the force employed to tame or exile wildness and the wild things that exhibit it.[37] Max's mischief carries some threats of minor violence in the sense that the book's first two images show him armed with a hammer and a fork, but this violence remains limited mostly to playful pretending. His mother's violence, on the other hand, is palpably real and carries with it consequences that are far from hypothetical. Her declaration that Max is a "WILD THING!" comes in all caps, and, after Max responds in kind with "I'LL EAT YOU UP!," she swiftly sends him to his room without dinner.[38] She only speaks these two words in the book, but both present readers with an entire world, one based upon a rigid sense of order. The words work in tandem. They distinguish Max's actions as wild, outside the boundaries of "social regulation." More importantly, however, her words show how, at least in her eyes, Max's actions strip him of his personhood and render him a "thing." Not a "wild boy" or "wild child," but a "WILD THING!" Her words also reveal her power to name, to distinguish human from beast, and her authority to provide or deny food as she sees fit. Thus, her violent reaction and severe punishment serve a twofold purpose: they aim to tame Max and shepherd him back to full personhood. By restoring him, she also restores the structure that stabilizes their life.

Blue Velvet also violently divides the world into the wild and the tame. Violence obviously governs Frank's world; however, the violence of sunny Lumberton is equally pernicious. Forceful taming is all over the town, from the aggressive control exerted upon each lawn to the efforts of law enforcement to ensure all wildness does not spill over to the "safe" parts of the city. Authority figures permeate the opening sequence that establishes the world as one of order: firemen, crossing guards, fathers, etc. Even the dividing street's name, Lincoln Ave., fuels associations with not only authority, law, and government but also sharp divides between good and evil that result in violent conflict. But there is also the softer violence steering the social order, the power that compels figures into conforming to societal roles and expectations. Most apparent here would be Jeffrey, whose entry into the adult and orderly world has ramifications beyond his own maturity: it immediately presses him into action as a civilizing force upon Dorothy. While I do not entirely agree with McGowan's reading of the film, we agree Blue Velvet depicts Jeffrey and Frank seeking to domesticate Dorothy.[39] Frank uses violent games to strip her of her family and identity until she becomes the passive maternal fetish object he desires. By delivering Dorothy from this wild fate, Jeffrey transforms himself into an errant knight who protects both the queen and the order she represents by slaying the dragon and rescuing her. By redirecting his violence from Dorothy to Frank, Jeffrey completes his initiation into the adult world and immediately becomes one of its chief representatives and enforcers, a model citizen.[40]

However, Sendak and Lynch seldom endorse the dichotomies they present. Rather, they employ the hierarchical ideologies represented by binaries to undercut them, "question[ing] the hierarchies of being that have been designed to mark and patrol the boundaries between the human and everything else."[41] The works repeatedly feature "scene[s] of unmaking" in which stable moments collapse to reveal the wildness within.[42] Both Max's attempts to construct the land of the wild things in his room and the camera's descent beneath the grass in Blue Velvet depict the placid order of the world unraveling. In these "scenes of unmaking," Lynch and Sendak depict wildness as a catalyst for growth rather than as a road to ruin. Although it may seem like a retreat from progress, Max and Jeffrey's rumpuses accomplish more than sowing wild oats: each gains a greater sense of self-awareness through direct confrontation with the wildest and darkest parts of themselves. As Halberstam notes, "only in the wild rumpus can monsters recognize each other," and both Blue Velvet and Where the Wild Things Are turn upon moments of recognition that interrupt the wild rumpus and direct it toward a final internal confrontation.[43] During their wild night out, Frank stops his car and turns to Jeffrey, hungrily takes a large huff from his tank as he gleefully looks deep into Jeffrey's eyes and says, with a hint of satisfaction and wonder, "You're like me." Jeffrey may initially reject Frank's assertion, but as he replays his violent encounter with Dorothy in his mind alongside Frank's abuse of her, their resemblance becomes undeniable. Jeffrey discovers who he is and what he is capable of and rejects it, making his development into a mature adult dependent upon the wild rumpus.

Max's moment of realization also rests upon the recognition of the antagonist within. At first, it seems that Max has found his tribe in the land of the wild things; however, recognizing himself in the wild things does not fill him with the same existential horror as Jeffrey's realization with Frank. The monstrous figure Max "recognizes" during the wild rumpus is not a figure of chaos but rather a figure of order: his mother. Consider the wild rumpus from a slightly different perspective. The wild things make Max their king, elevating him to a place of authority he does not enjoy at home. Embracing this authority requires him to discipline the wild things by calling a stop to the wild rumpus and sending the wild things to bed without their supper. In that act, he becomes his mother. Sendak does not spell this moment out beyond stating that "Max the king of all wild things was lonely and wanted to be where someone loved him best of all," but one can infer that his loneliness leads him to put himself in the shoes of his mother, who also feels lonely after disciplining her son.[44] This realization helps him to see "the challenging task of maintaining both social order and loving bonds in a chaotic context."[45] Max returns home because he wants to be loved, even though that environment places restrictions on his behavior that carry with them the threat of that love being denied him. The wild rumpus allows Max both to see the wild thing in himself from an outside perspective and to realize how alienating it can be to a caring authority figure. Rather than

FIGURE 2.3 Frank Booth, the most wild thing of all. *Blue Velvet* directed by David Lynch © De Laurentiis Entertainment Group 1986. All rights reserved.

having Max's mother turn to him and declare, "You're like me," it is Max who looks to his mother and admits to himself "I'm like you." Instead of being horrifying, this admission proves to be enriching. Through these encounters, Jeffrey and Max learn that wildness is not as wild as it seems: the wild is still a place with hierarchies and rules, "equal parts freedom and constraint."[46]

While the tame and the violent forces that maintain it certainly come under scrutiny in both works, this is not to suggest that Sendak and Lynch valorize the wild. The wild is in fact violent, frightening, and overwhelming in both *Blue Velvet* and *Where the Wild Things Are*. It is not a state or identity to aspire to but rather a site of "ruination, destitution, anarchy, and despair."[47] Sendak and Lynch separate wild from tame to demonstrate how the notion that one can be weeded out from the other by force constitutes yet another fantasy. Watching texts that confront the wild things without and within allows audiences to better apprehend the world that requires their expulsion.[48] Halberstam outlines the choice before Max, Jeffrey, and the audience quite well:

> [E]ither you settle in to the domestic prison you have been offered or you set sail for another, potentially more violent, terrain. The wild here is not a place and not an identity; it is neither sanctuary nor utopia. The wild is not heaven, hell, or anything in between; the wild is the space that the child and adult share in their antipathy to one another. The wild is entropic, cruel, and violent.[49]

The wildness performs a cathartic function by enticing and entertaining the audience while suggesting such wildness needs to be tamed, contained within the confines of fiction. This point explains why wildness is so prominent in children's literature: it instructs children on the types of repression they need to enact to be accepted into society as full citizens. However instructive such material may be, its instruction undermines the very boundaries it is meant to erect and enforce by showing how such boundaries are arbitrary and propped up by violence and denial.

Resisting Closure

Are the wild things truly defeated at the end of these works? Do the protagonists really learn to put wildness behind them? It is certainly tempting (and comforting) to think so, and while the resolutions to both works give audiences a decent amount of evidence to support claims that the forces of order and good have come out victorious, there are just as many pieces of evidence that suggest a more tenuous state of affairs. Formal analysis of the endings to *Where the Wild Things Are* and *Blue Velvet* shows how Sendak and Lynch resist tidy resolutions in favor of a more complex presentation of the relationship between wildness and order, one that subverts the traditional models of closure found in children's literature toward more unsettling ends.

Perhaps first it is best to look at the evidence that shows these characters taming themselves. In *Where the Wild Things Are*, rather than explode in a violent rage, Max channels his aggression into a fantasy in which he projects his anger onto a group of monstrous creatures whom he pacifies with stern language. These actions allow him to return to reality, with a twist: he finds himself welcomed back to the place where the tame things are and rewarded with hot food for sublimating his rage.[50] Most tellingly, the final image of Max shows him in the process of removing his white wolf suit, revealing his hair for the first time. This removal at the end suggests that Max is ready to stop being a wild thing and start being his mother's son, regaining his humanity along with her approval and love. In *Blue Velvet*, Jeffrey orchestrates a scenario that takes him back to the place where he discovered the wild thing in himself, Dorothy's closet, only instead of spying on Dorothy and Frank, he shoots Frank and rescues Dorothy and her son from his evil clutches. He returns to his normal life assured that the wild things have been exiled and he can become the person he always dreamed of being, only wiser. In the final scene, Jeffrey wakes up from a nap to hear Sandy tell him his lunch is waiting for him. Dorothy plays at a playground with her son and Jeffrey and Sandy look at a robin perched on a branch, a beetle writhing in its beak. The dream Sandy described to Jeffrey earlier in the film has now become prophecy: the robins have come, the trouble is over. Jeffrey and Sandy become full members of society and Dorothy sees her position as mother restored.

Both texts end with the kind of return to reality commonly found in the happily ever afters of children's literature. According to Gilead, these returns to reality take three forms. The first type, such as *The Wizard of Oz*, positions the return as the completion of growth that "neutralizes antisocial impulses" presented by fantasy and puts it in its proper place, as a site "where the wild things *were*" that is now stripped of its "anarchic, escapist energies."[51] In the second type, exemplified by Carroll's *Alice* books, the return rejects of fantasy's subversive potential without the logical progression of the first type, leaving the two forces in "an uneasy equilibrium." Finally, the third type, such as the ending of *Peter Pan*, does neither, making the meaning of the return to reality ambiguous, even tragic, because "the seductive force and dangerous potentiality of fantasy" remain.[52] A feeling of loss looms over this third type of return because without any playfulness to lighten the tone, the resolution's meaning lacks any legible set of cultural codes or ideologies, making it more difficult to discern.[53] These more ambiguous returns resolve little because they tend to provoke more questions than provide answers, making the resolutions anything but tidy.[54] Within this return, the ending, generally assumed to be a place where audiences can begin to "relax [their] interpretive energy," suddenly becomes the most demanding moment.

Where the Wild Things Are and Blue Velvet engage with these frames in more subversive ways than the aforementioned surface readings of their endings allow. Gilead reads the resolution to Where the Wild Things Are as an example of the first type in which Max overcomes his "antisocial impulses," and it would appear that, at least structurally, Blue Velvet follows suit. However, I argue that these texts' endings function as intriguing examples of the third type because each contains enough ambiguity about the nature of reality and the nature of wildness to suggest that, although ultimately dangerous and unsatisfying, the allure of wildness and fantasy remain ever-present, irresistible, untamable forces.

The resolution to Where the Wild Things Are ought to be open-and-shut: Max comes home. Max takes off the wolf suit. The wildness has been cast out. The end. However, such a reading fails to see the full picture, and I mean that literally. As discussed earlier, the reality Sendak establishes at the beginning of the book is framed by white space that shrinks as the wildness takes over. For things to have truly returned to normal, the white border would have to return as well, and the image would have to shrink to the size seen on the first page. Yet the final image of the book takes up the full page. Further, the night sky seen outside Max's window is much clearer than when he first entered the room, and we can see as many stars outside as we could when the room became a forest. We have not come full circle at the end. Max's fantasy has altered the size of his mother's world, making it larger and clearer than the one he left. Therefore, whether the wolf suit is on or off, Max has brought some of the wildness—and the knowledge that attended it—back to reality. The readings that see a complete victory for the forces of tameness indulge in a certain degree of wishful thinking governed as much by the demands of fantasy as the practical nature of reality. Even the piece of evidence that seems the most ironclad, the removal of the wolf suit, reveals itself to be motivated as much by wish as it is by logic. The ending gives the reader little guarantee that Max will not don the wolf suit again (or that he even completely removes it). Nearly all the indicators of wildness remain just as present at the end as they do at the beginning, if not more so. The fantasies do not cast out the wild things because wild things cannot be cast out by something as simple as a stern command or a threatening stare. Rather, one must become adept at negotiating between fantasy and reality, wildness and tameness, forever. Max does not so much grow out of his wild impulses as he learns how to mediate the clashing realities both within and without him, showing children how maturing involves accepting their "serious, burdensome positions as mediators between conflicting social and personal realities."[55] The place where the wild things are is the same place the wild things have always been: everywhere.

The ending to *Blue Velvet* has the promise to be an even more unqualified triumph than the ending of *Where the Wild Things Are*. Scholars such as James Lindroth read the optimism of the final sequence as Lynch backing down from the subversive potential of his work in favor of "a classical closure."[56] Jeffrey's return to the sunny side of Lumberton and the more normative relationship with Sandy does appear to represent a maturation or "waking up" from the dream of childhood; however, just like the opening sequence, these tropes are presented as just that: tropes, archetypes that audiences can easily recognize and affiliate with the scores of similar resolutions they have seen. This familiar material grants Lynch access to the audience's "unconscious terrains" so that he can destabilize and defamiliarize them via a resolution so excessively positive that it calls these archetypes into question.

The subversive nature of the ending comes into focus through Lynch's juxtaposition of sound and image. The film returns to the dreamlike intensity of its opening sequence with dazzlingly saturated colors and the soaring strains of Julee Cruise's dreamy "Mysteries of Love." Every character smiles broadly and offers wincingly sincere expository statements such as when Jeffrey's father says that he is feeling much better or when Jeffrey says "Maybe the robins are here" as he and Sandy stare at the robin on the windowsill. The film could not be any more explicit in asserting that everything is perfect now. However, this fairy tale ending feels incongruous with what the characters and the viewers have been through. The tonal shift rings false and unearned, and here the ambiguity of Gilead's third return to reality sets in. In his overcommitment to the happy ending, Lynch instructs the viewer to doubt the reality of what they see and read this reality instead as fantasy.

After all, the film has never presented viewers with a reality to return to: all it has offered are opposite and mutually reinforcing fantasies. This

FIGURE 2.4 The robins come to stop the wild rumpus. *Blue Velvet* directed by David Lynch © De Laurentiis Entertainment Group 1986. All rights reserved.

ending depicts less a "return-to-reality" than what McGowan calls a "restoration of the idealized fantasy."[57] This ending offers pure Reaganite wish fulfillment: if we can rid the world of "people life Frank," then there truly will be no "trouble in this world" and the dream of the opening to the film can be reality. However, as Coughlin notes, the previous events in the film "unequivocally stain" the fantasy of Lumberton to such a degree that it becomes an unsustainable "impossible" charade as phony as it is alluring.[58] After we see the robin with the captured beetle, Lynch cuts to familiar images from the opening sequence: the yellow tulips, the waving fireman, and the red roses. Now, however, they unfold in reverse order, enlarged and at a slower speed. This alteration constitutes less coming-full-circle than an unwinding, an unmaking of the fantasy.

But this excessive sincerity represents only the start of the unraveling. After we return to the images from the opening sequence, the film cuts to a slow-motion shot of Dorothy watching her son play in a park. Every loose end appears to be tied up in a lovely Main Street, USA bow. However, as Dorothy clutches him to her chest and fully embraces a normative vision of femininity, she opens her eyes and looks around her fearfully, as though disturbed by the unreality of her surroundings. A reprise of Isabella Rossellini's performance of "Blue Velvet" submerged in echo returns the soundtrack, casting darkness and fear across the triumphant sequence. With this one music cue, Lynch completes the unmaking of Lumberton's American dreamscape and subverts the return-to-reality framing most thoroughly, nullifying the optimism of Sandy's robins monologue and characterizing the happy ending as nothing more than an unstable dream. There is trouble until the robins come, and there will be trouble after the robins come. The robins and the beetles are part of the same fantasy. The final pages of *Where the Wild Things Are* also suggest these ideas; however, Lynch is able to extend Sendak's work because, as a filmmaker, he has more tools at his disposal than Sendak does as a

FIGURE 2.5 "Blue Velvet" returns. *Blue Velvet* directed by David Lynch © De Laurentiis Entertainment Group 1986. All rights reserved.

writer and illustrator. Where Sendak has only images and words, Lynch has the return of "Blue Velvet" to the soundtrack.

As much as *Blue Velvet*'s ending may constitute an ironic reversal, it is important to note that this is not a smirking ironic ending but another instance of Lynch's "sincerity-in-irony." The film still carries within it the wish that this dream would come true, but the final music cue of the film declares it an impossible one. As powerful as the imagery of the ending may be, Janet L. Preston argues that the earlier, darker elements of the film are powerful enough to overwhelm it. We may want to believe that the robin's arrival signals the end of evil in Lumberton, but the film has made clear that "evil does hide in the human soul; depravity is a condition of life in this world; and the irrational lurks within the ordinary."[59] To believe otherwise is to believe in a fantasy. Lynch includes this dreamlike ending so we can recognize this fantasy of the idealized American life *as* fantasy, "a mere sham [that] cannot be fully restored" and see the degree to which Americans live inside a dream that they mistake for reality.[60] In engaging with a genre as dedicated to clear and tidy resolutions such as children's literature, the irrationality of Lynch's ending serves as "the greatest crime" against closure.[61] Where the closing moments of the film should be saying "and they all lived happily ever after," it instead whispers "let the wild rumpus start!"

The Return to Fantasy

By returning to the imagery of the opening sequence, Lynch shows the desire of everyone to retreat into fantasy, for the awakened dreamer to go back to sleep. Jeffrey indeed has an up-close-and-personal encounter with evil and overcomes it; however, like Max at the end of *Where the Wild Things Are*, he "returns faithfully to his bed and to the good old house full of familiar objects."[62] Jeffrey does not seem intent on ushering in a new, more mature age in which he confronts reality directly. Instead, he reclines in the reveries of the dream world he stands to inherit. Even Lynch downplays the amount of growth Jeffrey experiences, calling what we see in the film only "a partial portrait" of Jeffrey that fails to capture the full extent of his thoughts, suggesting there may be darker depths to Jeffrey's psyche the film dares not plumb. His summary of Jeffrey's arc is so basic as to undermine it entirely: "he had an experience and he gleaned some stuff from it."[63] Lynch's comments underscore how Jeffrey is not as well-adjusted at the end as narrative logic may demand that he be, and the ending makes it appear that Jeffrey's maturation has been less into the reality of the adult world than citizenship in America's repressive fantasy. Further, this experience does not alter the world of Lumberton. The town continues to be the same dreamy fantasy of a postwar American small town it has always been. Just like Lumberton, there is so much more roiling beneath the surface of Jeffrey than what the film shows. He has "gleaned" a sense of just how much there is within him, but he does not investigate deeper. Instead, he closes the case, mistaking killing Frank with putting his own wildness to rest.

Lynch's juxtaposition of the iconography of America with disturbingly violent content throughout *Blue Velvet* interrogates the difference between American symbols and the real America they purport to represent. As Makarushka argues, *Blue Velvet* demonstrates the danger in mistaking the storybook images of America for the American reality and the violence inherent in forcing a population to live inside this fantasy.[64] The ending of the film does not resolve this dilemma. Jeffrey may wake up in the final scene of the film, but the ending suggests that he and the rest of Lumberton's populace remain asleep, citizens of the American Dreamscape. However, the return of "Blue Velvet" suggests that this restoration is far weaker than the images would have us believe. With the so-called wildness allegedly put down, *Blue Velvet* leaves us with only the unsatisfying fantasy and the suggestion that the social order around us is but "a mere frame around a more exciting and variable realm."[65] The final strains of "Blue Velvet" announce that audiences have one more dream to wake up from.[66]

In their rushed and too-pat endings, *Where the Wild Things Are* and *Blue Velvet* present resolutions that border on numbing, and the brisk nature of their presentation offers audiences a deliberately unsatisfying sense of reassurance that drives the audience to doubt the stability of reality itself and instead view the so-called normal world as the most escapist fantasy of all, and the more threatening. Closure never quite arrives; each terminal point of inquiry only opens other paths to explore. This can make for a perplexing or frustrating experience; however, this perpetual unmaking testifies to the vital sense of wildness at play in *Where the Wild Things Are* and *Blue Velvet*. All is not revealed in the end. Rather, their endings suggest that things will always lurk "beyond the grasp of language or conscious thought."[67] Depths even darker are more than merely suggested: the stories all but guarantee their return. For all the unveiling, for all the digging and clawing through the idyllic veneer, these works conclude with an even greater irony: the "unnerving impression" that this traumatic digging represents little more than "scratching the bright, shiny surface."[68] In this way, the works not only remain wild but employ wildness as a method, an ethos, a way of navigating the American Dreamscape with eyes wide open.

3

Lonelyhearts and Locusts in the Dream Dump

Cruising *Mulholland Drive* with Nathanael West

When *Mulholland Drive* premiered in 2001, critics were quick to note its tonal and stylistic similarities to Nathanael West's 1939 novel *The Day of the Locust*; however, none has traced out this connection at length, even though Lynch himself stated in an interview that he loved West's book.[1] Perhaps no one pursued this thematic lead because viewing Hollywood as "capital of corrupt, twisted fantasy" has become so old hat that one need not even mention it; repetition and overuse have made such a view a starting point for examinations of "the Industry," and as a result West's apocalyptic vision of Hollywood has lost much of the acerbic power or novelty it once possessed.[2] Even though West's critique may be so widely accepted as to make a passing reference to *Locust* seem like sufficient commentary, there exists a much deeper connection between West and Lynch beyond the generic depiction of Hollywood-as-dystopia. In fact, an intertextual reading of *Mulholland Drive* that traces the affiliating identifications between it and West's work reveals *Mulholland Drive* to be the fullest cinematic realization of West's fictional project.

Although *Day of the Locust* and its setting on the margins of the film industry stand as the most obvious touchstone for Lynch's film, the parallels between *Mulholland Drive* and West's earlier novels *The Dream Life of Balso Snell* and *A Cool Million* are even more striking. I agree with Jonathan Veitch that West, and by extension Lynch, regards Hollywood not as the disease but a symptom of a larger sickness "rooted in the cultural contradictions of advanced capitalism itself."[3] Both West and Lynch cast their net wider than Hollywood itself to focus on larger systems and institutions through their emphasis on the complicity of audiences in exploitative cycles of deception. Hollywood is "the capital of the corrupt, twisted fantasy" that is the American imagination, a factory that manufactures and sells dreams to millions; however, these two artists go even further to unmask the supreme American fantasy masquerading as the truth: the guarantee that one's dreams can become real if one only dreams big enough.

The prominence of dreams in David Lynch's films hardly needs to be established, but what is less obvious is the prominent place dreams occupy in the novels of Nathanael West even though none of his books contains a dream sequence with chipmunk-cheeked ladies doing song and dance numbers in radiators. West's first novel *The Dream Life of Balso Snell* certainly has roots in surrealism and dadaism, and Rita Barnard argues that all of West's work is heavily invested in what she calls "collective wishing and the social production of desire in an era of mass-mediated culture."[4] Others, such as Mathew Roberts, read West alongside Adorno's critiques of the culture industry, illustrating how Hollywood uses the irresistible-but-empty promise of wealth, fame, and eternal happiness as a means of controlling consumers.[5]

Miss Lonelyhearts, West's second novel, contains the best articulation of this sensibility. As the titular advice columnist looks at the abject people on the street with "broken hands and torn mouths" stumbling into movie theaters and fishing romance magazines out of the trash, he remarks that "[m]en have always fought their misery with dreams. Although dreams were once powerful, they have been made puerile by the movies, radio and newspapers. Among many betrayals, this one is the worst."[6] In reducing dreams to their lowest common denominator, an (allegedly) inherent requirement of mass communication, wholesome dreams become tawdry and tarnished to such a degree that West's narrator can only describe them as treachery. West's and Lynch's works frame this betrayal in a tight closeup with hard light and no glamour filters to show how it both practically and psychologically enchants and then destroys the miserable people who believe that they can wish their way to a better life.

In *Mulholland Drive* and West's novels, Hollywood has a dual identity, one John Springer describes as both "promised land" and "wasteland."[7] These categories render Hollywood as a terminal point in two senses: a place of fulfillment and realization and a place of ending and apocalypse. (Its location on the edge of a continent makes it triply terminal.) Mass media opts for the Promised Land image and presents Hollywood to the world as the modern paradise flowing with milk and honey. However, this act makes it also a land "littered with [these] unkept promises" that pile up alongside shinier, newer promises until "the presumably stable categories of fact and fantasy soften and melt into one another" and one can no longer distinguish real from reel.[8] This dual nature, therefore, offers the dream and violates the dream simultaneously until the violation becomes indistinguishable from the promise it violates. West and Lynch stake their claim in this liminal territory between fulfillment and abjection to show how Hollywood stands as the final destination not only for an individual or an industry but for a nation. As the major exporter of fraudulent dreams, Hollywood simply becomes a stand-in for larger betrayals and emptier promises that define the ultimate Promised Land and Waste Land: the United States itself.

West's first novel, *The Dream Life of Balso Snell*, distills "promised land" and "wasteland" into two useful symbols that he returns to implicitly throughout his subsequent work: the Trojan Horse and the *phoenix excrementi*. The former is the gift horse of Homer that promises peaceful bounty; the latter are residents of a wasteland devoted to the industrial reproduction of waste, a "race of men [who] eat themselves, digest themselves, and give birth to themselves by evacuating their bowels."[9] Together these two symbols encapsulate the cycle of imagination, deception, consumption, elimination, and regeneration that defines the Hollywood of *Day of the Locust* and *Mulholland Drive*. In West's and Lynch's fables of creative and romantic failure, the dreams (and bodies) of wide-eyed newcomers voyage to the Promised Land of Hollywood to receive the gifts that allegedly await them there, only for them to suffer a humiliating defeat that transforms them into the fertilizer that spawns the next batch of starry-eyed ingenues traveling to Hollywood convinced that their dreams will come true. As caustic as their critique of the Hollywood system may be, the film industry is but a symbol to West and Lynch, a stand-in for the ultimate Trojan Horse, the capitalist dreamland of the United States itself. Further, West's and Lynch's visions reveal how the audience's consumption of this abject spectacle renders them complicit in a capitalist cycle fueled by the destructive deferral of dreams.

All the Pretty Horses

The Trojan Horse towers over other symbols as the ultimate distortion of reality where menace poses as munificence, malicious reality masquerades as benevolent fantasy. Both West and Lynch choose Los Angeles as the location for their masterpieces reimaging the Trojan Horse to show the promised land's reality to be as arid and empty as its appearance is lush and full, a mirage on the edge of the desert. While critics often characterize Los Angeles as a place without any real attachment to history, Dennis Lim argues instead that Los Angeles does not ignore history but rather "encourages the conflation of history and myth," making it the ultimate locale for a remake of the siege of Troy because it too acts as a gift horse that lures its victims with promises of perfect happiness, only to destroy them by revealing the gift to be nothing more than a beautiful illusion.[10] According to Erik D. Curren, being rich and famous is not the true appeal of Los Angeles but rather the chance to participate in a fantasy, to become part of the Trojan Horse by playing a supporting role in the grand illusion.[11] Curren's point illustrates how the Trojan Horse may represent a deception that destroys, but West and Lynch also reveal it to be a deception that inspires the next dream to rise like a Phoenix from the rubble, ready to construct the next Trojan Horse.

Lynch and West shine the spotlight on Tinseltown's artifice in a manner that detests the lie as much as it admires the lie's beauty and effectiveness. *Day of the Locust* shows how the Trojan Horse's illusion is so total that it can even conceal its flaws from those constructing it. In the novel, set designer Tod Hackett visits a soundstage engaged in recreating the battle of Waterloo. As the crew begins another take, Tod watches as "the thickness of the cannon smoke" prevents the performers from noticing that crew members are still finishing the hill they are to charge and the raised set collapses, sending the cast crashing to the ground.[12] The moment presents the Trojan Horse in miniature: The façade and artifice of the scene were so strong that they obscure the dangerous reality and lure a crowd to a tragic fate. Put another way, reality cannot support the dreams it is tasked with propping up, not on the Waterloo set and not in the minds of hopefuls such as Hackett, *Mulholland Drive*'s Diane Selwyn, *A Cool Million*'s Lem Pitkin, or the supplicants of Miss Lonelyhearts. The grandeur generated by the dream factory's smoke obscures their vision until it is too late.

Both West and Lynch are highly attuned to the "pleasures and risks of believing in an illusion," though West arguably does not find the pleasures as pleasurable as Lynch.[13] West devotes a great deal of attention to pointing out the chaotic assemblage of ersatz styles, materials, and media in his fiction. The opening image of *Day of the Locust* depicts French and English armies marching along a Hollywood backlot, but the masquerade does not stop at the studio gates. Even the people on the street with "'platinum' hair" and dressed in Tyrolean hats and "sports clothes which were not really sports clothes" present false fronts to the world.[14] When these people go home, the homes, with their clashing styles from throughout space and time, play their role as actors in the main attraction. Consider this description of Homer Simpson's house in *Day of the Locust*:

> The house was queer. [...] This door was of gumwood painted like fumed oak and it hung on enormous hinges. Although made by machine, the hinges had been carefully stamped to appear hand-forged. The same kind of care and skill had been used to make the roof thatching, which was not really straw but heavy fireproof paper colored and ribbed to look like straw.[15]

The entire neighborhood exists in scare quotes, from the "gumwood painted like fumed oak" to the hinges that "appear hand-forged" and the straw thatching that "was not really straw": West describes Simpson's home as "'Irish'" in a block of "'Spanish'" cottages. Not to worry, though, because the interior of Simpson's home is also decorated in the "'Spanish'" style, in which "some of the plants were made of rubber and cork; others were real."[16] So much artifice exists that the narrator must take pains to note when something authentic appears, a move that indicates either a heightened form of realism or something far removed from it.

Not even the deepest human emotions are immune to inauthenticity and triviality in West. The heartfelt words of the lonely suffering masses who pour their hearts out to Miss Lonelyhearts are perceived as possessing all the originality of an assembly-line product "stamped from the dough of suffering with a heart-shaped cookie knife."[17] Even when Miss Lonelyhearts, overcome by the enormity of human suffering and humanity's cynical disregard of it, attempts to reach out to those around him with a genuine message about love and suffering, all he can manage is "a stage scream."[18] Artifice's victory, it appears, is total, invading the real world and laying waste to it so completely so as to have conquered even the interior of the cookie-cutter human heart.

As much as West's prose seethes at the pervasiveness of artifice, it also marvels at the labor and effort required for everything to continually be passing itself off as something else. Like Tod Hackett's massive painting *The Burning of Los Angeles*, West's fiction shows the ways in which the world conceals the horrors and emptiness of existence in a pleasing artificial package. His 1934 novel *A Cool Million* functions as a full-length depiction of the labor and maintenance required to keep the Trojan Horse functioning. Each brutal setback Lem Pitkin makes is met with an inspirational monologue encouraging him to deny the reality in front of him and persist in his dream because "America is still a young country" where "shipping clerks are still becoming presidents of railroads."[19] Pitkin's denial of reality may inspire him but it hardly benefits him, as each renewal of faith in the American Dream leads to further injury for him (and greater profit for others).

For West, believing in the illusion actualizes tragedy, whereas for Lynch, the illusion remains beautiful, even though it begets tragedy. From the moment Betty (Naomi Watts) arrives in Los Angeles, Lynch presents a Trojan Horse to the audience as Los Angeles opens its arms to her. Everything about her arrival in town is overly corny at best, too good to be true at worst. Strangers eagerly buy into her dreams without a dose of skepticism, and even the cab driver goes out of his way to load her bags into his cab before she even has to hail one. Lynch and cinematographer Peter Deming bathe LAX in a low-contrast angelic glow, rendering the city as a dazzling, frictionless glide toward a bright future. The tone of the sequence reeks of

Old Hollywood musicals, tipping viewers off to the fact that this scenario strains credulity; however, audiences stick with the film because the images, along with Angelo Badalamenti's soaring score, encourage them to let down their guard and embrace the fantasy despite their better judgment. Like Betty, they pounce upon any reason to believe the dream is real.

The most rapturous moments in *Mulholland Drive* are frequently the ones that foreground artificiality and deception. Many of these moments involve performances, especially auditions. Adam Kesher's (Justin Theroux) meeting with the mysterious financiers, Camilla Rhodes's (Melissa George) audition for *The Sylvia North Story*, Betty's audition, and Club Silencio all contain aspects of performance and artificiality. Auditions are a special type of performance that, while provisional or demonstrative in nature, contain elements of promise and artifice: one person (the auditioner) presents themselves and their talents to another (the director) to convince them that they are the person the director is dreaming of, assuring them that, when it comes time for the "real" performance, they will deliver the best version of it. Camilla Rhodes's audition scene and Club Silencio are foils of each other in which artifice and truth intersect in unexpected ways. Each takes artifice as its starting place—lip synching in this case—and shows how the truth is smuggled past us as we are deceived into mis-embodying a singing voice. In the case of Camilla Rhodes, the peppy singing voice proves to be a poor match for Camilla's wooden, almost terrified stage presence. She enters as if in a trance and then springs to life as though powered remotely, creating an eerie, menacing tone to the audition. Within the context of the plot, this mysterious figure represents a Trojan Horse for director Adam Kesher. She may appear to be just another young ingenue, but her pretty face

FIGURE 3.1 Camilla Rhodes auditions. *Mulholland Drive* directed by David Lynch © Universal Pictures 2001. All rights reserved.

conceals the dark roots of power controlling the film industry, and refusing her threatens to raze his career to the ground. She is a gift horse he must accept, meaning that he must accept the artifice that goes along with it and become a willing participant in the deception. If he wants his dream to come true, he must participate in the fantasy that "This is the girl."

The performance in Club Silencio, on the other hand, fools the audience into thinking that Rebekah Del Rio delivers a live Spanish-language rendition of Roy Orbison's "Crying." Her bold voice reverberates throughout the club and her eyes well with tears as her voice quivers. But the performance, like the glittery teardrops on her face, is an expertly executed piece of dramatic stagecraft only revealed when Del Rio, overcome with emotion, collapses to the ground as the tape recording of her voice continues to blare over the loudspeakers. The rupture bewilders the audience and destabilizes their relationship to the scene as the emotional rug they thought they were standing on proves to be suspended in mid-air, leaving them as lost and disoriented as the characters. Perhaps "fools" is not the proper word for this bit of deception because the club does not engage in any deception at all. Quite the contrary: the emcee (Geno Silva) clearly announces, complete with a demonstration, that the performance is only a tape recording. The audience has been told that they are about to receive a gift horse. Yet this moment is where Lynch demonstrates that, for him, the artifice remains impossibly alluring and irresistible. Even when in full possession of one's better judgment, one cannot help but be seduced by the dream.

Despite the inauthenticity of the scenario, Del Rio's pantomime becomes a vessel for authentic emotion—not hers, but the audience's. Her performance may be totally fake and the audience may be made overwhelmingly aware

FIGURE 3.2 Rebekah Del Rio's artificial performance. *Mulholland Drive* directed by David Lynch © Universal Pictures 2001. All rights reserved.

FIGURE 3.3 "There is no band!" *Mulholland Drive* directed by David Lynch ©
Universal Pictures 2001. All rights reserved.

of that fact the moment before she takes the stage, but the audience feels
something real nevertheless. In this way, Lynch's scene is a Trojan Horse in
reverse: it promises to be fake, and that is a lie. This Trojan Horse storms
the audience with something real, the very thing it said it would not deliver.
We see a similar dynamic at play in Betty's audition scene, where Betty leans
on the power of fakery to magically transform a trite, stilted scene into
high drama, leaving both the seasoned pros in the room and the audience
wondering where her performance came from and just how much of it is
real. In all of these examples, Lynch revels in the ambiguity that comes
not only from blurring the lines between the real and the fake but also by
simultaneously embracing and mocking cliché and artifice.

While the form of West's fiction and Lynch's film presents potent images
of the deception of the Trojan Horse, their strongest representations of
promise and betrayal come in the form of their characters. *A Cool Million*'s
protagonist Lem Pitkin and *Mulholland Drive*'s Betty represent "seeker[s] in
the country's ultimate frontier," classic rubes won over by Algeresque fairy
tales and inspirational posters the same way that the Trojans are fooled by
the horse.[20] Both are naive, wide-eyed idealists attempting to actualize their
dreams through sheer force of will, only to be taken apart and reassembled
as puppets of the system they yearn to join.[21] West and Lynch depict how
such rubes are the fuel that American capital runs upon the same way
someone who runs a Ponzi scheme needs fresh marks. In *A Cool Million*,
Mr. Whipple, an ex-president given to delivering cliché-ridden speeches
about the greatness of America, decrees to Pitkin that "America is the land
of opportunity. She takes care of the honest and industrious and never fails

them as long as they are both. This is not so much a matter of opinion, it is one of faith. On that day that Americans stop believing it, on that day will America be lost."[22] Quite clearly and explicitly, West shows how America runs on belief, on the mass participation in a fantasy dependent upon an unwavering faith in perpetually deferred promises. Pitkin is one of those true believers who is inspired by these words "just as similar ones have heartened the youth of this country ever since it was freed from the irksome British yoke."[23] It is Theodore Dreiser rewritten by Walt Disney.

The broad and brutal satire of *A Cool Million* demonstrates the persistence of this toxic American vision. As Lem Pitkin has all his teeth pulled and is imprisoned, characters reassure him that his big break awaits just around the corner, and they always come ready with a story of how someone just like him, or even worse off than him, made it big: "I read the other day about a man who lost both of his eyes yet accumulated a fortune." West shows the hollow nature of these inspirational stories by having the character, coincidentally named Betty, add "I forget how, but he did."[24] The dream does not even require specific details or evidence to persist. No matter how paper-thin the narrative is, its pull remains irresistible for the faithful like Pitkin, whose belief in the promises of America leads him down many a perilous path, costing him his money, his freedom, his teeth, his eye, his scalp, and some of his limbs, all because he refuses to lose his unwavering faith. Pitkin's suffering and death at a theatrical political rally become transformed into art by the audience who witnessed his abjection, and his quest becomes framed not as a hopeless fantasy he was conned into pursuing, but as being "in the honorable tradition of his country and its people."[25] Rather than being an example of the faulty promises of the American imagination, he becomes elevated as a sustainer of the very myth that kills him. The novel ends with Mr. Whipple standing over Pitkin's dead body and declaring him a martyr for the American Dream: "although dead, yet he speaks [...] of the right of every American boy to go into the world and there receive fair play and a chance to make his fortune by industry and probity without being laughed at or conspired against."[26] The rest, it seems, is not Silencio but rather a resurrection of the same dream that duped and destroyed Lem Pitkin. In short, the Trojan Horse swallows him whole and moves on in search of its next city to raze.

As broad as Pitkin's characterization may be, even he is not as abstracted a character as *Mulholland Drive*'s Betty Elms. Calling her an archetype almost seems generous. Betty lacks any characteristics that could be considered three-dimensional characterization; the only backstory Lynch gives her is that she won a jitterbug contest in Deep River, Ontario, and has an aunt living in Los Angeles who has some connections in the industry. Instead, she enters the story with all the innocence and naiveté of a newborn baby, complete with a wide-eyed fascination with everything that happens to her, all of which seems to be occurring for the first time. Will Scheibel argues that removing Betty's character from geography and history makes her a representation of "the myth of the city" of Los Angeles.[27] The city of Los Angeles, of course, is seldom the glowing, frictionless glide that Betty experiences when she arrives. Instead, as the film shows, the mythic veneer is a pleasant presentation of a nefarious reality; the city is a conspiratorial maze presided over by seedy characters who hold cryptic deliberations in dark rooms that determine success and failure, life and death for everyone basking in the sun's temperate glow.

The city is not the only bright beautiful Trojan Horse obscuring a harrowing reality, though: Betty acts as a Trojan Horse herself. Her story is a bright package containing the story of Diane Selwyn, a failed ingenue whose theatrical and romantic aspirations have been laid waste by the vagaries of the film industry. To cope with rejection from both Camilla Rhodes and Hollywood, she retreats into a fantasy in which all her dreams come true. For Martha Nochimson, the two are essentially so intertwined as to be indistinguishable from each other. Hollywood's Trojan Horse in *Mulholland Drive* presents itself to the industry professionals and the viewers alike in the form of the female performer because the industry "hinges on the exploitation of this disposable figure." Diane Selwyn's rotting corpse represents "the axle of disintegration," the sickening and deadly interior of the Trojan Horse that is Betty.[28] Sadly, Diane's dream strains credulity and, like the Waterloo set in *Day of the Locust*, cannot sustain the weight of its own illusion. As a result, her vision of success in Hollywood frequently reads as a parody of the rags-to-riches narrative, as though her failure to make it as an actress only illuminates for her the folly of her dream, proving that it cannot sustain itself even if it remains in the realm of fantasy. Betty's body stands as a symbol of Hollywood as the Promised Land, Diane's a Wasteland that also represents the disguised rot at the heart of the film industry.[29] Diane's reinterpretation of her dream as parody echoes M. A. Klug's reading of artistic failure in West's fiction, where the self-conscious artist either succumbs to ironic mockery as a means to express their deepest emotions or unlocks deeper creative energy through surrendering completely to an irrationality that would result in destructive madness.[30] In *Mulholland Drive* and *Day of the Locust*, the protagonists somehow manage to pursue both methods, fashioning their own creative, mental, and physical apocalypses.

Like the Waterloo set in *Day of the Locust*, the promises of American capitalism cannot bear the burden of those who wish to use it as a foundation for their dreams, and the failure of that system takes them all down. Todd McGowan's reading of *Mulholland Drive* in his article "Accumulation and Enjoyment" shows how capitalism may be the biggest Trojan Horse of all because, like the Horse, it "conceives of enjoyment in terms of the promise," on the guarantee that there is more pleasure ahead—or, in the case of the Trojan Horse, inside—and this promise causes things to happen.[31] "This is the girl" is the promise that, once uttered, irrevocably sets events in motion, making one star rise and the other fall. That girl who eventually appears on the screen becomes a Trojan Horse to the audience because in her excessive fullness on the big screen, she promises them that their fantasies are possible and available, theirs for the taking. Aspiring starlets accept this gift horse and come to Hollywood to live "just like in the movies," and the industry feeds upon her dreams to get her to participate in producing more illusions, only to discard her when she loses her allure and is replaced by yet another ingenue who comes to Hollywood believing the promise offered by this girl on the screen. They do not look at her and say, "This is the girl." They look at her and say, "The girl is me."

The Phoenix in the Dream Dump

In this regard, *Mulholland Drive* shows how The Girl is both the Trojan Horse and the *phoenix excrementi* described in *The Dream Life of Balso Snell*. She is the Promise and the fertilizer from which the Promise arises anew. The two symbols create an unending cycle in which promises are made, betrayed, and made again out of the waste of the previous promise. According to Deborah Wyrick, *The Dream Life of Balso Snell* depicts all Western culture as a "wasteland […] composed of the excretions and eliminations of humanity."[32] West's and Lynch's works evince a preoccupation with waste, not with literal waste per se, but with, as Nochimson puts it, "the transition from human hope to putrefication."[33] Their art—which West describes not as "nature digested" but rather as "divine excrement"—demonstrates the way that capital, particularly in the form of commercial art, drains reality of its substance and leaves empty, putrefied forms masquerading as the real, Trojan Horses that conceal a haunting, hollowed-out absence within.[34]

West and Lynch continually illustrate the cyclical nature of dreams. Dreams create art that inspires the populace to dream unattainable dreams, and these dreams rise out of the rubble of the dreamer's own failures like the *phoenix excrementi* to influence reality again. The fact that *Balso Snell* takes place entirely in the digestive tract of the Trojan Horse shows how no consumption takes place in this process, only the digestion of previously consumed material that then finds its way, miraculously, to the reproductive system. As the narrator of *Day of the Locust* assures us, "no dream ever entirely disappears." Rather, a dream initially "troubles some unfortunate person" somewhere, and that dream will fester until it winds up being filmed on a studio backlot "when that person has been sufficiently troubled."[35] West depicts Hollywood as a breeding ground for the *phoenix excrementi* of *The Dream Life of Balso Snell* in a sequence in *Day of the Locust* where Tod encounters a scrap heap. As he takes a stroll around the lot, Tod comes to a hilltop that overlooks a pile of discarded movie sets, a "final dumping ground" teeming with "partially demolished buildings and broken monuments." To Tod, the heap represents "a history of civilization [...] in the form of a dream dump" that "grew continually, for there wasn't a dream afloat somewhere which wouldn't sooner or later turn up on it."[36] This pile represents the once-useful "troubled" dreams of some "unfortunate" people that are no longer needed; however, the films made from these dreams will likely "trouble" others to dream dreams that will not go away until they are projected on a screen and then added to the pile, toxic runoff from the Dream Factory. West shows how the *phoenix excrementi* have found a physical location where they can do the work of dream production, distribution, and recycling on an industrial scale: Hollywood.

The Dream Dump scene contributes to West's emphasis on the artificial methods of construction found in his descriptions of Homer Simpson's home and the collapse of the Waterloo set. Taken together, these moments unmask Hollywood's depiction of abundance as "a false front" that literally cannot support the weight of the fantasy it is made to prop up.[37] As McGowan says of *Mulholland Drive*, West's fiction reveals the promises of capital to be flawed because they are simultaneously insufficient and excessive.[38] The excessive accumulation of empty promises—the empty calories of the imagination—results in excessive waste, heightened amounts of trash but also heightened levels of absence and lack; the trash piles as high as the promise remains unfulfilled, creating a flimsy, ramshackle Trojan Horse. Like the scene in Club Silencio, the Dream Dump of *Day of the Locust* deals directly with the interplay between presence and absence, accumulation and excess, lack and waste.[39] The intensity of Rebekah Del Rio's performance and the abundance of the Dream Dump assert the presence of emotional content; however, the reveal of the tape recording and the fact that Hackett is looking at used up, discarded material testify to an absence of feeling, a hollowing out of affect. Veitch reads the detritus of film productions piled high in the landfill as representative of the "excremental 'dream dump'" that is the modern world.[40] As spot-on as this observation is, I disagree with Veitch that the process comes to an end in the landfill. When we read *Locust* alongside *Balso Snell*, we see this "excremental dream dump" as being not only generative but integral to the process of fantasy production in capitalist America. The sets may wind up in the dream dump, but the film that uses them is coming soon to a theater near you to trouble another unfortunate dreamer with high hopes of making it in the City of Dreams.

Nowhere is the transformative power of the *phoenix excrementi* more evident than in Betty's audition scene in *Mulholland Drive*. Like many scenes in the film, this one happens twice, allowing us an opportunity to see how Hollywood recycles previously used images and scenarios to create something new. However, instead of repetition dulling its impact, this scene comes alive the second time around. We first encounter the material in

FIGURE 3.4 Betty's laughable rehearsal. *Mulholland Drive* directed by David Lynch © Universal Pictures 2001.

Betty's rehearsal of the scene with Rita (Laura Elena Harring). The dialogue and the scenario that attend it smack of laughably low-rent melodrama, the kind of tawdry *faux*-emotions that would barely pass muster for a third-tier soap opera or a 1990s direct-to-video erotic thriller. The material is so awful that even the *über*-sincere Betty cannot get through it without laughing at its overwrought tension. Lynch even shoots and edits the rehearsal scene in conventional shot-reverse shot coverage that cuts on dialogue, the kind of traditional approach to shooting and editing that he generally avoids. The scene is, dramatically speaking, crap. Everyone knows it. However, crap is no match for the power of a desperate dream. During the audition, when she feels pushed into a corner by the stakes of the audition and Woody's sexually forward performance, Betty turns this crap into dramatic gold and summons a side of herself heretofore unsuggested and unseen, unleashing a performance that elevates the material from execrable to spellbinding, the kind of moment that appears as a clip on an Oscar telecast. Although what we see is only a well-executed performance of poorly executed writing—something both artificial and manufactured—we are left with something we had ruled out any chance of receiving: genuine and dazzling emotion.

As in Club Silencio, we are wowed by something we have already recognized as fake. The scene becomes a true testament to the power of art by presenting what George Toles calls "sincerity hatched at the very core of artifice."[41] Toles goes on to note the dual nature of the scene's revelation: it serves to conjure not only genuine drama out of trite pap but also a star out of absolutely nothing. The star Toles refers to is not Betty Elms but Naomi Watts, as the scene is even more so a demonstration of her talents to the audience than it is Betty's to the jaded casting agent and clueless director.[42]

FIGURE 3.5 Betty's transformation. *Mulholland Drive* directed by David Lynch ©
Universal Pictures 2001. All rights reserved.

This scene showcases in miniature what Lynch and West depict throughout
their work and what Hollywood produces with clockwork precision: the
way that dreams facilitate the transformation of waste that disgusts and
depresses into art that invigorates and inspires.

This recycling of dreams spawned by the *phoenix excrementi* creates a
media feedback loop in which everyone inhabits a landscape permeated
with and determined by mass media, to the extent that any outside ceases to
exist. Thomas Strychacz describes the creative hopefuls who populate *Day
of the Locust* as "powerless characters who have been completely shaped by
the mass media" to such a degree that "they have become 'media' themselves,
capable only of projecting pre-existing fictions."[43] This dynamic defines the
central relationship in *Mulholland Drive*, where Betty and Rita become more
invested in discovering Rita's identity after Betty remarks that it is "just like
in the movies." Further, the objects of desire in Lynch's and West's worlds are
introduced as mechanically mass-produced and marketed objects of desire.
In *Day of the Locust*, Faye Greener is a character constructed completely
out of movie magazines whose manufactured unattainable persona drives
the men around her to pursue her as a fetishized Dream Object—"This
Is the Girl"—representative of all Hollywood dreams. Her introduction in
the narrative drives this point home: she is first seen in a movie still for "a
two-reel farce in which she had worked as an extra," as an image.[44] Even
though Rita does not get introduced via a movie still in *Mulholland Drive*,
her first scene does characterize her as the archetypal inaccessible starlet
who travels exclusively by limousine. Rita herself operates as a "projection
of pre-existing fictions" when she chooses her name from a movie poster
for the Rita Hayworth noir classic *Gilda*, unconsciously connecting her

FIGURE 3.6 Rita finds herself in an image. *Mulholland Drive* directed by David Lynch © Universal Pictures 2001. All rights reserved.

own identity and situation to the femme fatale of a noir story not unlike her own. The scene where she chooses her name emphasizes her image-based existence in a similar way to West's introduction of Faye in *Day of the Locust*. The camera focuses on Rita's face *in a mirror* as she spots the *Gilda* poster in the reflection, creating a *mise-en-abyme* of an image seen in a reflection seen in yet another reflection viewed through a camera.

While it could certainly be enough to read Rita as the film's central Dream Object (or Camilla Rhodes, her real identity, who is also introduced through an image in the form of a headshot), it is important to read Betty as a similarly crafted image. First, she is the mental projection of failed ingenue Diane Selwyn, but more importantly, she stands as the Dream Object for the audience, who must identify with a fantasy image for the film's critique of the culture industry to work. As Scheibel notes, Betty also functions as a media projection in the sense that she is "completely flat," with her character being defined through wardrobe references to blonde cinematic icons such as Grace Kelly, Kim Novak, and Tippi Hedren.[45] Further, the Betty-Rita portion of the film, like Diane's referential projection of Betty, is another media creation projected by Diane Selwyn in the sense that she recasts her tale of lost love and failure not as a romantic tragedy but as a genre mashup of an inspirational drama and a romantic mystery. This projection is an example of recycling in both works, as these hopefuls use the cultural detritus around them to fabricate their own star images to the extent that they "only [exist] as an already performed self, comprised of well-known star personalities and character types."[46] We see this dynamic in *Day of the Locust*, through the many stories Faye tells to enchant the men around her, which Barnard considers to be a dream even larger than Faye's dreams of stardom.[47] If Faye's acting dreams cannot come true, perhaps she can sell her dreams to someone else in the form of the stories she tells, which she thinks of less as dreams than as intellectual property to be profited from, providing yet another example of waste being recycled for a new aspirant audience: the *phoenix excrementi.*

West shows how this kind of recycling and rebirth can happen on a national scale thanks to mass media. At the end of *Day of the Locust*, mass entertainment becomes mass violence only to become mass entertainment again as the movie premiere devolves into a riot that gets broadcast over the radio.[48] From a far enough distance, say, for a radio listener at home, the premiere and the riot, the fake and the real, all become the same. The glitz and the glamour of the premiere and the chaos and violence of the riot all become part of the same siren song that will beckon an audience member to come to L.A. The reality will certainly not live up to the exciting promise of the broadcast, which will disappoint the dreamer even more and drive them to a violent outburst that will itself become a sensationalized story that will entice yet another dreamer to pursue their dreams only to become another member of the *phoenix excrementi.*

Complicit Capital

The cycle does not stop there. One character in *The Dream Life of Balso Snell*, John Gilson, describes his ideal staging for a play of his, in which "the ceiling of the theatre will be made to open and cover the occupants with tons of loose excrement. After the deluge, if they so desire, the patrons of [his] art can gather in the customary charming groups and discuss the play."[49] This scene, while graphic and hostile toward the audience, links artistic creation and reception to a waste cycle. Both the play and the audience act as *phoenix excrementi*, being covered in fertilizer to give rise to another round of artistic creation and discourse through a post-show analysis. In a similar way, *Mulholland Drive* (not to mention *Miss Lonelyhearts*, *A Cool Million*, and *The Day of the Locust*) covers its audience in the waste and despair of the film industry, only to provoke more artistic discussion that allows that waste cycle to continue. Perhaps we are even engaging in it right now.

Like the Trojan Horse, Hollywood relies on complicity. The gift horse must be accepted. By consuming media, the audience is encouraged to participate in and perpetuate their own disenchantment, to be entertained by it, to become *phoenix excrementi.* According to Curren, this complicity represents a stronger pull than even the expectation of fame and fortune.[50] Despite the clarity of West's and Lynch's critiques, the audience still fails to understand that these Trojan Horse narratives are the work of a system which, in the words of Roberts, "will always cheat us, even in the private projection room of personal (or literary) fantasy."[51] West and Lynch must participate in this cheating too. Their narratives "mobiliz[e] the force of frustrated desire" before revealing that those desires have been stoked under false pretenses.[52] After all, they cannot demystify Hollywood (and capitalist America) without mystifying it for the audience; they cannot get the audience to identify strongly and authentically with the members of "the Cheated" without first cheating them.[53] Their attack relies upon what Roberts calls "frustrated rage" fueled by "personal entanglement in mass-mediated desire" that comes from believing in an empty promise.[54] In order to participate meaningfully in Diane's or Tod's rage, the audience must share it.

And share in it they do. Betty's storyline may be transparently rife with clichés and impossibilities, yet the audience gets sucked into it all the same because it's their dream too. Even though its logic is paper-thin and it reeks of artifice, audiences believe it because they want to. It is simply too beautiful to resist. Thus, the reveal that Betty's charmed existence is only the dream of a defeated Diane Selwyn constitutes a betrayal of the audience's dream, a brutal return to reality followed by the realization that this betrayal was not perpetrated by the film but by the audience members themselves. The film, like the emcee in Club Silencio, has been fairly upfront with the audience that the story it has been telling is almost certainly too good to be true. And, just like in Club Silencio, the audience knew it was fake and bought it anyway because they still believe in the dream Hollywood has sold to them. "Life *is* a stage," as a character named Beagle writes in *The Dream Life of Balso Snell*, "and *we* are clowns. What is more tragic than the role of a clown? What more filled with all the great essentials of great art?—pity and irony."[55] As goes Hollywood, so goes the world, for Hollywood is but the industrial arm of the American imagination; it does not create the fantasy; it simply has found a way to mass produce it in such a way that demand will always outpace supply.

The new dreams sprout from the rubble of the previous dream's collapse. West's fiction is littered with one delusion giving birth to the other, from *The Dream Life of Balso Snell*'s narrative progression from defecation to ejaculation, *Miss Lonelyhearts* death to rebirth, *A Cool Million*'s continual reassembly of Lem Pitkin and his dream from his disfigured body and psyche, and the transformation of *The Day of the Locust*'s climatic riot into high art. Balso Snell's epiphany, if a novel such as *The Dream Life of Balso Snell* were to have such a traditional literary trope, comes when he realizes that the only way out of the Trojan Horse "inhabited solely by writers in search of an audience" is not to continue listening but to tell a story himself.[56] And here the circular nature of the artistic process becomes evident: a steady diet of other people's dreams and stories encourages the audience not only to dream on their own but to become creators themselves. The shit of writers in search of an audience becomes fertilizer that spawns other writers in search of an audience ad infinitum. In all these examples, the cycle requires an audience to participate, a new mark to keep the con going. As consumers of these dreams, the audience enables them to continue, and as viewers of *Mulholland Drive*, so do we.

"This Is the Girl"

The mysteries at the center of *The Dream Life of Balso Snell* and *Mulholland Drive* require descents into black holes: the black keyhole of the blue box in *Mulholland Drive* and the black hole of the Trojan Horse's anus in *Balso Snell*. For Wyrick, this pursuit of self-knowledge, to find out who one truly is as a person and artist, "sucks [the artist] into oblivion," destroying the very thing they seek to define.[57] This paradox does not apply to the artworks themselves, however, because West and Lynch, as superior artists, cannot help but create strong work that affirms the artistic process and the art form itself. In this sense, the works become a crucial piece of the very system they wish to denounce, making beautiful art out of abject waste, supreme *phoenix excrementi*.[58]

And this is where *Mulholland Drive*, perhaps inadvertently, becomes a Trojan Horse of its own. The film begins its life as a pilot for a television series, only for that dream to be canceled by ABC executives. Then, like the *phoenix excrementi*, the project receives a new lease on life via additional funding for Lynch to transform the rejected television pilot into a theatrical feature film. *Mulholland Drive* the feature film represents a triumphant birth from the discarded waste of the dream dump that is, like Diane Selwyn's fantasy, "rooted in a doomed yet irresistible urge to rewrite the past."[59] Although the attempt the film depicts results in failure, as do the attempts in West's fiction, *Mulholland Drive* the film is a real-world success, the exact kind of rags-to-riches story West parodies in *A Cool Million*. Like *Day of the Locust*, *Mulholland Drive* cannot help but elevate their evisceration of the industry into high art that itself becomes a fresh piece of inspiration for a new crop of dreamers on their way to joining the ranks of "the Cheated." The film, like the *phoenix excrementi*, "simultaneously produces and—through consumption—destroys itself, only to produce itself again," and, in doing so, resembles and transcends the exhausted, recycled, and reproduced commodities it consumes: "ever-renewed yet ever-the-same."[60] This is the transformation of Diane into Betty, Camilla into Rita, and *Mulholland Drive* the TV pilot into *Mulholland Drive* the film. We find ourselves repeating "this is the girl" forever.

4

The Water and the Well

Nuclear Media as Hyperobject in Cormac McCarthy and *Twin Peaks* (2017)

Even more than Hiroshima or Nagasaki, the Trinity test on July 16, 1945, ushered in our modern age. Jennifer Fay, building on the work of Jan Zalasiewicz, marks the Trinity test as the start of the Anthropocene in that it, more so than the subsequent attacks on Hiroshima and Nagasaki, is defined less by acts of war than "calculated act[s] of experimental science" in which elite scientists "colluded with the military" to create and test something capable of annihilating life on Earth.[1] This claim demonstrates how the impact of the bomb far exceeds the destructive effects of any single detonation; rather, it initiates a chain reaction that defines and shapes every moment afterward because the full scope of its impact cannot truly be measured because trace elements of it are present in every corner of the planet.[2]

The notion of an entity being so prevalent as to be too vast to measure corresponds with Timothy Morton's concept of the hyperobject. Morton defines a hyperobject as something that is "massively distributed in time and space relative to humans," such as the Everglades, black holes, the Solar System, or climate change.[3] Morton outlines several properties of hyperobjects, foremost of which are their viscosity and their nonlocality: "they 'stick' to beings that are involved with them" to the degree that "we are already inside" them, and they are so widely "distributed across the biosphere and beyond" in various discrete phenomena that "it's very hard to see as a unique entity."[4] Hyperobjects force people to consider their status on the planet and the universe, affecting our definitions of existence, Earth, and the social.[5] Radioactive material serves as a prime example of a hyperobject because it cannot be thrown away since no such thing as "away" exists with something that has a half-life of millions of years.[6] In this sense, hyperobjects are both inside us and all around us, "stickier than oil and as heavy as grief. The closer we get, the less we know," even as we become more intertwined with them.[7] Once such material appears in the world, it is immediately everywhere and part of everything, viscous and nonlocal, and can no longer be separated from the environment into which it has been introduced. The border that was once between these objects, what kept the water separate from the well, so to speak, no longer exists. Now they are the same. Now, this is the water and this is the well. There is no escaping them.

As Fay shows, nuclear weaponry's trace elements are not confined to radioactive material; they have also contaminated visual culture while simultaneously presenting "a crisis of representation."[8] Although the United States was hardly the only country to conduct such nuclear experimentation, Fay does show how the United States "inaugurated this regime and its visual culture" throughout the rest of the world.[9] Just like radioactive material, nuclear imagery has a long half-life and can be found all over the planet in all types of media, both those directly concerned with representing the atomic bomb and those that are not. Fay argues that a work does not have to directly mention or represent the Bomb in order to be suffused with its influence because the population has "absorbed the atomic spectacle into their DNA" through exposure to atomic test footage and safety films instructing citizens how to prepare for and behave during a nuclear attack, not to mention fictionalized representations of nuclear war or the threat of it.[10] This imagery of the atomic age has not only altered our existence at the visual, political, or psychological levels, but at the aesthetic level of representation. Jeff Wood goes so far as to say that, after July 16, 1945, "*Trinity is the culture.*"[11]

In some ways, representations of nuclear conflict are a necessity for understanding the power and meaning of the Bomb because after all, the real thing would leave few witnesses. Daniel Cordle argues in "Cultures of Terror: Nuclear Criticism during and since the Cold War" that "Global nuclear war" is "an entirely virtual construction that is accessible *only* through" representation.[12] The annihilating potential of the atomic bomb demands a representation beyond realism, yet, as Deborah Lovatt shows, there is a limit to this kind of representation in the "alarming discrepancy between the power of the Bomb and the descriptive powers of language."[13] Cordle sees this double bind as well: these representations must envision the annihilation of the very culture that they help constitute.[14] They must, in essence, "imagine [their] own non-existence."[15] Such representations help create a culture that calls upon people to live two lives: an ordinary one and another poised for the end of existence itself.[16]

Few texts actualize Lovatt's and Cordle's observations better than Episode eight of *Twin Peaks* (2017). An intertextual approach to the series lends insights into Lynch's work and his representation of the atomic bomb, particularly at the intersections of *Twin Peaks* (2017) and literature, specifically the work of Cormac McCarthy. The only sustained critical discussion of Lynch and McCarthy appears in the Jeff Wood's essay "Hurricane Bob," in which Wood uses McCarthy's recent essay "The Kekulé Problem" as a point of entry to understanding *Twin Peaks* (2017). According to Wood, McCarthy's statement that "the simple understanding that one thing can be another is at the root of all things of our doing" captures the duality of creation and destruction, doing and undoing, that one finds in *Twin Peaks* (2017) and much of Lynch's other work.[17] In *Twin Peaks* (2017), Lynch "drive[s] his surveyor's stake into the ground" at the Trinity test site, locating it as ground zero for this "the final fissure" in which "one thing can be another."[18] Wood's mention of McCarthy is astute; however, Wood misses that McCarthy has also "driven his surveyor's stake into the ground" in the exact same spot Lynch does, Trinity, in his 1994 novel *The Crossing*. Close examination of these two works (along with a brief consideration of McCarthy's 2022 novel *The Passenger*) shows not only how many of Lynch's thematic concerns can be accessed through the atomic bomb but the surprising degree to which his approach to representing the atomic age resonates with McCarthy's. Both works go "inside the bomb" to explore the core of the energy that makes and unmakes all things, and each work "re-enact[s] the trauma of the deployment of nuclear weaponry itself" that gave birth to the same fears as the wars the weapons were designed to combat.[19]

Read together, these works and their treatment of the relationship among the atomic bomb, broadcast media, and violence reveal each conceives of the Bomb and the fallout from its creation as hyperobjects, entities so immense and widespread as to elude not only time and space but understanding. Lynch's depiction of the Bomb and the abundance of media on display and in use throughout *Twin Peaks* (2017) extend McCarthy's ideas to suggest the Bomb finds not only representation but its ultimate potency in media, both through the content media disseminates and the apparatuses that transmit them. Consuming media shepherds us into the nuclear age and exposes us to its horrors, which we absorb unconsciously and which manifests itself as intimate personal trauma. Media becomes the viscous and nonlocal hyperobject through which the Bomb (and the creative energies and destructive evils that attend it) penetrates and permeates the world. McCarthy's and Lynch's seemingly imbalanced juxtapositions of the atomic bomb with intimate family dramas reveal that even though the Bomb may represent the cutting edge of science, its effects are as private, focused, and intimate as that of domestic violence.

"This Is the Water"

As Episode eight of *The Return* reveals, the story of *Twin Peaks* in many ways begins with the atomic bomb and represents an instance of advanced technological and scientific forces tapping into and unleashing ancient and primordial evil and destruction. Primordial evil and destruction are hardly foreign to McCarthy's fiction, and the Trinity test, which serves as *The Crossing*'s closing scene, signals not only the end of an era but the final blow that separates protagonist Billy Parham from family, country, nature, and perhaps time itself. The book is the second volume in McCarthy's Border Trilogy, and despite its singular title, *The Crossing* depicts multiple border crossings by Billy, whose encounter with a she-wolf on his family farm sends him on a series of quests into and back from Mexico, each of which, in their own way, attempts to return animals or people to some earlier point of departure in both space and time, first a she-wolf, then some horses, then his brother Boyd's body, and ultimately himself. Along the way, he meets several strange wise men who speak to Billy about the nature of reality, the will of God, and the reality of good and evil. With each crossing, Billy loses the object of his quest: the wolf, the horses, his brother, his family, and finally his sense of home and country.

The novel's final scene finds Billy aimlessly wandering the New Mexico countryside, malnourished, angry, and defeated. He stops to rest at an old gas station where he encounters a grotesque dog, "an arthritic and illjoined thing" with a "misshapen head," "milky half blind eyes," and "twisted legs" that "was wet and wretched and so scarred and broken that it might have been patched up out of parts of dogs by demented vivisectionists."[20] Horrified and disgusted by the dog, Billy curses at it and chases it off with a pipe before falling asleep. He awakens to "the white light of desert noon" but instead of remaining, "the light was drawing away along the edges of the world" until "there was no sun and there was no dawn […] and that noon in which he'd woke was now become an alien dusk and now an alien dark," an "inexplicable darkness" in which "there was no sound anywhere save only the wind."[21] Overcome by the strangeness of these events and his estrangement from humanity and the world, Billy lowers his head and weeps until, as the last sentence of the novel reads, "the right and godmade sun did rise, once again, for all and without distinction."[22] Critics triangulate the timeline and geography of Billy's journey in Book IV of *The Crossing* to read this double sunrise as an account of the Trinity nuclear test and the dog as a harbinger of the mutant "illjoined thing[s]" that will emerge from the creation of the "demented vivisectionist[s]" who gave birth to the Bomb.

The scene is an overwhelmingly sad conclusion to an adventure story marked by grief, loss, befuddlement, and alienation. Billy's angry reaction to this creature with "twisted legs [and] strange head agoggle on its neck" forms the tragedy of the moment (and the novel as a whole) because it represents a dramatic reversal of his attitude toward animals.[23] After all, he spends the novel's first section protecting a wolf from the kind of harm that he threatens to inflict on this grotesque dog. These earlier protective efforts, even though they ultimately fail, lead Billy into the liminal space of the US-Mexico border where he achieves a deeper connection to nature. As Billy lays the dead wolf to rest at the end of Book I, he touches the wolf's head and "could see her running in the mountains, running in the starlight where the grass was wet and the sun's coming as yet had not undone the rich matrix of creatures passed in the night before her."[24] "All was fear and marvel" in that moment, the narrator explains, as Billy experiences a worldview not dominated by anthropocentrism but rather a world that predates human action.[25] This final passage in Book I illustrates that, for all its predatory characteristics that bring it into conflict with humans, the wolf represents a creative, life-giving force that embodies the natural world in a way that humans do not. (Further, Billy discovers during their journey that the wolf is pregnant.) Billy's pursuit of the wolf differs from the other men around him because he does not seek to destroy the wolf but to shepherd it home and, perhaps, to understand it. His desire for understanding, though, is not for the purposes of dominating it but for accessing its unique knowledge, for communion with "the rich matrix of creatures" from "the world that was," the world that existed before humanity that humans can no longer grasp.[26] Billy's wanderings can be read as attempts to experience this kind of connection and understanding, and the distances he travels show how such opportunities are nearing extinction in the Anthropocene. Perhaps at some point human beings were more connected to nature, but by the novel's end, we see the Bomb standing in for their complete divorce from the natural world, the epitome of anthropocentrism. In the ruins of the gas station on July 16, 1945, fear and marvel have turned sour and malignant, and Billy can no longer relate to nature because human action has mutated it beyond his ability to comprehend. Rather than appearing natural, nature is now, like the dog's howl, "something not of this earth."[27] The "rich matrix of creatures" appears to be, like the wolf and like Billy's family, extinct, irradiated by the "white light of desert noon."

A novel that begins with a description of Billy telling his brother "features of the landscape and birds and animals in both spanish and english" and ends with a creature that cannot be named suggests the existence of a final crossing in which the natural world has been so altered by the Bomb that it can no longer be represented in language.[28] This final scene positions humanity's most advanced achievement, the Bomb, as "the ultimate appropriation of natural force that has threatened human health and the health of the desert land to the present time."[29] As an "uncanny intersection of geotrauma and human history," the dog at the end of the novel serves as the abject fruit of this appropriation, suggesting that gaining power over the fundamental building blocks of matter not only alienates us from them but also threatens to warp matter itself beyond recognition, perhaps even annihilate it.[30] While the fact that "the right and godmade sun did rise, once again, for all and without distinction" can suggest that the world will go on much as it had before, being remade each day under a new, second sun, the ending marks the dawn of a new age in which this other sun, the one that is not "right and godmade," precedes and permeates the dawn as a viscous and nonlocal hyperobject. It is now in and on everything, "stickier than oil and as heavy as grief."

These forces—the appropriation, alteration, and alienation from nature—are all attained through violence, making the Bomb a creative force of knowledge as well as a destructive force of violence. Violence is, as Timothy Parrish says of McCarthy's Western novels, "a necessary condition of knowing and the means through which characters confront [...] their place within a universe that may or may not be ordered according to God's will."[31] Throughout McCarthy's and Lynch's works, we can see the connection between violence and metaphysical knowledge as humans "[usurp] the power of the Creator" to create nothing out of something, using destruction as a means of "assum[ing] a knowledge that is unique and lay[ing] claim to possessing the origin of the world [they] explore."[32] This usurpation can take many forms, whether it be in the form of evil domestic acts such as those perpetrated by BOB or Mr. C in *Twin Peaks* (2017) or the various bandits and highwaymen in *The Crossing*, or as more far-reaching state-sanctioned violent actions such as the collaboration between the US government and the scientific community that produced the Bomb. Whatever form it takes, the Bomb is but the most spectacular example, the most extreme articulation of God's creative knowledge made manifest as violent destruction.[33] The knowledge, it seems, either comes from or finds its expression in violence. Once this knowledge is acquired, there is nothing that can be done to return to the moment before the destruction. A border has been crossed and there is no crossing back, no chance of return. "Once the atomic bomb has been unleashed from the genie's bottle," Walter Metz writes, "we must burn."[34]

While these spatial borders can be crossed and recrossed, drawn and redrawn, the historical border cannot; the larger the event, the more irrevocable the separation. Pierre Lagayette shows how borders are markers of time as much as they are space in McCarthy. Borders change over time and their drawing, their coming into existence, "separate[s] two historical universes."[35] Billy's journeys back and forth across the border are arguably journeys away from the civilized forces that lead to the creation of the Bomb. His encounters with city life overwhelm, frustrate, and confuse him. The fact that the Army repeatedly rejects him for service in the Second World War on account of a heart murmur is further evidence of his estrangement from his country and from civilization. The novel's final scene suggests that Billy has run out of places to escape to: where he may have previously been able to flee America by crossing the border to Mexico, now there is no border because there is no "outside" the Bomb. Billy's cries at the end of the novel are thus double-voiced in that he grieves for both his family and the advent of the nuclear age.[36] Billy's personal tragedy and the global tragedy are one and the same, both consumed by an eternal evil that can be confronted but not defeated; endured, but never known. Just as the timeline of *Twin Peaks* is riddled with the fallout of tragedies, the landscape of *The Crossing* is littered with ruins of earlier catastrophes—churches, airplanes, bodies—split pieces that cannot be reassembled or reconstituted. These final crossings of time provoke the yearning for and ensure the impossibility of return. The Trinity test in the novel is but the last in a series of border crossings that dominate the novel; however, unlike the border between states or nations, this border cannot be crossed twice. The final crossing of the novel is just that: final.[37] This is the water and this is the well.

"And This Is the Well"

Well on its way to becoming one of the most critically discussed hours of television, Episode eight of *Twin Peaks* (2017) attempts to display the aesthetic power of the Bomb and to depict the horror of living inside it. The nuclear bomb, particularly the image of a mushroom cloud, has been lurking as a hyperobject in Lynch's filmography. It is the only piece of art adorning the walls of Henry's apartment in *Eraserhead*, and an enlarged image of it fills the entire wall behind Agent Gordon Cole's desk in *Twin Peaks*. The sustained attention the Bomb receives in Episode eight invites a recontextualization of the Bomb's influence and importance in Lynch's work both visually and thematically.

The episode can roughly be broken into five distinct sequences:

1 Ray Monroe's (George Griffith) attempted murder of Mr. C (Kyle MacLachlan) and the Woodsmen's resurrection of Mr. C.

2 A performance at the Roadhouse by "The" Nine Inch Nails.

3 The Trinity test and the camera's journey into the mushroom cloud.

4 The Fireman (Carel Struycken) and Señorita Dido (Joy Nash) learning of the Trinity test and sending Laura Palmer into the world.

5 Two scenes from August 1956: a first kiss between two tweens (Tikaeni Faircrest and Xolo Mariduena) and the Woodsman (Robert Broski) violently taking control of a radio station and reciting a poem that lulls all of its listeners to sleep, including the young girl from the first kiss scene, who unconsciously ingests a mutant winged insect with frog legs as she sleeps.

Episode eight shows how the Bomb and its fallout already live inside of us not only through "illjoined thing[s]" such as the mutant creature but also through hyperobjects such as the waves and radiation that make broadcasting possible. Indeed, in Episode eight, media and nuclear energy converge to act as symbiotic hyperobjects: viscous and nonlocal entities that make up the water and the well from which we all drink full and descend.

Many critics have turned to *Twin Peaks* to discuss object-oriented ontology and hyperobjects. Anthony Ballas argues that *Twin Peaks* (2017) can "be considered object-oriented cinema" in that the forces of good and evil—embodied by Laura and BOB—are only rescued or defeated symbolically and eternally return.[38] Ryan Coogan views Lynch's work as "a world of object vitality" in which "there is no distinct hierarchy between the anthropocentric and the inert."[39] Morton even uses *Twin Peaks*' key elements to explain the uncanniness of hyperobjects, particularly BOB and the Black Lodge.[40] BOB shows how "hyperobjects are agents" that "straddle worlds and times" and have "causalities flow[ing]" through them "like electricity."[41] In that sense, *Twin Peaks* is "object-oriented" in that it focuses on these "relationships between entities" and seldom regards events, locations, characters, or objects as separate or unconnected from other events, locations, characters, or objects. There is always a relationship between, and it is through those relationships that the show derives its thematic and emotional heft across its many iterations.

The third sequence in the episode begins with an extreme wide shot from the air. A title card reveals the time and place as July 16, 1945, White Sands, New Mexico, 5:29AM MWT, as a voice over a loudspeaker counts down from ten. At zero, there is a bright flash of light punctuated by the

FIGURE 4.1 The Trinity test. *Twin Peaks* directed by David Lynch © Showtime Networks 2017. All rights reserved.

FIGURE 4.2 The Bomb arrives. *Twin Peaks* directed by David Lynch © Showtime Networks 2017.

opening, frightened strings of Penderecki's *Threnody for the Victims of Hiroshima*, after which the iconic mushroom cloud takes shape onscreen. As the detonation occurs and its blast wave expands upward and outward, the camera slowly zooms in until it enters the center of the mushroom cloud itself and appears to cross into another realm.

The camera's voyage into the Bomb blast represents the various kinds of crossings that originate with the Trinity test both in the series and in American history. As we have seen, the Bomb is a historical crossing that marks the dawn of the Anthropocene, but Lynch engages in narrative and aesthetic crossings in this sequence as well. First, a narrative crossing occurs here in that the Trinity test triggers a chain reaction within the universe of *Twin Peaks* that leads to the creation of Laura Palmer and the arrival of the Woodsman and BOB, setting most of the machinery of the show's plot and metaphysics into motion. Secondly, there is an aesthetic crossing in the sense that the episode crosses over into a more abstract, experimental style (even by Lynch's standards). Together, these two crossings leave an indelible mark that permeates not only the rest of the episode and the rest of *Twin Peaks* (2017), but also the entirety of *Twin Peaks*, altering not only what is to come over the next ten episodes but also interpretations and receptions of its earlier iterations in its 1990–1 broadcast run and the prequel *Fire Walk with Me*.

In this regard, the Trinity test functions as a hyperobject within *Twin Peaks* too: after Episode eight, the Bomb is viscous: it is everywhere in the series, demanding to be contextualized with events even when it is not visible, and it is nonlocal in that there is no separating it from any aspect of the show. It becomes a potential key to understanding *Twin Peaks* even as it resists easy or unified explanations. Its clear identification and representation produces an emotional and visceral reaction, but it is also abstract and remote, making it as distant as it is immediate. Thus, it works as a hyperobject in much the same way that Morton describes nuclear radiation's own hyperobjectivity: like nuclear radiation, Episode eight renders the world of *Twin Peaks* "more vivid and intense" while itself becoming more difficult to know and understand as a concrete entity.[42]

The role media plays in Lynch's handling of the Bomb cannot be understated. Most obviously, the Bomb blast and the voyage into its cloud can only be the work of mediation because, as Cordle explains, the Bomb is only safely accessible via representation. There is no "camera" traveling into the cloud: the entire shot is the work of computer animation and digital effects. More importantly, however, is the fact that the characters in the show only experience the Bomb and the effects of its existence through mediation. Like the rest of us, the Fireman and Señorita Dido encounter the Bomb through representation via a screen in a theater space. The Fireman produces a representation of his own (Laura Palmer) to combat it, which he sends to Earth through the screen. Thus, both the Bomb and its opposing force interact with the world through media objects. More obviously, the Woodsman, himself a representation of the Bomb's destructive energy, spreads his sinister narcotizing effectives far and wide through mediation via the radio station. After the egg containing the mutant insect hatches, the Woodsman appears in the desert and eventually marches toward a radio station, where he crushes the skulls of a receptionist and DJ before interrupting the broadcast of the Platters' song "My Prayer" to recite a cryptic poem. As the Woodsman says "this is the water / and this is the well /

FIGURE 4.3 Nuclear media and mediation. *Twin Peaks* directed by David Lynch © Showtime Networks 2017. All rights reserved.

drink full and descend / the horse is the white of the eyes / and dark within," the people listening to the radio—a mechanic in a garage, a waitress in a diner, and the girl from the date—drift off to sleep. The slumber that his poem induces allows for the mutant winged insect with frog legs to climb into the young girl's mouth as the credits roll, making media an accomplice in the atomic agenda.

While the atomic bomb and broadcast radio may not seem at all comparable, the radio, like the Bomb, represents another instance of humans harnessing control of the invisible parts of the natural world, waves, and radiation. The radio tower resembles the Bomb spatially in that it too is a towering object in the middle of a desert with a power and scope that radiate far beyond its physical location. The Woodsman's broadcast, while hardly as destructive as an atomic blast, also constitutes a technological transformation of the landscape by rendering the entire radio audience unconscious.[43] The cinematography of this sequence further links the radio broadcast to the Trinity test in that both the test and the images of each radio listener tuning in are photographed the same way, with a slow zoom-in. From these desolate spaces, the power of the Bomb and radio reshapes reality. Like radioactive fallout, the damaging effects of the broadcast infiltrate the listeners without their knowledge because the threat is as omnipresent as it is invisible.

McCarthy's and Lynch's treatments of the Bomb also illustrate the duality of the atomic bomb as both stimulating and numbing. Although we may be tempted to regard imagery of nuclear blasts as aesthetic experiences, Fay views them as uniquely *anesthetic* experiences in that they—perhaps by design—"numb the human sensorium" by separating the viewer from the actual reality of the blast and any emotion that may attend such an event.[44]

FIGURE 4.4 The Woodsman's lullaby. *Twin Peaks* directed by David Lynch © Showtime Networks 2017. All rights reserved.

Episode eight of *Twin Peaks* (2017) demonstrates this implicitly with the Woodsman's radio message and broadcast of "My Prayer." The Woodsman's incantation may seem to be the opposite of anesthetic in that it demolishes the smooth sway of "My Prayer" and all the dreamy heartwarming nostalgia the sequence produces, replacing it with a series of words that, in the words of Ashlee Joyce, "def[y] comprehension but suggest something ominous, elemental, and primal: water, well, horse, white, eyes, dark."[45] However, the confounding nature of the poem is anesthetic in the sense that overwhelms the listener and causes them to shut down: it lulls them into unconsciousness because it is simply too much to take in, too incongruous with the previous reality to be processed and understood, not unlike the Bomb itself. In this unconscious state, the media audience can be fed and become one with as many mutant horrors of the Bomb as can be broadcast. One could also view the Fireman's creation of Laura Palmer as an aesthetic reaction to the anesthetic of the atomic blast. In this reading, Laura becomes an idealized figure of goodness and beauty sent to awaken and enliven a catatonic citizenry, a reading which aligns well with Laura's wholesome and altruistic reputation. If that is the case, then her story only reinforces the all-encompassing damage that the Bomb creates: the golden aesthetic figure becomes so damaged by the forces associated with the atomic bomb that she herself seeks numbness and oblivion. In this respect, Metz argues, Laura Palmer is closer to "a symbol of an American tragedy" than she is a weapon to combat evil or "some angelic counter" for a ruptured universe.[46]

The mutant insect "conjures a vision of radioactive mutation" not unlike the dog that appears at the end of *The Crossing*.[47] Joyce reads the young girl swallowing the mutant creature as a corruption of the Edenic courtship

FIGURE 4.5 Consuming the atomic age. *Twin Peaks* directed by David Lynch © Showtime Networks 2017. All rights reserved.

scene that precedes it and "reinforces the event of the Trinity test as a moment of original sin for contemporary humanity—the manifestation of a forbidden knowledge we cannot unlearn," a final crossing from which there is no going back.[48] Broadcast airwaves and nuclear fallout know no borders, and together they have the power to shatter the man-made borders between nuclear horror and saccharine 1950s teen courtship. The black-and-white cinematography only advances these aims, conjuring feelings of nostalgia during the date that mutate into stark expressionistic horror at the radio station and then merge together as the mutant insect invades the young girl's room and then her body. The girl ingesting the bug in her sleep, followed by the credits rolling over as she sleeps peacefully, captures Morton's description of life during the time of hyperobjects: "uncanny and intimate," sincere and ironic simultaneously.[49] She ingests a foreign toxin without being aware, just like we do each day. This is what Morton would describe as the irony of "waking up inside a hyperobject": something wrong has already happened, and we are responsible for it.[50] We have drunk full of the narcotizing elements of the bomb and its media and now we descend into a state of poisoned slumber, lotus eaters of the atomic age. The music of Episode eight presents this contrast as well. Pendericki's jarring *Threnody* and the metallic clash and clatter of Nine Inch Nails' dirge "She's Gone Away" stand in stark contrast to the dreaminess of the Platter's "My Prayer," suggesting that music after the Trinity test will be abrasive and nightmarish, with nothing sounding as smooth or innocent as it once did. Further, Joyce sees a lyrical connection between the Trinity test and "She's Gone Away" in the line "spread the infection where you spill your seed," which one can read as referring both to Laura Palmer's abuse at the hands of her father and the force wrought by the atomic bomb.[51]

By ending Episode eight in a private and intimate space such as a teenage girl's bedroom, Lynch makes the connections between domestic transgressions and national transgressions ironclad. The violation this sleeping young girl experiences in her room is the result of the larger violation of nature epitomized by the Bomb, which was created "for the purpose of incinerating whole citiesful of innocent people as they slept in their beds."[52] Laura Palmer's violation by her father may occur in her home but is also a manifestation of larger and more numerous violations occurring throughout Twin Peaks and the nation as a whole. The narrative of the episode shows how the private tragedy has its roots in the national, with the Bomb serving as the apotheosis of warfare and BOB as the spectral embodiment of domestic assault.[53] In this sense, the bulk of Episode eight enacts the *Twin Peaks* narrative in reverse: rather than beginning with a domestic tragedy that gradually takes on a global, even inter-dimensional scope, its atomic narrative opens with the geopolitical and gradually works its way back to the private space to demonstrate how, much like the murder of Laura Palmer demonstrates, the two evils are not at all distinct but rather the same form of evil applied to a different scale, symbiotic hyperobjects operating at the molecular and the global levels.

Laura Palmer's abuse and trauma function as hyperobjects in the town of Twin Peaks in the same way that the atomic bomb functions as a hyperobject in the world: both are obviously destructive, dangerously prevalent; both have contaminated everything, and both were created by us, often in broad daylight. Further, both occur and are allowed to persist in tormenting their victims because they happen while everyone around is asleep. Episode eight depicts literal sleep but *Twin Peaks* (including the original run and *Fire Walk with Me*) amply dramatizes the figurative slumber that afflicts the citizens of Twin Peaks and, by extension, the nation as a whole: the somnambulism of willful ignorance and nostalgia. Like the radio audience at the end of Episode eight, the people of Twin Peaks are equally asleep to the evils of their town, ignoring the numerous red flags surrounding Laura Palmer, prominent men such as her father and Benjamin Horne, and the town's endless supply of lowlife drug dealers "because it was more convenient to ignore it."[54] Their slumber preserves the dreamy image of the town in direct proportion to the degree that it allows the continued predation, assault, and murder of young women, and this slumber is a manifestation of the numbing nostalgic comfort of the American Century ushered in by the Bomb.

The connection between the private violation of sexual trauma and the public trauma of the Bomb can be seen elsewhere in *Twin Peaks* (2017) through the character Naido (Nae). As an Asian woman with no eye sockets, she conjures the imagery of the physical mutations and birth defects experienced by Japanese survivors of the atomic attacks on Hiroshima and Nagasaki and the wounds left by atomic war. Naido cannot see or speak, which means she, like Laura Palmer, has no way to bear witness to the trauma she has endured.[55] Just like Laura Palmer, she cannot verbally testify to what happened to her, but, unlike Laura, her bodily presence testifies perfectly to her trauma and "the truth of trauma's inherent resistance to representation, both personal and artistic."[56] The reveal that she is actually the tulpa of Cooper's (previously absent) assistant Diane (Laura Dern), herself a survivor of sexual violence, again merges the two traumas, national and personal, into one figure, just as Lynch previously does with Laura Palmer and the girl at the end of Episode eight.[57] The abused and traumatized women of *Twin Peaks* are the true counterparts to the Bomb, not innocent opposites, but intimate analogues. The defeat of BOB has a healing effect on Naido, which implies that defeating the domestic evil could also lead to a triumph over the more global evil of the atomic age.[58] Such a suggestion, however, overlooks the destabilizing effects that such efforts have elsewhere in *Twin Peaks* (2017), most notably in Cooper's attempts to "save" Laura Palmer from her fate. Cooper's intervention apparently disrupts the entire space-time continuum, sending him and Laura (now Carrie Page) into an alternate timeline, perhaps even our own. It seems that reversing the effects of BOB and the Bomb is as Promethean as the Bomb itself. There can be no return, only further (and perhaps greater) displacement. Once again the traumas of the Bomb and Laura Palmer's murder dissolve into the same kind of viscous, nonlocal hyperobject: even when we can see it, as with Naido, or return to it, as with Laura Palmer in *Fire Walk with Me* or Episode seventeen of *Twin Peaks* (2017), we cannot defeat or remove the trauma. There is no return with hyperobjects just as there is no such thing as "away" with nuclear radiation.

The Crossing and *Twin Peaks* split the atom literally and figuratively—the literal building block of matter and the building block of postwar American life: the nuclear family, only to reveal that the two are one and the same. Like the split atom, once the split to the nostalgic image of the nuclear family occurs, it cannot be put together again, no matter how much one tries. While the concept of the traditional nuclear family hardly requires defining, Cordle goes so far as to read any image of a troubled household post-1945 as an indicator of "a shaping nuclear context," to the extent that one can discover "nuclear origins" within "literary and cultural representations of contemporary anxieties."[59] In essence, trouble with the nuclear family is trouble with the Bomb. The Palmer household in *Twin Peaks* most certainly qualifies as a disturbed home that represents "contemporary anxieties," and Episode eight's new origin story for Laura Palmer only intensifies Cordle's claim about the so-called nuclear family. The Parham family in *The Crossing* may predate the nuclear family, but their tragic dissolution over the course of the novel that culminates in Billy's estrangement from all aspects of American life on the day of the Trinity test prefigures the losses that visit and

FIGURE 4.6 Rancho Rosa as America's nuclear terminus. *Twin Peaks* directed by David Lynch © Showtime Networks 2017. All rights reserved.

continually haunt the town of Twin Peaks and the rest of the nation during the atomic age. This atomic knowledge that was intended to harness the creative energy of the world and usher in a new generative age only hastens dissolution and destruction in *The Crossing* and *Twin Peaks* (2017), starting with what is often held up as the generative force of postwar America, the nuclear family. There is no new life in either work that is not in some ways monstrous or abject, and the familial images of domestic prosperity, such as tract homes like Rancho Rosa, remain uninhabited and unfinished, model home ghost towns not unlike the makeshift neighborhoods built to be destroyed in nuclear tests to see what kind of damage the Bomb would do to America. In *Twin Peaks* (2017), we have our answer.

"Drink Full and Descend"

Just as Lynch returns to *Twin Peaks* twenty-five years later, McCarthy returns to the atomic bomb in his linked 2022 novels *The Passenger* and *Stella Maris*. These novels measure the fallout of the Bomb across the so-called American century and characterize the Bomb as a force that unleashes a primordial evil, an act in which "the very stones of the earth had been wronged."[60] McCarthy's return to Trinity pushes his characterization of the event even further than he did in *The Crossing*: the Trinity test, that Promethean event of a "mycoidial phantom blooming in the dawn" reveals "a truth that would silence poetry a thousand years."[61] This act comes to represent "a dubious investment" in the forces that make and unmake the world, ushering in an age in which "a past we hardly even knew" has been "rolled over into our lives" as we slept, permeating the air and the ground for millennia to come and making return impossible.[62]

Radio and the Bomb are modern examples of tools McCarthy and Lynch focus on to show humans' attempts to harness and manipulate the power of nature, but McCarthy's description in *The Crossing* of Billy's father setting a wolf trap demonstrates that these tools are as old as civilization itself and all derive from the quest to control and know what lies outside of humanity's grasp, with futile and damaging results. Silhouetted by the sun "against the morning sky" as he sets the wolf trap, Billy's father is described as "truing some older, some subtler instrument. Astrolabe or sextant. Like a man bent at fixing himself someway in the world."[63] The trap, in other words, is only nominally about catching the wolf. By "fixing" the wolf in place, the trap will also "fix" humans in a superior position to nature. This "fixing" suggests a kind of stasis, as though the trap will hold not only the wolf in place but time itself. The narrator pushes this line of thinking by describing Billy's father's work as "trying [to fix] by arc or chord the space between his being and the world that was."[64] However, McCarthy's narrator immediately injects doubt into the desire to "fix" by adding "if there be such space. If it be knowable."[65] While this notion of technology as a means of humanity asserting and extending its influence and control over nature is hardly unique to McCarthy and Lynch, the sense that such endeavors are futile, misguided, or destructive is more particular to the Border Trilogy and *Twin Peaks* (2017).

As a novel that uses personal trauma to dramatize a global separation, *The Crossing* is a novel of loss and mourning. Billy Parham's loss of his ties to family and country merely dramatizes "the alienation of humanity from the natural world," a separation that becomes fully apparent in the atomic bomb, which creates "a false sun" whose rising and setting renders the landscape no longer intelligible.[66] There are hints throughout the novel that searching for and acquiring the kind of knowledge that Billy and the nuclear scientists seek, which can be understood as a deeper knowledge of the inner workings of life and matter itself, can only be alienating at best, apocalyptic at worst in that both attempt "to hold what cannot be held."[67]

Early in Billy's travels, a character named Don Arnulfo compares Billy's search for knowledge of the world to catching a snowflake: "You catch the snowflake," he says, "but when you look in your hand you dont have it no more.[…] if you catch it you lose it. And where it goes there is no coming back from."[68] Like the snowflake, Don Arnulfo tells Billy that "el lobo es una cosa incognoscible" ["the wolf is an unknowable thing"] and that attempting to know it is "como preguntar lo que saben las piedras. Los arboles. El mundo" ["like asking to know the stones. The trees. The world."].[69] The real world, Don Arnulfo claims, lies "between [humanity's] acts and their ceremonies"; however "the world between is invisible to them" because humans "see the acts of their own hands or they see that which they name and call out to one another."[70] Don Arnulfo tells Billy that if he wants to know the truth of the world, he needs to "find that place where acts of God and those of man are of a piece. Where they cannot be distinguished […] Lugares donde el fierro ya esta en la tierra […] Lugares donde ha quemado el fuego" ["Places where iron is on the earth. Places where fire has burned."].[71] Few scenes in the novel foreshadow the final scene in the gas station as much as this one, for the gas station is where "acts of God" meets "those of man" in "places where iron is on the earth" and "fire has burned" in the form of the Trinity test. Like God, this is a place where mankind "sits and conspires in the destruction of that which he has been at such pains to create"; however, it does not grant Billy the knowledge that he seeks.[72] The only understanding of the world that this seems to bring to Billy at the end is that the connection to the natural world has been irreparably, violently severed. The more one tries to know, the more unknowable the world seems, and the more irrevocably alien it becomes. Even the epiphany he experiences with the wolf in which he senses "the rich matrix of creatures" is tinged with destruction and impossibility because he is touching the head of a dead wolf whose eye "[gives] back no light."[73] Atomic power is like a snowflake, "if you catch it you lose it. And where it goes there is no coming back from."[74]

The same is true of Laura Palmer. Lynch demonstrates this through his continual interrogation of the desire for control in *Twin Peaks* (2017) by denying both his characters and his audience the returns that they seek. *Twin Peaks* (2017) does not end with Cooper's triumphant return and the resurrection of Laura Palmer in Episode seventeen. Instead the series continues for another episode to show the misguided nature of Cooper's quest (and the audience's desires). Cooper fails because his pursuit of Laura, like humanity's nostalgic retreat from the terror of atomic power, represents an impossible desire to return to "the world that was"; along with the perplexities of *Fire Walk with Me*, Episode eighteen represents Lynch's argument that "the world that was" before Laura's murder is ultimately unknowable and inaccessible, just as a world before the Bomb is unknowable, and reexaminations of it prove more disturbing. Once one has "[drunk] full" of the water and the well of atomic power and "descend[ed]," a return is no longer possible.

Both *The Crossing* and *Twin Peaks* (2017) are concerned with trying to take things back to some earlier, more perfect state of being where they supposedly belong—the wolf, the horses, Boyd's body, Laura Palmer, the United States, etc. Each attempt requires the crossing of some border or boundary, and each attempt fails because, in crossing that boundary, one creates an irrevocable change. The border for McCarthy is more than a spot on a map but a symbol for the illusion of temporal permeability just as *Twin Peaks* is a nostalgic illusion of a return to a world "where a yellow light still means slow down instead of speed up," if such worlds ever in fact existed. One may be able to cross borders back and forth through space, but there is no such thing as a return. Both Cooper and Billy may have gotten to touch what they returned for, but, as Billy notes, "it sure as hell wasnt what [they] wanted."[75] Instead, to paraphrase a character in *The Passenger*, "the horrors of the past lose their edge" in the age of hyperobjects, "and in the doing they blind us to a world careening toward a darkness beyond the bitterest speculation."[76]

The Woodsman's attacks—themselves menacing intrusions into the innocent nostalgic 1950s so prevalent in Lynch's landscape—enact Fay's claim that "the price of symbolic freedom" in Atomic America "is submission" to the Bomb.[77] Everyone who comes into contact with him directly or indirectly submits to the iron grip of his hand or his broadcast. Similarly the "symbolic freedom" of the town of Twin Peaks requires a nation's "submission" to the Bomb on a national level and young women's "submission" to predatory men on a private level. This final sequence of Episode eight in which the entire populace succumbs to the Woodsman's cryptic lullaby recontextualizes this distinct Lynchian nostalgia as a kind of "historical amnesia," a somnambulant retreat into fantasies of an imagined lost past that can only be upheld through violence and repression, as seen through the violence of Mr. C., Leland Palmer, Frank Booth, and other Lynchian villains, or through complete infantilized innocence in the form of Dougie Jones.[78] More importantly, though, this reframes Lynch's cinematic project and offers a strong rebuke to critics of Lynch such as Fredric Jameson who see only reactionary impulses in this nostalgia. Instead, Episode eight positions this somnambulance as the nuclear reality of the United States. It is not something one yearns to return to, but rather something that *is*, something one is already in. The charm is always already malignant because, as *Twin Peaks* (2017) reveals, it comes from a great evil. The wholesomeness, even the desire for it, becomes a sign of being asleep, a dream lullaby heard on a radio. "My Prayer" becomes just that: the prayer one says before bed in which one prays "to linger" in the warm comforts of a vivid-but-numbing nostalgia.

PART TWO

"Let's Rock!":

Music

5

David Lynch at the Crossroads

Deconstructing Rock, Reconstructing *Wild at Heart*

"Finding Love in Hell"

Although the debut of *Twin Peaks* predates the release of *Wild at Heart*, I have decided to break chronology slightly to start this new part of the book with an analysis of *Wild at Heart* because it will establish many of the methods and ideas that the rest of the part will rely upon. David Lynch has called his 1990 Palme d'Or-winning film "a picture about finding love in hell," which may be the closest Lynch has ever come to saying what any of his films are actually about.[1] Despite his assertion, *Wild at Heart* is the Lynch film that scholars most often cite as a meaningless barrage of cynical postmodern signifiers, "a litter of quotation marks,"[2] "a parade of surfaces behind which is no significant depth,"[3] "a kind of cinematic vogue-ing that passes for the play of human emotions,"[4] "a violent collection of images and clichés in search of stability and meaning."[5] While the most vituperative condemnations of the film take aim at its love-conquers-all Hollywood musical ending, detractors save some venom for the two major motifs that unite in the film's happy ending, *The Wizard of Oz* and 1950s rock 'n' roll iconography. However, despite all the effort spent condemning these elements in the film, few investigate whether anything of substance lurks

This chapter first appeared, in slightly different form, in the journal *Music and the Moving Image*. Mike Miley; "David Lynch at the Crossroads: Deconstructing Rock, Reconstructing *Wild at Heart*." *Music and the Moving Image* October 1, 2014; 7 (3): 41–60.

beneath these allegedly empty signifiers. While there is no disputing that *Wild at Heart* reifies clichés, as Cyndy Hendershot describes in her critique of *Wild at Heart*'s allegorical style, I disagree with her conclusion that the film favors ironic allegory over sincerity.[6] Rather than brand Lynch as a mere ironist, Nicholas Rombes characterizes Lynch's predominant sensibility as "sincerity-in-irony": Lynch borrows from past forms "to build unstable narratives" rather than to parody or deflate those forms.[7] Rombes's claims about Lynch's sincere narratives are worth extending, and I wish to apply them to Lynch's use of rock 'n' roll music and its tropes, challenging the prevalent notion that *Wild at Heart* represents little more than "a sequence of forms without any real content."[8] Instead of functioning as simple Elvis impersonation, Lynch's use of cultural associations emanating from rock 'n' roll music and its iconic figures combine to formulate what may be his most complete (and sincere) statement on art's role in the world.[9]

Annette Davison, in her article, "'Up in Flames': Love, Control, and Collaboration in the Soundtrack to *Wild at Heart*," has already explored the ways in which Sailor Ripley and his ability to "generate music out of thin air" represent Lynch's ability as director to control the film's soundtrack, and, by extension, its narrative.[10] In fact, Sailor's connection to rock 'n' roll demonstrates Lynch's own Romantic ideals on the transformative power of artistic expression. Davison herself provides a window into this power in her article when she states that Sailor and Lula "gain release from the evils of the world through music and their bodily response to it."[11] Through this conception of rock as a force that delivers people from "the evils of the world," Lynch awards rock 'n' roll a transcendent, quasi-mythic status in *Wild at Heart* similar to the status Greil Marcus bestows upon rock in his book *Mystery Train: Images of America in Rock 'n' Roll Music*. For Marcus, rock serves as an organized form that provides the listener and the performer with a joyous, redemptive release from the terrifying chaos of the world. Lynch organizes the film around the blues rock tradition that "valorizes musical performance and active and bodily response" to music to create "thematic and physical relationships" among the narrative, the soundtrack, and the viewer.[12] Looking at *Wild at Heart* in this context reveals a filmic structure that uses rock music as more than a cynical stylistic reference in a pop-nostalgic lovers-on-the-run romance. Rock clichés and iconography in *Wild at Heart* become a structuring principle or code. Lynch reifies these clichés and iconography to illuminate a Romantic quest within rock 'n' roll to contain or transcend the forces that inspire it. The film's narrative atomizes rock to its core elements so that the story of Sailor and Lula, the emblematic rock couple played by Nicolas Cage and Laura Dern, functions as a synecdoche of rock 'n' roll itself, with Sailor representing a fledgling rocker in search of a new sound and Lula his muse. Starting with the speed metal of Powermad's "Slaughterhouse" in the opening scene, Lynch's film deconstructs and reassembles rock 'n' roll, working backward through American music stylistically and geographically to country and blues, and ending at the metaphorical crossroads where rock confronts its roots as the so-called devil's music. This development in Lynch's film inverts the progression of early rock 'n' roll as Marcus defines it: a hybrid of country and blues that seeks to triumph over a fatalistic worldview and becomes an exuberant creative force of love and passion. Through this journey, Lynch presents the Romantic ideal of art, and rock 'n' roll in particular, as an essential, generative force in a violent world.

Aboard the *Mystery Train*

It is easy to read *Wild at Heart* in terms of the contrasting visions of America presented by Marcus in *Mystery Train*. Marcus describes popular music as an attempt to reconcile "the American idea of paradise and the doomed facts of our history."[13] Marcus chooses two of rock's ancestors to embody this conflict in American music: "white country hokum singer" Harmonica Frank and Black bluesman Robert Johnson, with Harmonica Frank expressing the "pure delight of what was soon to be called rock 'n' roll," and Robert Johnson conjuring a world "without salvation, redemption, or rest."[14] These two visions, Marcus argues, formulate a cursed American character, filling Americans with a desire to exert control over a land that offers "too much to live up to and too much to escape."[15] Rock 'n' roll, Marcus claims, arises from a merger of these dialectical sensibilities and comes to be personified by the figure able to synthesize and transcend them: Elvis Presley. Even Marcus's description of Robert Johnson's music describes Lynch's film adroitly:

> half seduction, half assault, meant to [drive home] with enormous force [...] a loud, piercing music driven by massive rhythms and a beat so strong that involvement [is] effortless and automatic [...] a drama of sex, shot through with acts of violence and tenderness; with desires that no one could satisfy; with crimes that could not be explained; with punishments that could not be escaped.[16]

The world of the film is very much the same as Marcus's conception of Johnson's fear-laden America, populated by scheming, murderous perverts and psychos; a radio that only seems to report mutilations and necrophilia; and a dust-ridden landscape that rivals *Eraserhead* in its desolation. Lynch's choice to open the film in a location with a name as overdetermined as Cape Fear only further aligns Lynch's vision with Marcus's. This "aggressive and malignant" Southern American imaginary is what Sailor and Lula must travel across in order to achieve true freedom.[17]

While Marcus's writing and notions of rock's origins are compelling, I do not aim to suggest that Marcus's ideas on the history of rock should be accepted as what Mark Mazullo calls "transparent windows into rock 'n' roll's 'real history.'"[18] First of all, Marcus's writing does not offer the necessary distance to be received as a detached historical account. Marcus himself admits his book represents more of a "symbolic argument" about rock's origins than a bona fide history.[19] The section is worth quoting in full:

> The question of history may have been settled on the side of process, not personality, but it is not a settlement I much appreciate. Historical forces might explain the Civil War, but they don't account for Lincoln; they might tell us why rock 'n' roll emerged when it did, but they don't explain Elvis any more than they explain little Peggy March. What a sense of context does give us, when we are looking for someone in particular, is an idea of what that person had to work with; but for myself, it always seems inexplicable in the end anyway. There are always blank spots, and that is where the myths take over. Elvis's story is so classically American (poor country boy makes good in the city) that his press agents never bothered to improve on it. But it is finally elusive too, just like all good stories. It surrounds its subject, without quite revealing it. But it resonates; it evokes like crazy.[20]

Despite Marcus's somewhat glib dismissal of the necessity of a proper "sense of context," this in a way could explain the appeal that Marcus's history has on the popular imagination, despite its drawbacks: it, too, "evokes like crazy," thus allowing others like Lynch to further explore the resonances of the myths of both rock 'n' roll and America. Resonances and evocations remain the book's primary appeal and explain Marcus's preference for a "mythical stance" over a musicological one: his "musical analyses always [remain] subordinated to [his] mythical commentary."[21]

Second, there is a problem of contradiction: Marcus proposes an "authentic" rock 'n' roll that is by definition antiestablishment, yet in defining rock as such, the book creates its own establishment concept of rock that all future rock can only seek to conform to if it wishes to be viewed as "authentic."[22] Such a concept provides a view of *Mystery Train*'s purpose as well as the third challenge to viewing Marcus's text as historiographically sound: the book's purpose can be seen as being more concerned with dictating the future of rock than with accurately chronicling its origins. Mazullo shows how *Mystery Train* functions more as a "jeremiad for the generation of the 1960s": Marcus perceives rock as "undergoing a profound identity crisis" and in need of regeneration; therefore, his book seeks to "remove rock 'n' roll from the political failures of the 1960s" by recasting rock as "an expression of America's glowing past."[23]

Finally, the most significant "blank spot where the myths take over" in *Mystery Train* is race. It becomes difficult to view Marcus's and Lynch's valorizations of Elvis as a figure who triumphs over the despair of the blues as racially neutral. Marcus's conception of rock as reaching its fullest expressive potential when a white musician brings the primal violence and darkness of Black music under his careful control reads as a colonizer myth. This myth enabled rock's commercial success by repackaging "dangerous" music as safe and palatable for a larger (read: white) audience. One can see this notion reinforced by Marcus's celebration of Sly Stone, the only African American rock musician discussed at length in *Mystery Train*. Stone, whose band, Sly and the Family Stone, consisted of "whites as well as blacks, women [...] as well as men" and emerged from "a very white scene" in San Francisco with "a whole new thing" that "dismissed the simple, direct sound of the Black music of the day [...] but *took advantage of* its rhythmic inventions."[24] While Marcus asserts that Stone "was less interested in crossing racial and musical lines than in tearing them up," one can also see how Marcus attempts to, like he says of Stone, "[have] it both ways" with this argument: celebrate the musical blending of races without having to examine whether one side comes out better than the other in the exchange.[25]

Although Marcus's symbolic, ahistorical, and racially discomforting approach is problematic in several ways, his book nonetheless codifies ideas prevalent in the popular myth of rock history, ideas that inform the narrative structure and thematic content of *Wild at Heart*. Simon Frith points out that while these myths may not serve a proper historical function, they do perform a vital cultural function because "the importance of the myth of rock community is that it *is* a myth. The sociological task is not to 'expose' this myth or to search for its 'real' foundations, but to explain why it is so important."[26] Lynch's film, in leaning on the popular myths of rock history so extensively and uncritically, demonstrates their importance and persistence in the culture and contributes to one's understanding of what many see as the aggressive whiteness of Lynch's work. Reading *Wild at Heart* alongside Marcus's work requires one to entertain some of "the bad ideas running around out there," but it also provides the film with an order and coherence that many argue the film lacks and explains how Lynch arrives at both the film's transcendent ending and his unique approach to popular music throughout the rest of his career.

Wild at Heart's Rock Icons

Lynch leans on the rock 'n' roll's connection to America's mythic sense of itself so heavily in his film not to engage in postmodern winking but to ground and contextualize his narrative. As Martha Nochimson explains, *Wild at Heart* "is built on the inevitability of [the viewer's] subconscious connection [...] with the materials of the mass media."[27] Anahid Kassabian would call this "subconscious connection" to rock iconography an "affiliating identification," and her concept contains interesting parallels to Marcus's description of American cultural history, which resembles symbolic affiliation more than it does rigorous history: "cultural history is never a straight line; along with the artists we care about we fill in the gaps ourselves. When we do, we reclaim, rework, or invent America, or a piece of it, all over again."[28] While Kassabian's definition of affiliating identification applies to a film's compilation soundtrack, Lynch broadens his musical affiliating identifications to elements *beyond* the soundtrack, a practice that Ronald Rodman outlines in his article "The Popular Song as Leitmotif in 1990s Film." Rodman shows how directors like Lynch have capitalized upon the "semiotic and dramatic power" of compilation scores by "draw[ing] upon discourses around the musical work such as style and celebrity" while simultaneously retaining the functions of a traditional Hollywood film score, such as leitmotif.[29] In a postmodern compilation score such as *Wild at Heart*, "it is not the music, but the audience's perception of the music which matters."[30]

Wild at Heart's detractors might claim that these affiliating identifications only add to the "litter of quotation marks" piling up around the film; however, Lynch does much more than engage in a game of spot-the-signifier with the audience. Rather, these signifiers illustrate how a rock soundtrack can spill over into a film's narrative to the point that they become inextricably linked. Aesthetic depth enters *Wild at Heart* through this alleged superficial allusiveness, demonstrating Kassabian's idea that affiliating identifications expand interpretive possibilities and confirming Rodman's assertions that musical styles and celebrity figures inform an audience's perception of a film narrative or character.[31] Lynch merges the two styles Rodman outlines: Lynch not only associates particular music and musical styles with particular characters, but also associates particular singers and their mythic celebrity status with these characters. However, Lynch also goes beyond this merger. Sailor not only looks like the music and celebrities whose songs accompany his story, but also makes their music, becoming as creative as his rock 'n' roll hero, Elvis Presley. Lynch achieves this by affiliating Sailor with rock 'n' roll music and iconography at every level of his film: not just at the level of music and production design, but also at the level of cinematography, narrative, and meaning, to the point that the viewer cannot fully grasp Sailor without these associations. While this all could signify that Sailor (and the film) is little more than a derivative postmodern concoction, Lynch's use of these affiliating identifications in every aspect of his filmmaking makes Sailor Ripley the locus of meaning in the film. Unlike the affiliating identifications in other films, without these associations, Sailor (and the film) cannot exist. This perhaps also explains the failure of *Wild at Heart* for some critics: as the various signifiers broaden the interpretive field, the film runs the risk of alienating the viewer, as this method is "less tidy" than a conventional score, which means that some viewers will decline to engage with the film in this way.[32]

The musical style with which Sailor and Lula are associated most is 1950s rock 'n' roll, and the narrative of *Wild at Heart* has all the classic, archetypal elements one could ask for in a slick ditty by a ducktailed bad boy 1950s rocker: a sincere-but-damned rebel misfit and a sexually willing, independent girl fight her deranged, uptight Mama for a right to preserve their forbidden love; in order to escape the constraints put on them, they grab their cigarettes, snakeskin jackets, and bubblegum; hop in a classic convertible and hit a road littered with fatal car crashes, violence, and a doomed sense of romance; and their adventure climaxes in a lonely, remote place, where they meet a man in black whose presence will compromise their love for each other. In the end, despite being surrounded by loss and destruction, no one can keep them apart, not even themselves.[33]

Elvis Presley serves as Sailor's celebrity avatar. Hendershot describes Nicolas Cage's Sailor as little more than an "Elvis impersonator" and reads the beginning and ending sequences of *Wild at Heart*'s plot as an allegory for the Elvis film *Jailhouse Rock* (1957).[34] Hendershot outlines the parallels well: both films open with the hero killing a man in a fight, both films feature the hero going to jail for the crime, and both films end with the hero singing a love ballad to his beloved after they are finally reunited. John Alexander goes even further to claim that Sailor's transformation from the "wild untamed rebel" to the "compassionate sentimentalist" mirrors Elvis's career as his image becomes sanitized: "Like Elvis, Sailor's story begins with 'Mystery Train' and ends up as 'Teddy Bear.'"[35] While Alexander's observation is intriguing, I would argue that Lynch achieves a deeper significance through this so-called sentimentality than the real-life Elvis. Although Elvis is the most prominent rebellious rock figure Lynch associates with Sailor, it is worthwhile to note other icons contemporary to Elvis whom Lynch uses to create Sailor's overall rock 'n' roll image. In addition to Elvis and perhaps James Dean, Lynch also identifies Sailor with that other 1950s rebel icon Marlon Brando, who in Sidney Lumet's film *The Fugitive Kind* (1959) wears a snakeskin jacket "as a symbol of [his] individuality and belief in personal freedom." Brando portrays a guitar player in that film, and Sailor and Lula's journey, like that of Brando and Joanne Woodward in *The Fugitive Kind*, takes them on a road trip through the south in a classic convertible, terminating in similar trip to the Underworld.[36] The musical parallels go deeper, as that film is an adaptation of Tennessee Williams's play *Orpheus Descending*, and the Orpheus myth parallels what Lynch pulls off in *Wild at Heart* in many ways, even to the extent that the film rewrites the ending to the myth, where in this instance Orpheus and Eurydice escape the Underworld together as a result of turning *toward* each other. What these rebel characters have in common, however, is that their raging passions manifest themselves in violent and often criminal ways. Unlike these other narratives mentioned (and most depictions of the Hollywood hero), however, Sailor overcomes his need to control through violence and learns, through music, to relinquish control and thus "become receptive to life."[37] Only at that point is Sailor both able to accept a permanent life with Lula and create music wholly independently.

Of course, critics of the film like Kiel Hume look at these signifiers attached to Sailor and conclude "everything about Sailor points to a temporal and ideological disjuncture: he simply does not fit."[38] Although this is intended as a criticism of the film, this out-of-place quality is an important part of the film's engagement with rock as a cultural symbol. This same sense of disjuncture, according to Marcus, defined Sam Phillips's career at Sun Studios: "What Phillips was looking for was something that didn't fit, that didn't make sense out of or reflect American life as everyone seemed to understand it, but which made it beside the point, confused things, and affirmed something else. What? The fact that there *was* something else."[39] Like Elvis's music, Sailor embodies the spirit of rock 'n' roll in that his actions will point the way to a new vision of life, a way that begins as fantasy but comes to dominate reality. In this regard, his quest for music is also one for freedom of love and expression, and this quest takes place not only at the level of the plot of *Wild at Heart* but also in the interplay between the narrative and the soundtrack, for the conflicts present in the film do not resolve until the relationship between the soundtrack and the film is brought into harmonious synchronicity by Sailor. However, Sailor cannot perform this feat until he balances the polar forces within him: the violence of Robert Johnson's world of chaos and doom as characterized by Marcus and the world of love and dreams as endorsed by Glinda the Good Witch (Sheryl Lee).

Musical Geography

Sailor and Lula attempt, like Elvis, to escape Johnson's America, only to find it everywhere because it is part of the landscape, the very fiber of the country. There is no safe haven somewhere farther west or south, no utopia over the next mountain range; the road of *Wild at Heart* (and America) only leads to one place: the crossroads of blues mythology. When viewed in this light, the conflict of *Wild at Heart* plays out geographically. The geographical journey of the characters from Cape Fear, NC, to Big Tuna, TX, mirrors the musical journey of the soundtrack from late-1980s speed metal to early-twentieth-century Delta blues. The speed-metal song "Slaughterhouse" by Powermad, Sailor and Lula's favorite band, is the first (and most contemporary) rock song featured in the film. The song has all the stereotypes one would associate with the genre: it is fast, abrasive, and loud: Lynch presents the song in just that manner. "Slaughterhouse's" initial appearance accompanies a vicious assault, Sailor's manslaughter of Bobby Ray Lemon (Gregg Dandridge); however, another vicious assault occurs simultaneously on the soundtrack: "Slaughterhouse" interrupts (or perhaps "bandslaughters") Glenn Miller's prim, composed Big Band classic "In the Mood." Even though Lynch hardly needs to employ music to amplify the scene's violence, this harsh transition from Miller to Powermad, in addition to enhancing the surprise of Sailor's outburst, reifies rock 'n' roll's destruction of the smooth, syncopated sounds of big bands like Miller's with its raucous burst of primal emotion. While the song at this point appears to embody negative, destructive forces, Lynch plays into the common violent stereotypes of speed metal in this scene only to subvert them later in the film as Sailor abandons his violent impulses.

As Sailor and Lula attempt to escape Marcello Santos (J. E. Freeman) and Marietta Fortune, Lula's mother (and Laura Dern's real-life mother Diane Ladd), they leave the Carolinas and travel deeper into the south, passing through the Mississippi Delta region and New Orleans, the wellspring of jazz, blues, and rock 'n' roll. Three songs dominate Lynch's depiction of New Orleans: "Up in Flames" by Koko Taylor (and written by Lynch and Angelo Badalamenti), "Be-Bop A Lula" by Gene Vincent & the Blue Caps, and "Baby Please Don't Go" by Them. As Hendershot points out, Lynch uses these songs rather literally: "Be-Bop A Lula" plays over an extended scene of Sailor and Lula making love, and "Baby Please Don't Go" accompanies Johnny Farragut's (Harry Dean Stanton) fateful drive toward his death in "The Big N.O.";[40] however, rather than trying for a cheap, clichéd gag, Lynch's use of these two songs goes beyond the ironic or the literal when viewed in the context of rock 'n' roll style. "Be-Bop A Lula" and "Baby Please Don't Go" typify key features and themes of early rock 'n' roll, with "Be-Bop A Lula" expressing the romantic aspects of rock soaked in Sam Phillips's signature "backslap" reverb, and "Baby Please Don't Go," with its searing, distorted guitar sound and raspy lyrics, communicates rock's sense of danger and madness. Lynch pairs each song with the appropriate scene not to put quotation marks around them but so that "Be-Bop A Lula" comes to represent one of the last intimate moments for Sailor and Lula, and "Baby Please Don't Go" foreshadows not only Farragut's death but also Marietta Fortune's breakdown and Sailor and Lula's journey into the Underworld that gave rise to rock itself. In this way, the soundtrack, through Them's song, shepherds in the narrative's downturn as it descends beneath the geographical birthplace of American music in New Orleans into rock's thematic origins at the crossroads.

"Up in Flames" works to advance this decline even further. No scene set in New Orleans would appear complete or authentic without a jazz number, but this track, the only on-camera vocal not performed by Nicolas Cage or Powermad, represents an odd, twisted choice at best, as this possesses neither the jubilant syncopation of Dixieland nor the smooth composure of "In the Mood." This is something darker, a tune oozing desire, menace, and doom. Musically, the composition features the typical bassline Badalamenti utilizes in *Twin Peaks*, only here rather than walking briskly along with fingers snapping, the beat practically crawls, dirge-like, as though he and Lynch want to take apart each note to find its structure or roots, its connective tissue. Lyrically, things are not much different: the words speak of relationships ending, exploding, being consumed from within. This imagery connects to the death of Lula's father, which Sailor participated in, but it also connects to the second half of the film, where all the joy and freedom our rock couple gains from breaking parole and running away from home too goes "up in flames." Marcus writes of music depicting a world whose "promises and dreams [...] are too much to live up to and too much to escape," and although he is specifically referencing the music of Robert Johnson in that sentence, he could have been speaking of the imagery of "Up in Flames."[41] This tension between damnation and Eden, the excess of Saturday night and the piety of Sunday morning, is one that Lynch and Badalamenti cannot resolve with a jazz tune, only submit to, and from this point forward, the film itself plummets into the abyss of the Underworld and threatens to be consumed by it unless the soundtrack (and Sailor) can guide the narrative out of chaos and despair into order and life.

Outside of New Orleans, Sailor and Lula wind up on the margins musically. As they head farther west, they encounter the aftermath of a grisly car accident where one of the victims (Sherilyn Fenn) dies before their eyes. After this scene, pop music vanishes from the film altogether, and the soundtrack of the second half of the film consists mostly of Lynch's trademark drones and blasts of Penderecki. As we will see in the next chapter, the fatal car accident is a common trope in early rock songs and rock's worldview, which finds its most succinct expression in Nicholas Ray's film *Knock on Any Door* (1949): "Live fast, die young, and leave a good-looking corpse." The car crash in *Wild at Heart* fits this dynamic in several ways: it sets up the downward spiral that is the second half of the film, and it also serves as the moment in the film that the climax must refute in order to resolve the conflict. Lynch calls these moments in his films "eye-of-the-duck" scenes, meaning the scenes where the protagonists "lose their will in the

FIGURE 5.1 The "eye of the duck" scene. *Wild at Heart* directed by David Lynch © Polygram Filmed Entertainment 1990. All rights reserved.

flow of narrative events." "Eye-of-the-duck" scenes provide the "necessary prelude to closure," and although they do not operate as climaxes in and of themselves, from this scene forward, Lynch's protagonists face a choice: surrender control and be saved or cling to control and lose everything.[42]

Although it may not be a rock song about car crashes, Chris Isaak's "Wicked Game" functions as an "eye-of-the-duck" song for the "eye-of-the-duck" scene. Including Isaak on the soundtrack reinforces the influence Elvis has over every moment of *Wild at Heart* because Isaak's image and singing style clearly refer to (or even channel) those of Presley; however, Lynch uses Isaak's similarities to Elvis to make the content and placement of "Wicked Game" all the more unsettling. Like "Up in Flames," Isaak's song overflows with fire imagery and a similar sense of being consumed. While nominally a love ballad, the song portrays love as anything but romantic. Rather, love represents a destructive force, the malevolent energy of a world that "is only gonna break your heart." Although the speaker alternately claims he does and does not "want to fall in love," the mood of the song and Isaak's performance make abundantly clear that he has no say in the matter: love, that wicked thing in an even more wicked game, will trick the speaker into destroying himself. "The world is only gonna break your heart" because, as the song says in its final phrase, "Nobody loves no one." Even though the song is drenched in the kind of reverb a listener would expect to hear in an Elvis homage, the content of the song contradicts the cultural image of Elvis described by Marcus. Where Marcus views Elvis's music as an attempt to get away from anxiety and despair, the gloomy and despondent "Wicked Game" openly courts doom and dread. Viewed as such, "Wicked Game" in fact sounds like a Robert Johnson song covered by an Elvis impersonator, and the song appears at the moment in the film when all the promise of Sailor's break from society comes crashing down underneath the weight of his past (he admits to being involved in the death of Lula's father) and their circumstances (they are being pursued and set up by evil killers). The dream, in effect, is over, if it ever existed in the first place. Sailor and Lula enter Big Tuna, TX, in this vulnerable state, and the movement of the narrative grinds to a halt as they wait for Sailor's car to be repaired, making them the ultimate prey for the "black angel" Bobby Peru (Willem Dafoe).

Peru's arrival signals that Big Tuna in fact functions as the crossroads, and music precedes and defines both the space and Peru himself. For a strange film full of strange music, Lynch saves his strangest track for Peru's entrance. The track, which begins on a close-up tracking shot of Christmas lights, sounds like a song endlessly sliding downhill toward doom. In fact, it hardly sounds like a song at first: the rumbling, muted bass notes, and stray guitar chords more closely resemble a Lynch drone, something more suggested or subliminal than actually scored. There is little-to-no development in the song; it wallows in the dark, swampy groove it creates, and even Peru's appearance cannot rouse it save for a few additional distorted guitar lines. As a result, the scene becomes infused with a dread and foreboding from which the viewer fears the film will never return. Although it may only be the middle of the film, the viewer suspects it is in fact the end.

This strange song is incredibly hard to place (and track down) because it is not a swampy dirge at all. It is, in fact, a fast-tempo, driving rock song: Chris Isaak's "In the Heat of the Jungle," which Lynch manipulates substantially by slowing it to half-speed.[43] What we think to be notes on the bass are actually the song's tribal drum pattern, and the slow, sinister guitar chords in reality sound much more like a traditional, driving rock riff. The song as found in the film sounds unnatural and unnerving precisely because it is unnatural, altered, deconstructed, with all the momentum stripped away and replaced with menace. Here Lynch finds the ultimate contrast to the speed and vitality of rock 'n' roll, for this dirge represents the undoing of rock's great creative power; the malevolent forces that inspire rock surge to steal the transcendent triumph from rock's grasp, slowing its driving vigor down to lifelessness. In the case of "In the Heat of the Jungle," this is done figuratively as well as literally, thus the development of the narrative and the soundtrack converge and reinforce each other at their final destination. Lynch's modification of "In the Heat of the Jungle" contextualizes both Big Tuna and Peru's arrival as the terminal point in deconstructing American music: we have traveled across the American South and in the process delved underneath rock to arrive at the source, the crossroads, the place where we will confront the forces that rock music in fact has been trying to keep at bay, only now we must do so without the curative power of music.

Rock 'n' Roll Liminality

Thus, the course of Sailor and Lula's journey represents a confrontation with the space between the promise and the terror of America, transforming Big Tuna, TX, the terminus of this journey, into the crossroads of blues lore. Lynch has been developing this conflict since the first scene of the film. In detailing the opening scene in Cape Fear as "somewhere near the border between North and South Carolina," Lynch characterizes his world and his protagonists as figures in a state of transition, who exist within a liminal space from which they will find either redemption or damnation. This liminal "space in-between," Christopher Smith argues in his analysis of blues in contemporary cinema, is the gap between good and evil, salvation and damnation, "the cash for drinks on Saturday night and the tithes for church on Sunday morning."[44] It is the liminal territory of the blues where this tension becomes "ritualized and resolved, [...] creat[ing] social states permitting the transformation of identity or behavior."[45] Where Smith views the blues itself as liminal territory, Lynch and Marcus believe that rock 'n' roll constitutes the liminal territory. They associate the blues, particularly the music of Robert Johnson, as one of the poles, along with the "white country hokum" of Harmonica Frank, that rock 'n' roll sits between; the blues symbolize, in effect, "the cash for drinks on Saturday night" that, when not balanced by the "tithes for Church on Sunday morning," threaten to destroy the rock musician.

The transformation Smith describes depends upon the outcome of the bluesman's crossroads encounter with a figure called Papa Legba. Samuel A. Floyd describes Papa Legba as "guardian of the crossroads and grantor of interpretive skills,"[46] though most of us would recognize him more as the devil to whom bluesmen sell their souls in exchange for musical genius.[47] The musician/artist encounters Legba at the crossroads, the liminal space, where Legba offers him/her a deal: "move forward toward transformation" through music or "retreat into the *brutal mundanity* of Delta life."[48] In this respect, Smith explains, music becomes transformative, "magic," for it creates a "sacred space out of which new possibilities [...] become reality."[49] Because Smith views the blues as liminal territory, the supernatural figure that the bluesman encounters at the crossroads is actually Legba, a liminal figure who *assists* in confronting and overcoming alienation. Lynch, however, appears to subscribe more to Marcus's more problematic vision of the blues, which prefers rock 'n' roll as the liminal, "sacred space" because while "blues made the terrors of the world easier to endure, [it] also made those terrors more real."[50] Johnson's blues, according to Marcus, are doomed to failure, and knowingly so, because no song Johnson sings will be powerful enough to overcome the world's horrors.[51] For Lynch and Marcus, the figure at the crossroads is not a creative deity like Papa Legba but simply an old-fashioned conception of Satan: a destructive, chaotic figure without any musical talents whose malevolence must be kept at bay by art.

Lynch applies Smith's vision of blues music to rock 'n' roll in the film, to the point that the narrative journey of *Wild at Heart* serves as a rock 'n' roll analog to the bluesman's search for a new identity, an identity that offers more possibilities, an identity that can capitalize on the liminal space of rock and preserve the triumph of Saturday night and the spirituality of Sunday morning in a way that dissolves these dichotomies and thus eschews the threat of damnation. Lynch and Marcus see Elvis as the figure who succeeds in bridging this gap, thus enshrining white rock 'n' roll as a generative force that transforms the darkness of existence, an attempt that is ongoing for Marcus and one that is successful for Lynch at the end of *Wild at Heart* when Sailor merges his Saturday night sense of wildness with his Sunday morning sense of love.[52]

If Sailor stands in as the bluesman/artist, then the "black angel" Bobby Peru clearly represents the "devil at the crossroads" of the Robert Johnson legend (he even emerges from the depths of darkness in his first appearance). Lynch sets up Peru as the anti-artist, the destructive force

FIGURE 5.2 The "black angel" Bobby Peru. *Wild at Heart* directed by David Lynch © Polygram Filmed Entertainment 1990. All rights reserved.

that Sailor must overcome in order for the world to come alive again. Peru is all Saturday night juke joint, the antithesis of Sailor, the direction Sailor will go if he turns away from love and succumbs to the "bad ideas running around out there." Like Sailor, Peru is right at home in rock mythology, defined by a black leather jacket, with some added fringe to suggest angel wings. Also, his slick, shiny hair, pencil-thin moustache, and flamboyant attire bear some similarity to rock 'n' roll wild man Little Richard. Of course, Lynch's metaphor becomes obvious when we get a glimpse of Peru's teeth: for all the slick coolness on the outside, Peru is rotten at the core; his smile reveals the devil within. When we first meet Peru, we learn of him through his work in pornography, but Peru is a pornographer in more ways than one. In addition to making porn films, Peru creates a figurative porno when he forces (or directs) Lula to say "fuck me" to him. Furthermore, Peru not only creates a plan for a robbery but, like he does with Lula, he corrupts Sailor's mind by cajoling him into participating in the robbery, using the knowledge of Lula's pregnancy he gained during the rape scene. The robbery itself is not intended to be a robbery at all: it is in fact a ruse that will enable Peru to trap Sailor, kill him, and collect on Santos's contract. Therefore, like his symbolic rape of Lula, Peru's efforts in creating a robbery never have a material result because creation is not his intention: instead, Peru uses his powers to rob others of their creative potential.

The scene where Peru ropes Sailor into his robbery contains the most bare-bones blues in the entire film, "Buried Alive" by Billy Swan, and thus constitutes the perfect soundtrack for a tempting meeting with Papa Legba. The title risks being as on-the-nose as Cyndy Hendershot's characterizations of Lynch's use of "Be-Bop-a-Lula" and "Baby, Please Don't Go," but in this instance Lynch uses "Buried Alive" to represent American Music's Ground

Zero, springing out of the crossroads. The track is an all-acoustic guitar solo straight out of the Delta governed by a seemingly aimless strumming, as though the song awaits someone or something to point it in a direction, in any direction. The song and the scene appear to merge: both travel to the crossroads in search for a viable path forward, hoping to meet a man or a force that will give them the creative skill to organize the chaos of existence into music. Christopher Smith would view this encounter as latent with redemptive potential for the bluesman, but Lynch and Marcus see it in purely negative terms, for nothing good can result from a meeting with the devil. Peru has no musical or creative abilities, and taking what he has to offer will strip the recipient of not just their soul but their talent as well, robbing them of the very thing they come to the crossroads to enhance. Sailor must learn to negotiate the divide between himself and Peru if he wishes to escape from Marcus's concept of Robert Johnson's America: his success will inject "a fresh charge of energy" into the culture, while his failure will create "a hole which opens in despair beneath [his] feet."[53] This is where Sailor becomes most closely aligned with his musical inspiration, Elvis Presley, who, through his rejection of the negative energy that, according to Marcus, characterizes the blues, liberates rock 'n' roll from the more despairing aspects of its cultural roots, sidestepping the darkness and offering redemption in its place with a refusal to succumb to the pessimistic vision that Johnson offers.[54]

Even though the Legba figure here is white, Lynch's portrayal of him as a devil with no musical talents, as well as Peru's association with darkness, the crossroads, and a Black rocker/preacher like Little Richard set him up as the (predominantly) African American bluesmen like Robert Johnson whose chaos and dread the white Elvis renounces in order to attain musical supremacy and mastery. When Peru is contrasted with the blonde-haired white female of the Good Witch who serves as his foil in the film, the contrast between Saturday night and Sunday morning could not be more Black and white. The notion that Peru's Legba lacks any musical talent casts this contrast in an even starker light, as does the fact that Lynch's rock 'n' roll soundtrack selections, with the exception of the on-camera performance of "Up in Flames" by Koko Taylor, feature white singers exclusively. It is not that the force of the blues is merely destructive or demonic: it is not legitimately musical; it is simply noise that cannot offer redemption to anyone, only damnation. In order for American music to be redemptive, if we are to follow the implications of Marcus's and Lynch's portrayals, then it must be purified of its "dark" origins in the blues. This quest for purification, in many respects, symbolizes a quest for control in which the Saturday night juke joint, with its African rhythms and its tendency toward depravity, must be subjugated by the white rocker.

Lynch's Speed-Metal Romanticism

Apart from sex with Lula and his outbursts of violence, music is the only area in the film where Sailor enjoys a superior level of control and mastery. Davison outlines these moments where Sailor successfully manipulates the soundtrack: at the Hurricane, Sailor not only stops the band (Powermad itself) mid-song, but also becomes their bandleader in an impromptu cover of Elvis's "Love Me"; Lula searches for music on the radio to distract her from all the accounts of gore and mutilation, but only Sailor can locate a station playing music (Powermad's "Slaughterhouse," again adding a certain level of magic to Sailor's command of the soundtrack); and Sailor even has the ability to "generate music out of thin air" at the end of the film when he sings "Love Me Tender" to Lula.[55]

Initially, however, Sailor's power and passion express themselves as violent and destructive forces, and Powermad's speed-metal track "Slaughterhouse" serves as a leitmotif that establishes the intensity of Sailor's erratic, unreformed passions.[56] As mentioned earlier, describing "Slaughterhouse" as a leitmotif can appear potentially problematic at first because its abrasiveness seems to mirror the violence of the world around it, thus cementing Sailor as a figure of the violent world rather someone in pursuit of a way out of it.[57] Although Lynch uses "Slaughterhouse" to violently disrupt the calm status quo in the opening sequence, Michel Chion believes the song ultimately performs a different, more creative function in the film. Chion relates "Slaughterhouse" to another song Lynch uses as a leitmotif, Strauss's Im Abendrot: he claims that Lynch does not include these two songs to set up a snobbish contrast between high and low culture but rather as dual leitmotifs that complement each as "two expressions of the same power of love."[58] In fact, "Slaughterhouse" and Im Abendrot even fade into each other during a key scene in the film where Lula feverishly scans the dial in search of something positive, finding nothing but vivid accounts of brutality. She exclaims "It's Night of the Living fuckin' Dead!" and demands that Sailor find music on the radio "this instant." Sailor succeeds in finding "Slaughterhouse," and their visceral physical reaction matches their equally vigorous dancing from the scene at The Hurricane. As their dancing continues, the camera cranes and tilts up to reveal a dazzling sunset as "Slaughterhouse" fades into Strauss's Im Abendrot, thus positioning Sailor and Lula's point of view in line with that of the Romantics and marking their jubilation as a celebration of "the life-affirming energies of nature."[59] Not only does the music change, but so does Sailor and Lula's behavior: by the time Strauss takes over the soundtrack, Sailor and Lula have stopped their aggressive dancing and embrace.

For a film so focused on the grotesque, right down to its desolate, almost post-apocalyptic landscapes, this scene sticks out as a high point of sorts, a brief moment of aesthetic transcendence before the "eye-of-the-duck"

FIGURE 5.3 Speed-metal Romantics at dusk. *Wild at Heart* directed by David Lynch © Polygram Filmed Entertainment 1990. All rights reserved.

scene initiates the plot's downturn. This can be seen as an expression of the Romantic sensibility, which Kenneth Kaleta and Chion agree applies to Lynch, particularly in *Wild at Heart*.[60] In the radio scene, Sailor and Lula, through rock 'n' roll, succeed in suppressing the horrors of the world and thus make the world over in their image, bringing the world "over the rainbow" into their own. (The brilliance and multiple-hues of the light only serve to advance this notion.) The scene stands in stark contrast to the first use of "Slaughterhouse," where the song jarringly overpowers "In the Mood" during the killing of Bobby Ray Lemon. Lynch underscores this difference by using a different section of "Slaughterhouse" for the radio scene. Where previous section of "Slaughterhouse" accompanies scenes of sex or initiates moments of violent destruction, here the song ushers in a successful moment of Romantic transcendence. Lynch uses this section of "Slaughterhouse" once before in the film, and to a similar purpose: during the scene at the Hurricane, this part of the song also gets interrupted when a clubgoer begins dancing with Lula, thus giving Sailor "an opportunity to prove [his] love for [his] girl" by subduing the man and then singing Elvis's "Love Me" to Lula. In both cases, this same section of "Slaughterhouse" succeeds in signaling a transition away from violent, physical expressions of love and toward tender, musical expressions of love. This success is temporary in both scenes; however, what is crucial for later is that Lynch shows this can be done, that art has the power to transform the world around it, no matter how temporarily. In this regard, Chion and Nochimson each show how the film can be viewed as a journey of letting go of aggressive expressions of the power of love and instead being "overcome" by tender expressions of the power of love, from "Slaughterhouse" to "Love Me Tender."[61]

This transformation can only be attained, Lynch suggests, through a journey that deconstructs cultural norms, an odyssey to the roots of both the creative and destructive, the liminal space. The journey that Sailor and

Lula make in the film, both geographically and musically, represents a confrontation with liminality in which one encounters both a "base element in our involuntary energies" and a higher, generative, "maternal matrix of narrative and cultural renewal."[62] In the film this is the liminality of rock 'n' roll itself that Sailor carries within him and must learn to embrace. It is within this space that the seeker can find the power to merge culture and nature, Saturday night and Sunday morning, fantasy and reality in a manner that offers "the hope of a real offer of something of more permanent value" in a world that is "wild at heart and weird on top."[63]

Which brings us to the much-derided musical ending of the film. In it, Sailor reunites with Lula after serving his sentence for the robbery he commits with Bobby Peru, only to walk away from her and their son because he views his condition as hopeless, claiming that he will always be wild at heart and thus could only have a detrimental effect on Lula and Pace's lives.

FIGURE 5.4 Sailor commands the band. *Wild at Heart* directed by David Lynch © Polygram Filmed Entertainment 1990. All rights reserved.

FIGURE 5.5 Sailor summons music out of nothing. *Wild at Heart* directed by David Lynch © Polygram Filmed Entertainment 1990. All rights reserved.

After an improbably multicultural street gang pummels him, Sailor receives a visit from Glinda the Good Witch, who tells him that, despite his being wild at heart and lacking in parental guidance, Sailor must not turn away from love. If Sailor is truly wild at heart, Glinda says, then he will follow his dreams. Sailor then awakens from the trance, apologizes to the street gang for his homophobic insult, shouts "Lula!" (much like Brando's "Stella!") and chases after her. He finds her stuck in the midst of a traffic jam in the wake of a terrible car accident and pulls her to the hood of her car. At this moment, background music arrives out of nowhere, and Sailor, despite having a horribly broken nose, manages to sing "Love Me Tender," a song he promised he would sing only to his wife, warmly and sincerely, as the credits roll and the lovers slowly dance on the hood of the car.

Jeff Johnson provides a succinct version of the common criticisms of this ending, claiming that Lynch "drive[s] *Wild at Heart* into the wreck of a happy ending to satisfy his all-American longing for a return to Edenic purity."[64] Eric Wilson reads the ending even less favorably, describing it as a parody of traditional Hollywood movie endings that

> doesn't redeem so much as divert; it is not a romance as much as it is a send-up. If the film does indeed invoke romantic love, it does so only to make fun of Hollywood versions of affection. The film, in the end, seems to suggest that real love is impossible—only fake love, artificial movie love, can exist [...] [the film] reveals the total artifice of Hollywood joy.[65]

And the ending is most certainly sudden, clichéd, unexpected, and unconventional; however, it is not ironic in the cynical, postmodern sense that critics would have one believe. Rather than serve as "a knowing wink at happy endings," *Wild at Heart*'s climax presents the viewer with a "sincere invitation to an actual happy ending."[66] These very clichés that critics find so ironically repulsive are for Lynch a means of escape from the darkness of the world.[67] Although I appreciate that Johnson finds something resolutely American about this ending, I find a marked difference between a "longing for a return to Edenic purity" and a refusal to submit to a fatalistic worldview. Where the former is fanciful and impractical, the latter is willful and empowering. The ending reveals not only Lynch's commitment to passionate sincerity but also his Romantic vision of the transformative power of art. Lynch underscores this Romanticism by featuring *Im Abendrot* again in this scene as Sailor climbs over cars toward Lula. While abrupt, this ending does not negate any of the ideas in Lynch's film; rather, it offers the radical break Lynch sees as possible when one succeeds, through art, in creating an image of the world that contains and overcomes the "bad ideas" lying in wait. This final sequence places the creative power back into Sailor's hands: Sailor not only has regained his power to control music, but also has it stronger than ever because he has the power to conjure music out of silence without the assistance of a backing band or car radio.

It is no small accident that this final musical performance takes place in a traffic jam caused by a car wreck: this final scene undoes the destructive power of the earlier crash scene (the "eye-of-the-duck" scene), for now rather than slipping into nonsense and death, the film coalesces into order and life not through "a deeper immersion in the fantasy itself" but through an openness to the curative subconscious as embodied in rock 'n' roll.[68] Its strangeness shows how powerful Lynch believes his Romantic vision to be: when the wild at heart follow their dreams, they have the power to make over a world even as vile and brutal as the world of *Wild at Heart*. With the ending, Lynch reveals that, despite so much evidence to the contrary all around him, he refuses to accept the futility of art in the face of death and horror. This refusal is one that Marcus, writing about rock 'n' roll, believes is ultimately based on faith in the power both of love and art, "a faith meant to transcend the grimy world it call[s] up."[69] This is how Marcus describes the triumph of Elvis's rock 'n' roll: "the rhythmic force that was the practical legacy of Robert Johnson had evolved into a music that overwhelmed *his* reservations; the rough spirit of the new blues, city R&B, *rolled right over* [Johnson's] *nihilism*."[70] This quintessentially American idea, Marcus claims, "had to begin with an honest refusal of doubt and fatalism."[71] This refusal is what Lynch explores as the province and purpose of art. Where Robert Johnson and others may give up and be consumed by the terror and the dread, Lynch sees an opportunity for music to do what Marcus says about rock 'n' roll in the Prologue to *Mystery Train*: both *Wild at Heart* and rock music try "to create a world where we feel alive, risky, ambitious, and free […] dispensing with the rest of the American reality if we can. […] there is an attempt to create oneself, to make a new man out of what is inherited and what is imagined; each individual attempt implies an ideal community."[72]

FIGURE 5.6 Undoing the damage of the car wreck. *Wild at Heart* directed by David Lynch © Polygram Filmed Entertainment 1990. All rights reserved.

Lynch finds the American equivalent of the Romantic spirit in his portrayal of rock 'n' roll in *Wild at Heart*, for, as Marcus shows, rock functions as a liminal space that emerges victorious over the dread and despair of the blues to inject a creative, American spirit back into the world where the tension between Saturday night and Sunday morning resolves into a raucous celebration of individuality and personal freedom. Where Robert Johnson offers a vision of America that is doomed and dead, Lynch responds with "an unmatched version of an America that is full of life."[73]

Lynch's New Pop Signature

With *Blue Velvet*, Lynch established an approach to compilation scoring that many view to be one of his trademarks, in which he places seemingly innocuous pop ballads from the early 1960s underneath surreal scenes of disturbing violence and transgression. This practice strips the pop gloss off these allegedly safe songs to reveal the darkness at the root of both the song and the culture that produced it. Louise O'Riordan calls this a "conflicted" approach and views it as Lynch's "cheeky nod to the artifice of [his] scenes."[74] While Lynch does use rock music, particularly "Slaughterhouse," in the conflicted, performative way O'Riordan describes, he employs this signature style to quite different ends than he has in the past. Yes, "Slaughterhouse" initially functions as yet another brutal evocation of destructive sex and violence rupturing the surface calm of ordinary life; however, Lynch's efforts to associate the song with other musical styles such as *Im Abendrot*, challenge that initial, conflicted understanding of "Slaughterhouse" to promote a Romantic transformation from destruction to creation, beginning with an ironic expression of dissonance and guiding the audience through the film toward a sincere expression of harmony.

Therefore, in this case, Lynch portrays his signature style as the *superficial* understanding of the song that needs to be deconstructed by the film; his signature style, not the song, becomes conflicted, to the point that Lynch can present a pop ballad like "Love Me Tender" sincerely and without any conflicted meanings by the film's end. The fact that Sailor foreshadows the performance of "Love Me Tender" as a song he will only sing to his wife further prepares the viewer for such a sincere expression. While one could say this also occurs on the soundtrack at the end of *Blue Velvet* when the robins come, there the sincere musical expression comes from a Lynch-Badalamenti composition, not from a previously existing song. Further, as we have seen, *Blue Velvet* problematizes any sense of sincere comfort the viewer feels at the end of the film as title track continues to haunt the film as it echoes over the final fade-out, implying, through its conflicted meaning, that the world's wickedness may return. For a filmmaker as steeped in the ironic, contrapuntal use of pop music as Lynch, presenting a romantic surface uncritically represents quite a departure.

This strategy could be seen as a critical misstep for Lynch, a moment when he is not being adequately ironic, detached, or Lynchian; however, I prefer to assert that Lynch does this not to be naïve or insincere but rather to offer a more comprehensive, overt expression of his Romantic sensibility than he offers anywhere else in his *oeuvre*. Viewing Lynch's musical signature in this way reveals a more complex and nuanced practice than the predominant perception of it currently allows. This is not to say that his signature use of pop music has been wholly misinterpreted; however, the general trend of reading his compilation scores has perhaps led to an oversimplification of his overall sensibility because that use of music is so powerful and iconic. His changed tactic in *Wild at Heart* not only offers a new dimension to his use of pop music but also invites a deeper and more polyvalent way of looking at music in all his work. What follows will apply this more polyvalent approach to more of his work.

6

The Ballad of Laura Palmer

Since its premiere on ABC on April 8, 1990, scholars and critics alike have filled countless pages and column inches pointing out the myriad genres and styles *Twin Peaks* participates in, from soap opera to police procedural to postmodern neo-noir to pop surrealism and everything in between. While these comparisons are most certainly apt and fit neatly into discussions of David Lynch's broader cinematic project (especially the surrounding works *Blue Velvet* and *Lost Highway*), they seldom stray far from the literary, televisual, or cinematic. This limited focus overlooks the deep relationship *Twin Peaks* has with musical forms and traditions.

This claim is not to suggest that scholars have not been talking about music in *Twin Peaks*. Far from it. Angelo Badalamenti's finger-snapping jazz lines and swooning operatic arrangements have become as central to the show's identity as coffee and cherry pie and have been the subject of much scholarship, including an entry in the popular *33 1/3* book series. In fact, unlike Badalamenti's other work with Lynch, his score for *Twin Peaks* is so iconic that it obscures the ways that *Twin Peaks* interacts with pop music and pop music forms, especially pop from the early 1960s. John Richardson comes the closest to conceiving of *Twin Peaks* in musical terms in his article "*Laura* and *Twin Peaks*: Postmodern Parody and the Musical Representation of the Absent Femme Fatale." He writes that the parodic gestures in the music of the series create an image of Laura Palmer as "fragmentary, internally inconsistent, and unfathomable" to such a degree that "conventional narrative substance is eclipsed," leading one to conclude that the series "can be perceived as *nothing but music*."[1] Richardson discourages this reading to some degree; however, a sincere reading of *Twin Peaks* as "nothing but music" illuminates how 1960s pop music styles and forms subconsciously inform and steer the series' emotional and narrative course.

Although it may seem like *Twin Peaks*' connection to 1960s pop remains at the iconographic level of wardrobe and set decoration (1980s teens in poodle skirts, saddle oxfords, and leather jackets), its use of 1960s pop is not as limited as what we hear on its soundtrack may make it seem. According to Mark Mazullo, this era of pop music, with its heavy reverb and swelling vocal harmonies, features "a certain 'abnormality' in the sound [that] provides a disconcerting foil to the song's almost unbearably naïve sincerity, the often-saccharine 'normality' of its emotional message, harmonic structure, rhythm, and musical form." In Lynch's hands, these needle drops become "a portal to the uncanny" and give each film "a unique and expressive sound signature."[2] The style, tone, rhythm, and feelings of *Twin Peaks* bears a 1960s pop sound signature from one genre in particular: the teen tragedy ballad. Even though no instances of it ever appear on the soundtrack in the series, *Twin Peaks* uses the sensibility and iconography from this genre to stir genuine feeling in its media-savvy audience so much so that *Twin Peaks* itself could be viewed as another entry in its canon and a part of its legacy. With its recreation of the teen tragedy ballad and its "clashes between innocence and desire, between the comforts of sincerity and the unfathomable dangers of authenticity," *Twin Peaks* itself is, in the words of Mazullo, "a *new* song that tells us something about *old* songs" in a way that renders it a coherent, consistent, and fathomable depiction of a postwar America still reeling from the loss of its idealistic vision of itself.[3]

Teen tragedy ballads, also known as coffin songs, splatter platters, death discs, and other derisive terms, were a pop ballad fad of the late 1950s and early 1960s. These songs present sentimental narratives of teenage love, loss, and death, most commonly in a fiery car wreck, often sung from the point of view or the lover left behind, although some notable examples are narrated from the point of view of the dying or deceased lover. While there are several songs from this genre that have achieved classic status, such as the Shangri-Las' "The Leader of the Pack" and Jan and Dean's "Dead Man's Curve," critics generally dismiss teen tragedy songs as commercial schlock from the musical Dark Age between 1958 and 1964 that R. Serge Denisoff calls "an uncomfortable way station from Elvis Presley to Lennon and McCartney."[4] The tone and content of these songs can certainly make them appear to be outside the boundaries of good taste; however, one should hesitate before claiming that the "morbid sentimentality" of these songs renders them little more than crass novelty recordings.[5]

While some of these songs are indeed too morbid and melodramatic to be taken seriously, the artistic merit and social function of these songs remains largely underappreciated. As David Inglis notes, teen tragedy ballads do not differ much from other pop songs: they are at their heart "laments for lost or unfulfilled love" and unique primarily in the sense that a tragic death is the reason their love remains unfulfilled or lost. The depiction of this loss comes off as overly emotional because the characters in these songs (and their audience) are almost always teenagers. This detail is more than merely coincidental. The arrival of teen tragedy ballads shortly follows the emergence of the teenager, youth culture, and car culture in the American imagination (and media market), all forces that figure prominently in teen tragedy songs. These cultural shifts gave young people new ways to enjoy and define themselves, but they also gave them new ways to meet an early end or to lose someone close to them too soon. Within the confines of the three-minute pop song, teen tragedy ballads depict a maturing generation's first encounters with death in all its "sudden, unfair, and, above all, disruptive" power.[6]

Such disruptive deaths were increasingly ubiquitous in the popular imagination in the late 1950s and early 1960s, from fictional tragedies serving as plot points in teen melodramas to real-life catastrophes such as the Day the Music Died, the deaths of James Dean and Marilyn Monroe, or, most traumatically, the assassination of John F. Kennedy. The ubiquity of these figures in mass media created an illusion of closeness between them and the public, making their deaths less abstract than they might have been for teenagers of previous generations. These sudden deaths rattled emotions on a national level the same way the unexpected tragic deaths of young loved ones did the hearts of teens on an individual level. The aftermath of these events, both personal and national, left the bereaved reeling and adrift, compelling them to cherish and romanticize the time when their lives were not marked by sudden tragedy. This impulse inspired people to process this trauma in the form of art, producing songs and other kinds of tributes in which the deceased were romanticized as images of youthful vigor and exuberance who escaped the corruption and decay of adult life by never growing old.[7]

In order to better understand the impact and influence that teen tragedy ballads have on the American imagination, we must look beyond the genre, beyond even music. As strange as such an approach may seem, David Atkinson argues that it is a necessary one because like the murder ballads from which they descend, teen tragedy songs have an intertextuality to them that cannot be limited to music alone: it "extends to other texts, especially those occupying something of the same field of cultural production and cultural discourse."[8] If one wants to examine another text that embodies and extends the discourse of teen tragedy ballads, one can find no better example than *Twin Peaks*. Although Lynch has hardly made a secret of his fondness for the Shangri-Las, he has never used a teen tragedy song in any of his films.[9] In a sense, he hardly needs to: the sensibility and style of teen tragedy ballads permeate most of his work, but none more so than *Twin Peaks*, whose affiliating identifications with teen tragedy ballads demonstrate how Lynch's series is not just an extended teen tragedy song but the fullest, most extensive expression of the genre to date.

Teen tragedy songs bear all the sound signatures of David Lynch's own music: heavy reverb, simple, direct lyrics that border on (or at least indulge in) cliché, and melodies that wallow in soaring and disarmingly naked expressions of emotion. These songs also come from the exact same time period and share a fascination with the same kind of American iconography as Lynch's work. The wholesome, innocent American wonderland rattled by horrific tragedy that we see in *Blue Velvet, The Straight Story*, or *Mulholland Drive* is exactly the kind of world conjured up by songs such as Del Shannon's "The Prom," Mark Dining's "Teen Angel," or Cathy Carroll's "Jimmy Love." However, rather than use teen tragedy songs directly, Lynch uses them as a discourse, treating them as what Katherine M. Reed describes as "artifact and part of collective memory."[10] Mazullo claims that Lynch's use of other 1960s pop songs such as Roy Orbison's "In Dreams" or Linda Scott's "I've Told Every Little Star" "reimagin[es] their history" in a manner that "calls into question our culture's peculiar sublimation of the pop song, and particularly of the sincerity expressed in these often taken-for-granted cultural texts."[11] The *Twin Peaks* universe is just such an example in the sense that it not only traffics in the collective memory of American musical culture but also becomes both artifact and memory itself, creating a "shared history" and network of affiliating identifications for viewers over its three incarnations that imbue the people, songs, sounds, and objects that appear repeatedly in the series with symbolic weight and, most importantly, feeling. Reed's and Atkinson's conceptions align well with Kassabian's idea of affiliating identifications, extending Kassabian's concept by showing how Lynch's soundtracks draw audiences into a more active viewership to construct the film's meaning via an "active dialogue" with these affiliating identifications that goes far beyond that of a mere needle drop.[12] This active dialogue in *Twin Peaks* achieves a greater level of affective expression because it engages with the audience's "collective memory" of an entire genre of music *without ever using any of its representative songs on its soundtrack*.

As is the case with much Lynch's work, *Twin Peaks* and teen tragedy ballads use the energy inherent in the tension between sincerity and irony, art and kitsch, to resurrect genuine feeling within a commercial space of consumption such as the pop song or primetime network melodrama. However, where Lynch's use of 1960s pop songs elsewhere often creates a sense of "estrangement," in *Twin Peaks*, the form of the teen tragedy ballad becomes a key tool of *engagement*, a resurrection of those very feelings of raw, sincere emotional intensity the culture has worked tirelessly to mock, deny, or suppress.[13] Like teen tragedy ballads, the emotional register of *Twin Peaks* is simultaneously a cliché of and catalyst for genuine feeling.[14] The speakers in teen tragedy ballads fit a melodramatic archetype that Justus Nieland describes as "radio-active" in the sense that they are less realistic representations of human behavior as they are "receivers and transmitters in a mediated network of affect and action."[15] Their lack of three-dimensional psychological realism makes it easier to disregard their emotional outpourings as the stuff of cliché; however, in so thoroughly and wholeheartedly committing to the cliché, in such open expression of sentiment, they reanimate the feelings numbed by cliché and allow an attentive and sincere listener to receive "radio-active" transmissions of feeling from inside themselves that they seldom tune into.

In their over-the-top and startling inclusion of non-musical elements, the production of teen tragedy songs itself is even more "radio-active" than the uncanny pop hits Lynch uses elsewhere in his films. Chock-full of sound effects ("The Leader of the Pack"), spoken narration or dialogue (Bernadette Carroll's "The Hero"), graphically vivid narratives (Johnny Cymbal's "The Water Was Red"), and reverb-drenched harmonies (Jody Reynolds's "Endless Sleep"), teen tragedy ballads feature a more dynamic and complex sonic landscape than many of their pop contemporaries. These elements are often the ones critics cite as proof that the songs are little more than silly novelty recordings, but these same elements are also the ones that make the songs sound remarkably cinematic.[16] In asking listeners to experience the tales these songs tell in widescreen Cinemascope Sensurround, teen tragedy ballads themselves become "radio-active," transmitting far and wide in search of something beyond what music can express, something that can produce images, dramatic lighting and visual effects, and, above all else, intense feelings. Ironically, they achieve this feat through a focus on the kitsch status of the "mortified cultural materials" themselves, which they treat seriously as outpourings of genuine feeling rather than soulless commercial cashgrabs.[17]

Such qualities can be difficult to discern by looking directly at a mawkish teen tragedy song, which is why *Twin Peaks* serves as an essential statement on the teen tragedy genre that extends its ideas and repositions it in the public imagination. With *Twin Peaks*, Lynch expands the emotional and aesthetic scope of the teen tragedy ballad to show how these ballads of loss and lament mourn the horrific loss of not only a love interest, but also the ideals of beauty and excellence that love interest has been made to embody. Through the "resignification of cultural material," *Twin Peaks* resurrects one of the most kitschy, mocked, and forgotten forms of music, the teen tragedy ballad, and makes it a "meeting place" for genuine emotion "where recycled culture may be reinvested with subjective values."[18] With each point of view shift in the series, from the focus on the grief of the sweethearts left behind in the ABC run, to the victim herself in *Fire Walk with Me*, and, with *Twin Peaks* (2017), to the viewers of the original seasons and the current residents of a disillusioned, desiccated America, *Twin Peaks* uses the teen tragedy form to critique the retreat into nostalgia and the romanticization of the tragic deaths of young beautiful people to confront a culture that refuses to look squarely at tragedy and its complicity in it. In doing so, the *Twin Peaks* universe offers a panoramic view of Lynch's vision of America: a seemingly innocent lover mourning the tragic loss of their ideal beloved and the innocence that attended that love, until all that they have left to hold onto is that sense of loss itself.

Mourning the Teen Angel:
Twin Peaks (1990–1)

It might seem like *Twin Peaks*' contribution to the teen tragedy ballad is that it takes it into the supernatural realm via the Red Room, Project Blue Book, and Glastonbury Grove, but the presence of the supernatural in tales of beautiful dead young women goes back at least as far as Child Ballads.[19] More recently, Dickie Lee's 1965 song "Laurie (Strange Things Happen)" details a narrator falling in love with a ghost. The speaker walks a beautiful girl named Laurie—note the name—home one night. She complains she is cold, so he gives her his sweater. The next day, he realizes he forgot to get his sweater back from her, but when he returns to the girl's house, her father tells him that she died a year ago last night, which also happened to be her birthday. When the narrator goes to her grave to confirm the father's story, he finds his sweater draped over her tombstone. His response is a line straight out of a David Lynch film: "Strange things happen in this world."

Although other teen tragedy ballads do not feature the dead returning from the grave for a night, all are about people in love with ghosts, and this love drives them to attempt a kind of musical resurrection. The songs are fueled by a desire to reanimate and reclaim a lost loved one by telling the story of their death in song and, as in J. Frank Wilson's "Last Kiss," the Everly Brothers' "Ebony Eyes," and several other songs, to dream of the day when they will be reunited in the afterlife. (In some songs, such as "Endless Sleep" or Kip Tyler's "Eternity," the speaker plots to take their own life to expedite their heavenly reunion.)

Of course, efforts to resurrect and reanimate a body through song or any other means are impossible, but we can resurrect our emotions through bestowing totemic power on an object or through representational acts such as photographs, songs, and, at its most extreme and literal form, taxidermy. Sherri Ayers turns to taxidermy as the central metaphor for how *Twin Peaks* speaks in the "dead language" of allegory to "[resurrect] feeling."[20] With its uncanny appearance and location on the outskirts of good taste, taxidermy becomes a similar intersection of death and kitsch that teen tragedy ballads represent musically.[21] Plastic kitsch objects such as pop songs, television soap operas, and sentimental tchotchkes are the media equivalent of taxidermy in the sense that all are attempts to freeze time, to preserve life and sentiment, to keep the absent present. As an object itself, a song fixes these internal emotions in an external form—a song, a record—that can be touched and repeated endlessly, preserving the memory of the lost love as well as the speaker's grief, to freeze them in time at the moment they are lost. Martha Nochimson notes the totemic power that superficial objects acquire in *Twin Peaks* through their association with Laura Palmer and her murder, such as her sunglasses, diaries, and other items. These objects become what Nochimson calls a "meeting place between social constructs and the larger energies" in the sense that they become symbols upon which people can project their complicated and unresolved emotions about Laura and the tragedy of losing her.[22] Brooke McCorkle Okazaki makes this connection explicit in describing Laura Palmer as "a vinyl record [...] run down by the weight of her repeated trauma" and the viewers' repeated viewings of that trauma in the same way that playing a record gradually destroys the disc itself.[23]

These songs use objects as tokens of both the power of love and the tragedy of the lovers' separation, making these objects meeting places in the song for the tragedy and the grief and mourning that attend it. Like taxidermy, these songs are "artificial construction[s] made to appear real" that are often criticized for their tackiness in turning suffering into an object of consumption; however, they also imbue this suffering with genuine and intense emotion, making them meeting places for similar energies thanks to how they use objects as catalysts for feeling.[24] In "Teen Angel" and Ray Peterson's "Tell Laura I Love Her," rings become symbolic objects of love and grief. Tommy, the speaker in "Tell Laura I Love Her" dies in a stock car race that he entered in the hope of using the prize money to purchase a ring for his girlfriend Laura. The speaker in "Teen Angel" successfully pulls his love out of their car after it stalls on the railroad tracks as a train approaches, only to lose her when she runs back to the car to retrieve his high school ring he gave her as a symbol of his love.

As these synopses demonstrate, some of the derision surrounding teen tragedy ballads comes from the fact that these plots and the music's unrestrained, naked, and direct expression of intense emotion often makes them difficult to take seriously, a sentiment which should sound familiar to viewers of *Twin Peaks*. As Michel Chion notes, *Twin Peaks* faced similar criticism due to "the way it deploys tears" to an almost embarrassing extent in its early episodes.[25] The pilot episode of the series features several scenes of extended crying as each character learns of Laura Palmer's death. When combined with the iconic chords from Badalamenti's "Laura Palmer's Theme," Donna Hayward's (Lara Flynn Boyle) silent wail, Leland Palmer's shocked moan, and Sarah Palmer's (Grace Zabriskie) seemingly incessant load groans approach the level of melodramatic excess until they sound almost like songs of grief in their own right. Such unrestrained wails set to music sound remarkably like the end of Ray Peterson's "Tell Laura I Love Her." With each appearance of the song's chorus, Peterson's voice grows shakier and less composed, which, when combined with the echo, makes it sounds like Tommy is so close to breaking down in tears that he

FIGURE 6.1 AND 6.2 Excessive tears. *Twin Peaks* directed by David Lynch ©
Lynch/Frost Productions 1990. All rights reserved.

will not be able to continue, but the fade out as he repeats "tell Laura I love her" suggests that he will repeat this request for all eternity. Such prolonged portrayals of grief cross the line of what most audiences feel is acceptable, prompting them to dismiss the show's treatment of sorrow as "too much"; however, in going beyond the boundaries of what is generally regarded as acceptable displays of emotion, teen tragedy ballads and *Twin Peaks* unlock another "emotional dimension" that provokes audiences to accept these seemingly excessive emotional outpourings as the only reasonable responses to tragedy.[26]

Lynch and co-creator Mark Frost's engagement with the logic and style of teen tragedy ballads shows us how these pop objects transcend their kitsch status as taxidermy to generate and sustain real feeling. However, these efforts never can resurrect the lost love, only one's feeling about that lost love, thus the object accumulates more emotion while simultaneously drifting further away from what it was created to represent until all that remains is "a sense of endless lamentation."[27] Every mourner's cries in *Twin Peaks* say the same thing: "tell Laura I love her." They are engaging in public testimony in an attempt to externalize their intense internal feelings, with each character, each viewer joining into a symphony of feeling where the chorus is "Laura." This practice confronts and indulges in their grief but at the expense of Laura Palmer, whom they turn into an object, a symbol of their lost love. Laura Palmer may not take spectral form to haunt residents of Twin Peaks from beyond the grave as the girl in "Laurie (Strange Things Happen)" does, but she does not have to: she haunts the show in the form of the many media forms that stuff her hollowed-out identity—the photographs, videotapes, evidence bags, etc., that transform her absence into artifact.[28]

However, these songs and the weeping on *Twin Peaks* also serve as symbols of a deeper, more abstract loss: the loss that occurs when a culture's structuring symbols and myths fall apart. What the residents of Twin Peaks really lament when they mourn Laura Palmer is the time when they could believe that the fictions they created were true, a time when they did not have to admit they lived in a dream. Without the culturally fabricated image of Laura Palmer—the blonde homecoming queen from the nuclear family dating the football star in the quaint, heartwarmingly innocent small town—can no longer sustain this nostalgic image of itself and must now confront what it always has been: a place that has used nostalgia and kitsch objectification to obscure corruption, abuse, and trauma. As such, this mourning only highlights the loss of something that was not real to begin with, thus only the mourning becomes real. Such illusions play out in teen tragedy ballads on a personal and a national level. They capture the shattering of the teenage illusion of invincibility, but the historical context of teen tragedy ballads coincides with a shattering of American innocence in the early 1960s best exemplified by the Kennedy assassination, a cultural moment when America can no longer believe that things are always getting better or that things will always turn out for the best. After losing the symbol that has propped up that myth and obscured the reality, be it Laura Palmer, Camelot, or one's first love, the bereaved then must choose whether to face the reality of the situation or to attempt to revive their lost love through some kind of object. By tapping into and broadcasting these raw feelings of grief, pain, and sorrow, *Twin Peaks* demonstrates how teen tragedy ballads are the sonic equivalent of *garmonbozia* that can be replayed, resurrected, and reenacted indefinitely until everyone is walking around feeling like they are part of something that used to be alive, a taxidermied America.

Last Kiss at Sparkwood and 21: *Fire Walk with Me*

Fire Walk with Me makes for a subversive entry in the teen tragedy genre. Even as it fulfills many of its tropes, it rebukes the kind of nostalgic romanticization that teen tragedy ballads traffic in. Denisoff, Inglis, and Atkinson all note that teen tragedy and murder ballads pose a challenge to existing power structures, even if it is ultimately a dubious one. Denisoff is the most generous of the three, noting that teen tragedy ballads at their root depict a rebellion against the adult world and all that it represents, with the tragedy being that "immediate adversity can be overcome with the absolute of death."[29] Inglis extends this argument to classify death as an "act of resistance"; however, he concludes that, in the implicit approval of parental authority that their sadness and regret represents, teen tragedy ballads are "fundamentally conservative texts" that act as moral fables for any teens considering rebelling against authority.[30] Atkinson also argues that these murder ballads only seem to subvert dominant ideologies but function more as carnivalesque inversions of existing power structures that, in the ballad's desire for order and closure, the song ultimately reinforces.[31] *Twin Peaks* faces similar charges of conservatism, as does Lynch's work in general. The show's entire goal in solving Laura Palmer's murder is to restore order after a traumatic rupture in the existing balance of the sleepy town where a yellow light still means slow down instead of speed up. However, *Twin Peaks* repeatedly reveals the adult world to be corrupt, and with *Fire Walk with Me* and *Twin Peaks* (2017), we can see the subversive potential of the teenage tragedy ballad because these challenges to existing power relationship do not get resolved. Rather, everything becomes more destabilized and indeterminate to show how the real destabilizing force is the desire for closure, resolution, and order. Lynch himself has characterized closure as a tool of forgetting when he told the *Los Angeles Times* that "as soon as a show has a sense of closure, it gives you an excuse to forget you've seen the damn thing."[32]

FIGURE 6.3 Sparkwood and 21. *Twin Peaks: Fire Walk with Me* directed by David Lynch © CIBY Pictures 1992. All rights reserved.

The setpiece within the world of *Twin Peaks* that bears the closest resemblance to a teen tragedy ballad finds its fullest depiction in *Fire Walk with Me*: the scene where Laura hops off James Hurley's motorcycle at the stoplight at Sparkwood and 21 and disappears into the forest. This scene is one that *Twin Peaks* returns to in every iteration, with each return shifting the context not only of the scene itself but the series of which it is a part. In the pilot of *Twin Peaks*, James Hurley (James Marshall) recounts these events to Donna Hayward. His description sounds like the spoken narration that would play as the bridge in a teen tragedy song with background ooohs or the Lynchian sound of wind through the trees playing underneath:

> It was kinda like a nightmare. Donna, she was a different person. [...] It all made some kind of terrible sense that she died. ... Half the time she wasn't making any sense. I couldn't calm her down. I couldn't keep her on the bike. When we came to the light at Sparkwood and 21, and she put her hands around my neck and she screamed she loved me. I looked into her eyes: they were clear. It was like she was Laura again. She was so sad. She sounded so desperate. And she ran off.

This incident has all the hallmarks of the teen tragedy ballad. There is the dark road at night that is a staple in over a dozen songs, there is a lover running away from the speaker toward their death as we see in "Teen Angel," there is a motorcycle, and finally there is the poignant last embrace.

Fire Walk with Me returns to Sparkwood and 21, and in doing so provides an alternate perspective of the scene, one in which James's narrative from the first season of *Twin Peaks* is revealed to be heavily romanticized. *Fire Walk with Me*'s rendition of this scene demonstrates that James is not the Brandoesque bad boy his bike and leather jacket suggest he is but rather, like the speaker of "Teen Angel," so wrapped up in his love and infatuation for her as an idea that he let her run back into the wreck instead of holding her close. Laura and James's conversation on this dark road at night is not a tender exchange between parting lovers but a bitter and disturbing battle between lovers where insults collide with professions of love or distress, with each party changing emotions like a hairpin turn on a dead man's curve. Their actual parting at the light at Sparkwood and 21 carries this to tragic, operatic proportions, as Laura wails "I love you, James" as she staggers toward her horrible fate.

Like the bulk of *Fire Walk with Me*, the scene demonstrates in miniature how the film can be viewed as a response song to the tragedy ballad that is *Twin Peaks*, a response song in which Laura reclaims her voice and chastises everyone around her for turning her into a piece of taxidermy while still alive. At first glance, Lynch's stated desire to see Laura Palmer walk and talk appears to be a retreat into nostalgic fan service; however, any expectations that Lynch will use *Fire Walk with Me* to bask in the quirky glow of *Twin Peaks* quickly disappear. Instead, viewers are treated to a confrontation with all the forces that allowed Laura Palmer to be victimized. To accomplish this, Lynch leans into a motif common to murder ballads that Mazullo dubs "the drowned virgin-whore model."[33] However, much like P. J. Harvey does in her album *Dry* (also released in 1992), Lynch does not employ this trope to tell a cautionary tale about the dangers of female sexual awakening but rather to craft a more ambivalent and powerful dissection of the forces that construct this model and use it to prey upon its victims, consuming them from the inside out. Instead, Lynch, like Harvey, "provides simultaneously both the myth and the thing itself" in order to "act out disorienting and sometimes disturbing tales of identity, sexuality and power" as a vehicle for "a uniting of forces in the excavation of a troubled past."[34]

In choosing to have *Fire Walk with Me* be told from the point of view of the victim, Lynch rebukes not only the throng of so-called admirers within the world of the show who neglected and objectified Laura while she was alive only to profess love and devotion after her death, he also takes viewers to task for giddily fetishizing the quirkier aspects of *Twin Peaks* and forgetting the traumatic story at its heart that revealed the quirky nostalgia to be a lie. Such a move places *Fire Walk with Me* in the same camp as other teen tragedy response songs such as "Tell Tommy I Miss Him" or "I Want My Baby Back"; however, where those exist at the level of novelty tie-in or straight-out parody, *Fire Walk with Me* operates as a response song that critiques. Like "Tell Laura I Love Her," *Fire Walk with Me* allows the dead love object to speak and reject her fatal romanticization with every breath. The film shows how often her words are tuned out because they conflict with the romanticized image of her that the environment around her has erected. In fact, their love songs are perhaps trying to keep her voice from being heard by subsuming it into their love and grief for them.

As Todd McGowan argues in his book *The Impossible David Lynch*, Laura Palmer is the "structuring absence" of *Fire Walk with Me* in much the same way that the dead love objects of teen tragedy ballads and the beautiful female murder victim are.[35] Elevated to the status of a "Teen Angel," Laura Palmer has been hollowed out and stuffed with every contradictory fantasy about women that patriarchal culture has to offer.[36] This status is not lost on her; however, as much as Laura may attempt to craft a response song of her own, she finds that she is no match for the power of the cultural image she has been turned into. She tells James in their first scene together in the film, "I'm long gone, like a turkey in the corn," and she reiterates this point to him at Sparkwood and 21 on the night of her murder when she says, "There's no place left to go, is there, James? You know it and I know it. [...] Your Laura disappeared. It's just me now." This exchange, like much of Laura's interactions with her peers in *Fire Walk with Me*, is a dialogue between image and reality, a dialogue that *Fire Walk with Me* forces viewers to engage in, not only with the world of *Twin Peaks* but within themselves as fans of *Twin Peaks*. As viewers of *Fire Walk with Me*, we must "experience" and "endure" the emptiness of objectification.[37]

The objectification that *Fire Walk with Me* critiques finds its apotheosis in a teen tragedy ballad: J. Frank Wilson and the Cavaliers' "Last Kiss." In it, the speaker of the song swerves to avoid a stalled car and crashes. He comes to and finds his girlfriend barely alive and he kisses her one last time. In that last kiss, the speaker says that he "found the love, that [he] knew

FIGURE 6.4 "Laura's gone away." *Twin Peaks: Fire Walk with Me* directed by David Lynch © CIBY Pictures 1992. All rights reserved.

[he] had missed." Rather than mourning a lost love, "Last Kiss" portrays her death as a fulfillment of love, a love only achievable with her death. Unlike Sleeping Beauty, the kiss does not bring the woman back to life but becomes the act that objectifies its recipient and grants the speaker's love a kind of immortality that is inextricable from the fascination with their lover's death. While "Last Kiss" does this unconsciously, *Fire Walk with Me* addresses this objectifying impulse head-on, revealing that the Laura Palmer that Twin Peaks is in love with is a lifeless image, the taxidermied Laura Palmer.

"The Ballad of Laura Palmer," that is, *Fire Walk with Me*, finds its central theme song in Laura's "Falling in Space" monologue. In an early scene in Donna's living room, Donna (Moira Kelly) asks Laura, "do you think that if you were falling in space that you would slow down or go faster and faster?" Laura responds rather chillingly, "faster and faster. And for a long time you wouldn't feel anything. And then you'd burst into fire. Forever. And the angels wouldn't help you because they've all gone away." This monologue presents Laura as abandoned and adrift, plummeting to a death no one is willing to save her from because they only see the "Teen Angel" of their fantasies rather than the real woman in trouble. However, Lynch goes much further than simply mounting a critique of romanticized teen tragedy ballads: he attempts to stage an intervention for Laura. At the conclusion to the film, the horrific ordeal of Laura's murder abruptly halts as the abrasive soundtrack cuts out and an angel appears in the train car. While the angel does not stop Laura's murder, the angel escorts Laura to the Red Room. Here, Laura discovers the angels have not gone away but rather have arrived to deliver her from her suffering, to catch her as she falls in space. This reversal bears some resemblance to the sentiment teen tragedy ballads express where the

FIGURE 6.5 Laura falling in space. *Twin Peaks: Fire Walk with Me* directed by David Lynch © CIBY Pictures 1992. All rights reserved.

lovers dream of being reunited in the afterlife; however, where that wish for a reunion seeks to release the living from their grief, Lynch reaches out in *Fire Walk with Me* to console the real victim, to release her from her suffering and offer a dream of peaceful reunion, perhaps twenty-five years down the road, maybe even back at the light at Sparkwood and 21.

Laura's Gone Away: *Twin Peaks* (2017)

That impossible reunion came to pass in 2015 with the announcement that a new season of *Twin Peaks* was entering production. Along with that announcement came fans' hope for closure and answers to all the questions lingering after the end of the series' run on ABC. With *Twin Peaks* (2017), Lynch critiques not only nostalgia (as he did in *Fire Walk with Me*) but also the demand for closure and order that memorialization pursues. As Joshua Jones shows, the desire for closure in characters and viewers alike leads to Laura Palmer being reobjectified in *Twin Peaks* (2017) as Agent Cooper becomes a vehicle for the viewers' desire to save Laura (and, by extension, the rest of the town) from their tragic fate.[38] However, in *Twin Peaks* (2017), this attempt to resurrect Laura is no longer figurative: now Agent Cooper himself returns to the night of her death and attempts to pull her away from her tragic fate, redeeming her and the rest of America by extension. Across its eighteen episodes, *Twin Peaks* (2017) deftly indulges in, frustrates, and ultimately rejects these efforts for resurrection and closure, resulting in a chilling and horrific variation on the impossibility of going home again.

FIGURE 6.6 "The" Nine Inch Nails. *Twin Peaks* directed by David Lynch © Showtime Networks 2017. All rights reserved.

Although it may seem like the teen tragedy form has largely disappeared from *Twin Peaks* by the time *Twin Peaks* (2017) arrives, the appearance of Nine Inch Nails' "She's Gone Away" in Episode eight does more than simply contribute to the mesmerizing audacity of this staggering hour of television: it revives the teen tragedy ballad as a haunting industrial dirge. Or, perhaps more accurately, it unearths the darkness and horror buried within these songs. The song, which the band wrote expressly for *Twin Peaks* (2017), reads like a thesis statement for the series that rebukes the show's characters and viewers alike for their attempts to resurrect Laura Palmer and the nostalgic impulse that she represents. The lyrics may be more poetic and abstract in their imagery than most teen tragedy ballads, but it could not be more direct in its message. Residents of Twin Peaks and fans of the show can "dig in places till [their] fingers bleed" and "can keep licking while the skin turns black," but nothing will resurrect the feeling they crave, as Reznor repeats "She's Gone Away." What have also gone away are the soothing, soaring melancholy melodies that make a pretty object out of grief and loss. No chords, no riffs, no comforting formulaic structure, even for those accustomed to Nine Inch Nails' abrasiveness. Here all that remains is pounding percussion, screeching guitars, and a numbed chorus serving as the most conventionally musical moment. The song makes it clear: all that is left now is the loss; it is the only thing left that makes sense.

The show might have been released under the name *Twin Peaks: The Return*, and the series certainly capitalized on Laura's prophetic line, "I'll see you in twenty-five years" and the promise of revisiting some favorite characters and seeing some beloved plotlines resolve. However, for all the attempts at a "return" in *Twin Peaks* (2017), there is an equal amount of evidence that such returns are impossible: time moves in only one direction, and no amount of nostalgic objectification can bring back the dead. The most moving and poignant examples of this sentiment would be the "In Memoriam" dedications in the closing credits of many episodes that acknowledge the actors who either died before the series went into production or passed away shortly after their scenes were shot. These incomplete returns activate real feelings of true loss in the audience. With each new installment of *Twin Peaks*, Lynch ushers viewers through clichéd nostalgic romanticization to confront the feeling everyone, characters and audience members alike, has been trying to avoid. Each confrontation grows more intense for the viewer because each time is more personal. They have developed more attachments to objects and characters, making their losses more deeply felt.

Three key sequences in the final episodes of *Twin Peaks* (2017) drive this point home. The first represents the most satisfying and uncritical instance of fan service in the entire series: the kiss between Big Ed and Norma in Episode fifteen. The scene, captured from one camera angle and set to Otis Redding's "I've Been Loving You Too Long," acts as not only the ideal resolution of one story arc in the series but also a release of pent-up frustrated energy in fans hoping for a "return" to the original run's more emotive and sentimental moments after fifteen hours of delayed gratification. This scene, combined with Cooper's triumphant resurrection in the next episode, sets up the viewers' expectation of further wish fulfillment as the series winds to a close, wishes that the last two episodes will initially indulge only to violently strip away.

Twin Peaks' (2017) next "slight return" is to Sparkwood and 21 in Episode seventeen. In an amazing feat of recontextualization, Lynch takes Agent Cooper back in time to the woods of Twin Peaks and makes him the trigger for Laura's blood-curdling scream as she clings to James Hurley before running away. Cooper then rendezvous with Laura in the forest, attempting, like Orpheus, to lead her away from her fate and into an alternate future. He is, it seems, only partly successful. Later in the episode, we return to the banks of the river the morning Laura's body was found, only we do not see Laura Palmer wrapped in plastic: she's gone away. Perhaps she has not been murdered by her father. Perhaps this local tragedy and all the other, more abstract tragedies that attend it have been averted. Perhaps a return to innocence, a true sense of closure, is possible. However, as the remainder of Episode eighteen shows, this reset does more than merely resurrect Laura Palmer: it might alter the course of time and space itself. Although one must be cautious in positing any definitive interpretive claim here, at least on initial viewings, because, like Agent Cooper, viewers can never be totally sure of what they are seeing. As Episode eighteen of *Twin Peaks* (2017) shows, Cooper and Laura Palmer *doppelgänger* Carrie Page (Sheryl Lee) now roam some alternate, uncanny America where everything simultaneously looks familiar and is not how it is supposed to be. While we want to take refuge in Agent Cooper, his usual Boy Scout assurance is no match for this bizarrely familiar world. Lynch delivers viewers the triumphant return of Cooper only to immediately reduce him to the same level of ignorance as Dougie Jones: staggering around in a kind of shellshock in search of something that reminds him of where (and who) he used to be, only animated by fleeting encounters with objects he once knew. As such, Agent Cooper becomes the embodiment of the viewer's sense of loss watching the series, which traps them with little that is tangible to hold onto but also with, in the words of Amanda DiPaolo, "no way to forget."[39] Like characters in a teen tragedy ballad, all anyone has left is the memory of what they have lost, the love they know they have missed, so they keep returning to those objects that remind them of what they used to have so close to them for one last kiss.

Carrie Page's scream at the end of Episode eighteen represents the final return, a return to the original horror that set the series in motion, a return to the loss that nostalgic wish fulfillment was intended—and failed—to reverse, a return to impossibility. In doing so, it reveals "this quest for reanimation" exemplified by the series and by teen tragedy ballads to be an empty

FIGURE 6.7 Carrie Page screams. *Twin Peaks* directed by David Lynch © Showtime Networks 2017. All rights reserved.

endeavor, a fool's errand.[40] The series ends exactly as it begins: with blood-curdling screams and cries at the reality that tragedy cannot be undone. Like "She's Gone Away," the series strips away all the sleepy nostalgia from the *Twin Peaks* universe to expose the desiccated center and the foolishness of trying to reanimate the dead dream. This is most fitting for the series, which repeatedly demonstrates to viewers that the "structuring absence" of *Twin Peaks* (2017) is no longer limited to Laura Palmer; it is nationwide. The Twin Peaks Cooper returns to is indistinguishable from the hollowed-out neighborhood Rancho Rosa. In fact, Rancho Rosa best exemplifies the world the entire series occupies: the shell of an idealized American community that Twin Peaks used to represent.

America's Endless Sleep

Twin Peaks resurrects feeling from dead commercial forms, not by ironic comment but through sincere engagement with the emotions that these media objects are dealing with, transforming a world and a musical genre overrun by kitsch and consumption of all kinds into a "meeting place for sincere emotional engagement" that cultivates "an empathetic awareness of [...] tragedy" in its viewers.[41] Within this dynamic, nostalgia can be a vehicle for resurrecting a deadened feeling just as much as it can be used as a retreat from feeling. Teen tragedy ballads and *Twin Peaks* demonstrate the allure of nostalgia as a coping mechanism for the present, while *Fire Walk with*

Me and *Twin Peaks* (2017) cast this nostalgic turn as a malignant force in itself. DiPaolo argues that *Twin Peaks* is not anti-nostalgia but rather a work that advocates for a more thoughtful deployment of nostalgia.[42] This more honest approach allows one to adopt a more sympathetic reading of the teen tragedy ballad as something both kitsch and more than kitsch. As he does throughout his work, Lynch continually allows the nostalgic kitsch of Eisenhower-era iconography to coexist with the genuine horrors that nostalgia attempts to obscure, which allows us to see how the two interact and how our own yearnings for closure and order sustain this energy.[43] Teen tragedy ballads demonstrate how this conflict can persist indefinitely. As Dave Marsh says of the tragedy ballad "Barbara Allen," "The answer is not blowing in the wind. The answer is that we will never find the answer, and never stop seeking it. And so we sing the song."[44]

7

"You'll Never Have Me"

Covering *Lost Highway*'s *Chansons Fatales*

While many critics and scholars have written insightfully about the soundtracks of David Lynch's films and their blend of jazz-inflected Angelo Badalamenti scores, nostalgic mid-century pop, and handcrafted drones and soundscapes, the music of Lynch's 1997 film *Lost Highway* remains underexplored, despite the fact that its soundtrack is Lynch's most commercially successful one to date.[1] *Lost Highway*'s music may not have received much scholarly attention because, unlike Lynch's other soundtrack work, its kitchen-sink assemblage of such popular mid-1990s alternative music acts as Nine Inch Nails, Marilyn Manson, and Smashing Pumpkins (along with 1970s glam giants David Bowie and Lou Reed) can appear like a brazen attempt by Lynch and his producers to secure funding and a teen audience for their inaccessible "21st-century *noir* horror film."[2] A closer examination of how Lynch uses this music in the film, however, reveals a more intricate and meaningful strategy than merely opening an additional revenue stream for a noncommercial film. Indeed, this abrasive music gives the film what Mark Mazullo calls a "unique expressive sound signature" that drives the film's central narrative strategy.[3]

Scholars have investigated the identity crisis generated by the *doppelgängers* and alter-egos at the heart of the film's plot, along with

This chapter appeared, in slightly different form, in *Music and the Moving Image*: Mike Miley; "'I Put a Spell on You': Affiliating (Mis)Identifications and Toxic Masculinity in David Lynch's *Lost Highway*." *Music and the Moving Image* October 1, 2020; 13 (3): 36–48.

how this doubling interrogates and revises the femme fatale and film noir's patriarchal logic; however, none discusses how the soundtrack amplifies these ideas. According to Mazullo, Lynch frequently selects songs that feature "a certain uncanniness in their sound" so as to shepherd viewers into a more receptive, dreamlike state, and *Lost Highway* offers viewers a more intense exploration of uncanniness by prominently featuring cover songs in scenes crucial to the narrative.[4] The presence of cover songs in a film overflowing with doubles and imagined identities calls for closer scrutiny of how these songs function in this film and how they may broaden one's understanding of how cover songs and compilation scores work.[5] Like a *doppelgänger*, cover songs destabilize viewers' experience by courting familiarity and estrangement in equal measure. These covers partner with the shifting, uncertain identities of the film's characters to create a shifting, uncertain cinematic landscape that explodes the possibility of locating a stable subject position. By blending the pleasurable and the discomforting, the soundtrack services the film's larger project of depicting the familiar logic of patriarchy as toxic, violent, and deranged.

Gabriel Solis defines a cover as "a new version of a song in which the original version is a recording, and for which musicians and listeners have a particular set of ideas about authenticity, authorship, and the ontological status of both original and cover versions."[6] This "particular set of ideas" invites increased engagement with listeners because the song thrives upon the contrast between what listeners hear in the cover and what they expect to hear based upon their familiarity with the original recording.[7] Similarly, viewers' prior knowledge and experience with a previously recorded song will affect how they receive any film that uses the song on its soundtrack because the song has a history and identity outside of the film it appears in.[8] By using cover songs in *Lost Highway*, Lynch taps into the "collective unconscious" of American popular music even deeper than a traditional compilation score would, summoning the viewers' awareness of a particular song's history while also presenting it in an altered form, or what Greil Marcus describes as "new songs in old skins."[9] Rather than limiting the range of interpretations and impressions available for interpretation in the film, these cover songs and their affiliating identifications open "the psychic field" by "evoking memories of emotions and subject positions" within viewers and "inviting [them] to place themselves on their unconscious terrains."[10]

Such a strategy only makes viewers engage more deeply with *Lost Highway*'s narrative of identity crisis by creating an uncanny sonic landscape that drives the audience further down the narrative's road of alienation and estrangement. Three covers appear (or reappear) in *Lost Highway* at crucial points in the plot: Lou Reed's 1995 cover of "This Magic Moment," written by Doc Pomus and Mort Shuman and originally recorded by The Drifters in 1960; Marilyn Manson's 1995 cover of Screamin' Jay Hawkins's 1956 song "I Put a Spell on You"; and This Mortal Coil's 1984 cover of Tim Buckley and Larry Beckett's 1970 track "Song to the Siren." Just like Fred Madison transforming into Pete Dayton and Patricia Arquette playing two roles in the film, these covers confuse viewers more than they comfort by shifting the genre of the original track. These songs twist Kassabian's concept of affiliating identifications to a disorienting degree, creating affiliating *mis*identifications among viewers in which their recognition of a song fails to provide them with a sense of pleasure. Each cover song accompanies a moment of recurrence, resurrection, repetition; and each moment centers upon a man's pursuit of a woman: her body, her mind, her secrets. By placing cover songs in these moments of the film, the soundtrack enhances *Lost Highway*'s critique of masculinity by characterizing masculinity as an inauthentic and frantic quest for control and mastery.

Further, the cover songs in *Lost Highway* reveal how these notions of desire and agency in rock music and cinema have been coded to satisfy and maintain a patriarchal order. The film's visuals indulge heavily in macho rockist iconography, particularly in its fixation with cars, pornography, pinup fashion, and, most of all, aggressive (and aggressively white and male) rock music.[11] This visual iconography partners with the sonic abrasiveness of the covers to suggest that what Martha Nochimson calls the "midcentury cultural fantasies about families, love, and male identity" have, like Fred Madison (Bill Pullman), undergone "painful transformations" and become caustic, manic, and violent.[12] By the end of the film, Lynch's covers and their affiliating misidentifications fulfill Kassabian's claim that compilation scores "challenge dominant ideologies" such as patriarchal authority by preventing viewers from being "tightly tracked into identification with a single subject position," even if the film does this by cultivating discomfort.[13]

While the film represents a departure from Lynch's earlier work in that it does not conclude with what Nochimson describes as "a liberating vision in the midst of the most constricting cultural systems," it does thoroughly and forcefully dissect the most constricting cultural system—toxic patriarchy and the male pursuit of dominance and mastery—revealing it to be an exhausted loop that has nothing left to offer the culture but violence and madness.[14] By subverting audience identification with the soundtrack, Lynch shows cover songs and compilation soundtracks can be vehicles for undermining and resisting control, *chansons fatales* whose identities are as fluid and beyond viewers' control as the femme fatale is from the male noir protagonist.

"We've Met Before, Haven't We?"

In what is perhaps the most memorable scene in *Lost Highway*, Robert Blake's character the Mystery Man approaches Fred (Bill Pullman) at a party. As he walks up, the music and background noise from the party fade out until it feels like the Mystery Man and Fred have entered a separate time

FIGURE 7.1 "We've met before, haven't we?" *Lost Highway* directed by David Lynch © CIBY 2000 1997.

and place. "We've met before, haven't we," the Mystery Man asks him. Fred denies it, but the Mystery Man insists they met at Fred's house. In fact, the Mystery Man says, he is at Fred's house that very moment. He even gives Fred a phone and tells him to call him at his home, which he does. And the Mystery Man answers. He has a conversation with Fred on the phone while also standing directly in front of him, saying nothing. He occupies two places at once.

In addition to being a terrifying demonstration of the power of cinema, this scene captures the uncanny experience of hearing a cover song for the first time. A listener encounters a song in the present that they have never heard before, yet the song also feels like something from their past. This sense of déjà vu disorients listeners just as Fred's encounter with the Mystery Man disorients him.[15] *Lost Highway*'s covers intensify this disorientation by undergoing sonic transformations. The swelling strings and smooth vocals of The Drifters' "This Magic Moment" become the distorted groaning guitar feedback of Reed; Screamin' Jay Hawkins's manic, obsessive waltz "I Put a Spell on You" mutates into Marilyn Manson's brutally percussive industrial rock freakout; and Tim Buckley's jazz folk ballad "Song to the Siren" transforms into This Mortal Coil's goth dream-pop reverie. Michael Rings calls this tactic of transporting a song into a new genre "generic resetting."[16] Recognizing a cover as a generic reset surprises any listener who did not anticipate hearing the original song transposed into the genre they are hearing, and even once they have identified the original song from its generic reset, their expectations simultaneously rise and get defied as they wonder how the upcoming changes in the original song will sound in a new genre.[17] These generic resets are dramatic and jarring, making them a perfect analogue for Fred Madison's transformation into Pete Dayton (Balthazar Getty) or Renee Madison's (Patricia Arquette) return as Alice Wakefield (again, Patricia Arquette).

Solis, building on the work of theater scholar Marvin Carlson, argues that covers, like theatrical productions, are "haunted by memory" of other recordings; even when the cover represents a significant departure from the original, the original haunts the cover because the cover "echo[es] and evoke[s]" the original, creating a kind of "co-presence."[18] Likewise, *Lost Highway* is a haunted text that depicts characters who are recognizable but, in the words of Greg Hainge, "estranged from the very context in which [they are] situated" because there is another version of them that haunts viewers: Pete Dayton is haunted by Fred Madison, Renee Madison haunts Alice Wakefield, etc.[19] To intensify this haunting, Lynch places songs that themselves are, as Solis says of covers, haunted by "the intense presence of [an] original" as well.[20] Like the characters styled after pinup queens, femmes fatales, and rockabilly bad boys, these covers are, as Anne Jerslev says, "recycled as a floating audio-visual iconicity," shifting the style and genre of a familiar song in a manner that disorients and discomforts viewers and resists being received as familiar, pleasurable, or innocuous.[21] Although Rings and Kassabian describe generic resets and affiliating identifications as pleasurable and empowering for listeners, Lynch's use of covers demonstrates that recognizable songs can also cause disorientation and be laden with menace because all of the orienting, pleasant comforts have been stripped away.[22]

Lost Highway's affiliating identifications disrupt feelings of affiliation the moment they are evoked. In doing so, the soundtrack advances the film's larger project of disrupting feelings of identification with male power, identity, and authority, tricking viewers into misidentifications that highlight the unorthodox nature of what they consider comfortable, normal, and natural. These songs, like the film they support, "explore the perils of personal authenticity under the conditions of postmodernity" and challenge patriarchal notions of an authentic self in favor of a conception of identity and autonomy that is more elusive, fluid, and subjective.[23] Rather than employing film music to propel the events and emotions of the images on the screen, Lynch uses songs to signal a crack or "rupture" in modernist definitions of selfhood and masculine claims of autonomy to depict the necessity for abandoning a toxic masculine desire for control and all visual and sonic expressions of it.[24]

"You Liked It, Huh?": Covering Toxic Masculinity

With two important exceptions that will be discussed later, *Lost Highway*'s covers occur entirely in the Pete Dayton storyline, which makes a great deal of sense because Pete's story acts as a cover of Fred's. According to Todd

McGowan, the Pete storyline demonstrates how "fantasy is not an escape from an unsatisfying social reality but a way of repeating it," or, viewed another way, covering it.[25] Pete's story essentially functions as a generic reset that, like the covers that appear in it, shifts genres and the identity of the lead singer in pursuit of a new, more virile identity. The greasy-haired rock rebel Pete is everything that jazzy noir-movie Fred is not: young and cool in his leather jacket and effortlessly able to command automobiles and women alike. Pete's story is a more vivid, fleshed-out version of the events of Fred's life because it represents masculine wish fulfillment; it is an attempt to imagine an idealized, improved version of reality that delivers on all the promises reality cannot, offering sense and order to Fred's confused and impotent existence.

Lost Highway's scene featuring Marilyn Manson's cover of "I Put a Spell on You" dramatizes this impulse. In it, Alice tells Pete the story of the first time she met Mr. Eddy (Robert Loggia) and one of his goons put a gun to her head to force her to undress for Mr. Eddy. This scene begins with a déjà vu moment where Alice repeats Renee's dialogue from the scene where Fred asks how she came to know Andy (Michael Massee). In both scenes, Arquette's character says, "It was a long time ago. I met him at this place called Moke's. We became friends. He told me about a job." Viewers receive no additional information to flesh out Renee's vague story the first time they hear it, but Alice's statement prompts a flashback in which she bears all, literally and figuratively. Thus, Alice's flashback acts as a cover of Renee's original monologue, a generic reset that places Renee's vague and mysterious story within a specific and familiar genre. Where Renee is as dark and shrouded in secrecy as her story, the platinum blonde Alice and her shiny garments

FIGURE 7.2 A Lynchian tableau for "I Put a Spell on You." *Lost Highway* directed by David Lynch © CIBY 2000 1997. All rights reserved.

radiate visibility. Frida Beckman discusses how Hollywood storytelling equates the urge to impose narratives on events with patriarchal control, especially in film noir. Solving the mystery surrounding the woman through a "gradual unmasking of [her] sexual power" frequently fulfills traditional filmmaking's demand for narrative continuity and logic— explaining the seemingly inexplicable in three tidy acts.[26] As much as film noir may appear to subvert Hollywood's traditional American values in its worldview and subject matter, the films nevertheless end with traditional heterosexist morality being restored by silencing, punishing, or neutralizing the chaotic femme fatale.[27] This formulaic approach suggests that the narrative logic of Hollywood strives to make patriarchy the result of cause and effect: logical, proper, just.

Beckman adroitly shows how Alice's sexuality may appear to be more dangerous than Renee's, but Alice's highly visible allure and desire constitute an effort by Fred/Pete to neutralize and explain away Renee's mysterious and unknowable desire, rendering her past and her secrets into a sadistic fantasy where she is forced to put everything on display to satisfy the male gaze and Fred/Pete's need for total knowledge and control of her. Unlike the mysterious, unknowable Renee, Alice's sexuality neatly conforms to, as Beckman writes, "the universe of male desire, order, and possessiveness" because her involvement in pornography seemingly provides an answer to the riddle that her desire poses to men and strips her identity of any mystery at all.[28] According to Beckman, Alice becomes as "a version of Renee that [Fred] can handle": a woman who desires to be humiliated and controlled sexually.[29]

Marilyn Manson's recording of "I Put a Spell on You" captures the brutality of this misogynistic need to control. Any expectation that the band will duplicate the dreamy sway of Screamin' Jay Hawkins's original evaporates immediately with the arrival of grating strings in the intro, followed by pounding toms that turn the waltz time of the piano, horn, and drum in the original from a lilt into a forced march. The druggy drawl of Manson's vocals in the first verse provides listeners with the only real opportunity to connect the track with Hawkins's original or any of its other notable covers. Such as it is, this familiarity is short-lived as Manson erupts into a feline wail at the end of the verse that gets crushed by a blast of discordant drums and distorted guitar that dominate the remainder of the song. Like their entire musical persona, the band's interpretation of the song seems self-consciously designed to unsettle, distress, and disturb, with most of the focus being devoted to force, volume, and impact. It becomes difficult to discern whether the band seeks to "ruin" the song or whether their interpretation unearths madness latent in the original. Regardless, the track performs a kind of coercive violence on the song, stripping its hypnotic mystery and replacing it with violence, chaos, and rage. The song rises in volume in a manner that threatens to overpower Lynch's provocative images, bombarding listeners with the speaker's maddened pursuit of reasserting his own lost sense of control over the object of his desire. Manson's increasingly unhinged delivery that begins as a barely audible groan and deteriorates into throat-scraping moans, howls, and wails leaves no doubt that it is the speaker, not the addressee, who has been put under a spell they cannot break. The song casts a spell upon viewers as well in that it transports viewers to a place they have been before (the original song) but do not quite remember this way (the cover). What ought to serve as an affiliating identification that orients viewers and invites them to fold their own experiences with music into the film instead becomes a moment of disorientation in which their knowledge of music makes it more challenging for them to make sense of events because the original song has been rendered unrecognizable by Marilyn Manson's blunt-force trauma.

This musical violation reinforces Alice's physical violation in the scene. Mr. Eddy controls Alice's movements with only the violent spell of his gaze, which makes the scene into a demonstration of male sexual dominance and the threat of violence lurking in the male gaze that cinema often serves as a manifestation of.[30] The lyrics promote this feeling as well by performing a kind of narration in this scene: Manson sings "I put a spell on you" at the same moment one of Mr. Eddy's thugs points the gun at Alice's head, connecting the "spell" in the song to Mr. Eddy's sexual violence. When paired with the music, the staging and editing of this scene in sync with the music give it the feel of a music video, as though the film halts all narrative progress for this violent burlesque. The scene ends when the scene cuts from Alice reaching to touch Mr. Eddy to Alice reaching to touch Pete's face. This cut and the dialogue that follows it underscore how this fantasy is employed to empower Fred/Pete. "Why didn't you just leave," Pete asks her, blaming her for her humiliation. Alice lowers her head, allowing Pete to complete her story for her with an explanation that reinforces his fantasy: "You liked it, huh?" Alice does not answer. In forcing Alice to expose her past sexual history and admit she desires domination, Pete assumes the position and power of Mr. Eddy.

Lynch's camera placement implicates viewers in this domination by gradually moving the camera into to Mr. Eddy's point of view. In reaching toward the camera, Alice's outstretched hand reaches for the viewers as much as it does for Mr. Eddy and Pete, all of whom are seated in comfortable chairs as they watch Alice's degradation. The scene may establish its point of view as Alice's in that it is her flashback, but its staging and gaze remain luridly male, subtly reminding viewers that the story is Pete's fantasy (perhaps even Fred's). The scene, then, serves as a powerful, multilayered example of Laura Mulvey's assertion that a woman's cinematic presence is a creation of the male ego made to please that same ego and that audiences become complicit in through their engaged spectatorship.[31] The song as placed in the film dramatizes the spell that the patriarchal narrative casts over Hollywood's imagination and women's identities, and its intensity demonstrates the power that this narrative has in viewers' lives. The scene operates like a standalone scene because it is, both visually and musically, *Lost Highway* in miniature in that it represents, as Jerslev states, "another staging of the impossible masculine desire to master the female."[32]

"I Like to Remember Things My Own Way"

Artists cover songs in an attempt to flesh out something in themselves that they believe their reworking of the song will provide them; however, their cover seldom manages to escape or supplant the original. No matter how transcendent the cover may be, its original lingers in listeners' memory. Similarly, the covers in *Lost Highway* remind viewers how reality haunts fantasy just as a cover is haunted by the co-presence of the original song.[33] The covers in the film mirror Fred's desire to create an authentic sense of self through the refashioning and appropriation of preexisting materials. This new self cannot be sustained because, as with covers, the original's intense presence haunts the fantasy.

No moment of *Lost Highway* typifies this kind of haunting more than Alice Wakefield's entrance in the film. Pete is working under a car when Mr. Eddy pulls up in a vintage Cadillac with a platinum blonde in the passenger seat.[34] The camera cuts to a medium shot of the blonde seated in the car, and viewers see that the blonde is played by Patricia Arquette, who also played

FIGURE 7.3 The arrival of Alice, or the return of Renee. *Lost Highway* directed by David Lynch © CIBY 2000 1997. All rights reserved.

Renee, Fred's brunette (and dead) wife. The grinding hum of Lou Reed's cover of The Drifters' "This Magic Moment" floods the soundtrack as she gets out of the car and walks into another one in supremely slow-motion. The film even goes so far as to intercut the lyrics of the song to the looks Alice exchanges with Pete. This combination of a song about love at first sight shot in slow-motion and set (and cut) to a song about love at first sight causes the entire moment to teeter on the edge of an embarrassing cliché, leaving viewers uncertain of how seriously to take Lynch's directorial choices.

Reed's cover adds to this confusion. It works against the sentimental quality of the song by drowning it underneath layers of feedback in a way that sounds simultaneously reverent and violent. This devoted attack on the song follows Kassabian's thinking about affiliating identifications in that an affiliating identification "crosses over the boundaries between unconscious and conscious processes" and demands viewers consider a wide variety of positions as they watch the scene.[35] As viewers recognize the song, the performer, and the hackneyed nature of the cue, they confront a series of baffling affiliations that frustrate as much as they please: "Is that 'This Magic Moment'? ... Is that Lou Reed? .... Is this meant to be sincere?" These moments of identification lead to more confusion and intensify the most confounding question in the scene, "Is that Patricia Arquette? Is this woman Renee?" Thus, the song's generic reset from its original pop idiom to Reed's drone-laden rock reproduces the film's identity crisis sonically, making viewers experience the surprise of this plot twist—or the magic of the moment—at every cinematic level.[36]

The song and Arquette's return to the film evoke George Plasketes's assertion that a cover "strik[es] a familiar chord" and "engag[es] the [viewer] in a historical duet with lyric and lineage. A distant dialogue. A delicate and dichotomous dance between past and present, place and possibility."[37] However, Lynch shows how this same "rousing residue of musical memory" Plasketes rhapsodizes can generate (or perhaps leads to) dissonance, confusion, and psychosis.[38] Despite their familiarity, neither Arquette's return nor Reed's song comforts viewers by conjuring a nostalgic trip down memory lane. Instead, both offer viewers a grating, jarring, aggressive return of a toxic past that refuses to stay past. Reed's cover—and Lynch's use of it—demonstrates Marcus's claim that covers are not merely "containers for nostalgia": The song is no longer "an innocent object" or "a kind of toy" "rubbed smooth by decades of overplay" but an aggressive text that slips loose from the safety of nostalgia and becomes once again the strange object it always was, harkening back to a simpler time while also thrusting listeners further into the present, fulfilling a fantasy while actively undermining it to amplify its malignance.[39]

Lynch's representation of the fantasy of the man eyeing the platinum blonde in the shiny Cadillac renders it an improbable construction that alienates viewers from what has traditionally been presented as a comforting, satisfying fantasy. Estranging viewers from what Alistair Mactaggart characterizes as "an allegorized cliché of American car fetishism" serves the film's larger critique of toxic masculinity and makes the destructive effects such masculine fantasies have on the real world visible again to viewers, who have grown accustomed to them through their repetition and overuse.[40] The scene needs to be startling and frustrating and to fill viewers with the urge to make sense of the narrative because if viewers find pleasure in Fred's fantasy as Pete, or even smoothly enter into it, then they are engaging with and taking pleasure in the same kind of toxic drive to impose their will over events. Viewers of *Lost Highway*, Todd McGowan asserts, must confront the "deadlock of desire" in fantasy to realize that fantasy does not deliver on its promises but only "provides the illusion of delivering the goods" that reality fails to provide.[41] Mistaking it for anything else poses a danger to others.

"You'll Never Have Me"

When the last cover appears in *Lost Highway*, it seems that Fred has succeeded in constructing a fantasy self (Pete) capable of mastering and taking possession of a highly sexualized female (Alice) and restoring a patriarchal logic over an out-of-control narrative. After Pete and Alice rob and kill the pornographer Andy, they drive out to the desert to sell the loot. When the fence is not there to meet them, they make the perfectly realistic and logical decision to have sex in the glow of the headlights of a vintage red Mustang as This Mortal Coil's cover of Tim Buckley's "Song to the Siren" swells on the soundtrack. As the scene nears its close, Pete repeats "I want you" to Alice. "Song to the Siren" abruptly fades, Angelo Badalamenti's ominous score returns, and Alice leans over to Pete and defiantly and definitively whispers "You'll never have me" in his ear before disappearing into the desert cabin, never to be seen again. The car headlights fade out and the film is once again cast into the darkness in which Fred Madison lives. When Pete stands up to go after Alice, he turns to face the camera and viewers see that Pete Dayton has transformed back into Fred Madison.

The dreamy reverb of the guitar and the rich, trebly echo of Elizabeth Fraser's vocals on "Song to the Siren" work with Lynch's visuals to lull viewers into the same passive stupor as Pete. The slow-motion photography, sweeping camera movements, and lengthy dissolves contrast the style of the rest of the film so much that the scene feels even more removed from narrative time and space than the previous two appearances of cover songs discussed above. As McGowan notes, the style of the film changes completely in this scene to match Pete's sense of romantic accomplishment, with "the screen becom[ing] so bright that the audience can barely continue

FIGURE 7.4 "You'll never have me." *Lost Highway* directed by David Lynch ©
CIBY 2000 1997. All rights reserved.

watching."[42] However, this moment of triumph proves to be a chimera, a
trap set to instill a false sense of security into Pete and viewers to destroy
both their fantasies, making it a true siren song.

If creating narrative sense in Hollywood storytelling involves stripping
a woman of her agency, then *Lost Highway* uses music and imagery to
reject Hollywood's representations of femininity as male projections of
their own inadequacy and lack of coherence. In saying, "You'll never
have me," Alice rejects not only Pete but Fred's macho fantasy and the
patriarchal continuity and logic that govern it.[43] While Lynch's treatment
of femininity often leans on stereotypes of the sacred feminine and film
noir's depiction of sexually empowered women as symbols of boundless
excess and unknowable mystery, *Lost Highway* remains focused on
pathologizing masculinity by, as Nochimson writes, "link[ing] the poison
of a debased imagination [...] to a denial of the importance of feminine
energy."[44] "You'll never have me" directly addresses Pete but can also be
read as what Jerslev calls a "meta-commentary" in which the femme fatale
addresses the film that attempts to control her, and the film's viewers,
who also will never possess the kind of control over her that the male
protagonists seek.[45]

This song is one that has captivated and eluded Lynch for some time, and
the backstory behind the use of This Mortal Coil's cover of "Song to the
Siren" advances my argument even further. In his memoir *Room to Dream*,
Lynch reveals that he originally wanted to use the song in *Blue Velvet*
but could not because licensing it was too expensive. Lynch says he was
reluctant to write his own song (what became "Mysteries of Love") because
"I wanted 'Song to the Siren,' so nothing was going to come up to that."
He recounts telling his producers "there are twenty-seven zillion songs in

the world. I don't want one of them. I want this song. I want 'Song to the Siren' by This Mortal Coil."[46] His story features echoes of *Vertigo*, a film which takes on an increasing importance in Lynch's work post-*Twin Peaks*. The song in *Lost Highway* becomes a substitute for the song in *Blue Velvet*, which mirrors Alice's function as a substitute for Renee, Pete's for Fred, Judy for Madeline in *Vertigo*, Kim Novak for Alfred Hitchcock's original choice Vera Miles, and so on.

As singular as this cover's appearance in this scene may seem, it is not its first appearance in the film. Even though it is not present long or loudly enough for most viewers to recognize it on a first viewing, "Song to the Siren" plays during a dark sex scene between Fred and Renee when Fred fails to perform. As Fred and Renee start to make love, ominous music by Angelo Badalamenti casts the scene in a dreadful light. Then a bright light flashes on the screen as Fred moves on top of Renee and the scene switches into slow motion; however, the scene does not play out like the subsequent slow-motion musical moments in the film. "Song to the Siren" appears as only a faint echo and competes with Fred's labored breathing. Fred's final exhale silences the song entirely and it is replaced by grating cymbals and frantic strings simmering low in the mix as Renee gives him a demeaning pat on the back. This scene directly contrasts the brightly lit sex scene in the desert both visually and sonically, casting one as the failed reality drowning in darkness and terrible sounds and the second as the triumphant fantasy bathed in bright light and lush music. Michel Chion describes *Lost Highway* as being structured around these two sex scenes, both of which feature the same music cue, and when one considers the second appearance of "Song to the Siren" in the film, Chion's reading becomes even more persuasive.[47] Lynch includes the song the moment before Fred begins his transformation into Pete. Fred stares at the walls of his prison cell and has a vision of a cabin in the desert exploding in reverse. "Song to the Siren" rises in volume as the cabin comes back together and abruptly ends as soon as the cabin becomes intact. The Mystery Man steps out of the cabin, matches eyelines with Fred, and walks inside the cabin. Immediately afterward, Fred transforms into Pete.

Taken together, these three occurrences of the song cement the film's throughline as a psychosexual drama about a man whose failure to please his wife sexually drives him to a psychotic breakdown in which he reimagines his life as a young, virile stud who is effortlessly irresistible to multiple women, only to see that fantasy crumble before him at what should be his moment of triumph. When one considers that these major turning points all feature the same cover song, first faintly and then at maximum volume, one sees more clearly how Pete's storyline represents Fred's attempt to reenact, or cover, his sex life to more favorable results. Thus, the cover song's historical use to establish a musician's authentic identity becomes literalized in *Lost Highway*—recall that Fred is a musician—to the point that each key moment in the film that deals with identity—Fred's sense of masculinity, Fred's sense of self, Patricia Arquette's reappearance, Alice's past, Pete's switch back into Fred—is backed by a cover song that also destabilizes the identity of the song.

"Dick Laurent Is Dead"

Through continually creating narrative puzzles that demand to be decoded, Lynch frustrates viewers, luring them into a state of agitation that stirs up an angry urge to interrogate events, to force them to explain themselves.[48] This disorientation allows viewers to appreciate the film's critique of violent masculinity on a visceral and psychological level because their own urge to have all mysteries solved according to logic, continuity, and the needs of their gaze resembles Fred's toxic, solipsistic need to fashion people and events the way he wants them to be rather than how they actually are. *Lost Highway*'s compilation score problematizes viewers' relationships with songs they believed they were comfortably affiliated with, turning these initial identifications of songs into a series of unpleasurable and bewildering misidentifications. Like the film, the affiliating identifications of the covers alienate audiences from themselves and their own contexts in the same way that Fred becomes alienated from himself.[49] The film puts the nostalgia of all versions of the song on display and asks viewers to confront their own subjectivity and visions of autonomy and mastery to realize that complete knowledge or control is not possible. One will not be able to master the song, the plot, the characters, the film, just as men should not attempt to master women.

The film's affinity for abrasive alt-industrial noise bands becomes more than a nod to a youth market—the sound viewers hear is the sound of toxic masculinity being abraded.[50] The film and the soundtrack work in concert to deconstruct "traditional and phallocentric" identities by "visually and aurally representing the multiplication of enunciators" without privileging "a single, all-encompassing enunciator."[51] Reed's and Manson's alienating covers do not "lull the listener into a mode of passive reception"; the raw sound reawakens them to the violence latent in the original songs.[52] Conversely, This Mortal Coil's cover adopts a soothing atmosphere only to have that comfort violently stripped away and the fantasy revealed to be a masculine fantasy of domination. Together, the covers and the story disrupt the single-subject orientations of most films and film scores to awaken viewers to new ways of seeing, hearing, and navigating a narrative that need not conform to a logic or symbolic order that frequently works to affirm the kind of patriarchy that the film critiques.

Lost Highway, as Tom O'Connor writes, "undermines any representation of an absolute male power," and it does so visually and sonically by defining masculinity as the haunted cover version, not the authentic original—always repeating itself in search of an original and displacing its sense of inauthenticity onto women.[53] There is no narrative progression to the film; rather, it is a loop in which the femme fatale escapes explanation and punishment, remaining in the same body, and the male protagonist suffers a complete identity collapse, mutating into another body and back again repeatedly, ultimately being unmasked as an incoherent, powerless object in a world beyond his capacity for understanding.

8

David Lynch's Old, Weird America

Straight Folk

The folk revival of the 1950s and 1960s was a brief flash in American popular culture filling the gap between Elvis getting drafted into the Army and the Beatles touching down on a New York City tarmac. It is the era that made Joan Baez and Bob Dylan household names, brought legends such as Pete Seeger, Leadbelly, and Mississippi John Hurt back into the spotlight, turned songs like "Blowin' in the Wind" and "I Shall Not Be Moved" into the soundtrack for the Civil Rights Movement and the New Left, and turned events such as the Newport Folk Festival into cultural flashpoints for a youth culture energized by "the intersection of social movements and the culture industry."[1] After being driven into the "momentary obscurity" of university halls and socialist summer camps by the tyranny of the Red Scare, folk music reappeared at the dawn of the New Frontier as young middle-class, mostly white Americans searched for ways to respond to the rapid changes of postwar life. To them, these old folk songs, along with folk instruments and proletarian fashion, functioned as an antidote to a mass-produced Americanist culture that they viewed as plentiful but poisonous.[2]

While the timeframe of 1958–64, from the Kingston Trio's "Tom Dooley" to the Beatles' "I Want to Hold Your Hand," set by Robert Cantwell in his book *When We Were Good: The Folk Revival* certainly fits the commercial and mainstream popularity of the folk revival, I would like to reimagine the timeframe as bookended by two musical texts that capture the style and themes of the folk revival, starting in 1952 with the release of *The Anthology of American Folk Music* and having its coda in 1967 with Bob Dylan and the Band's recordings that would become known as *The Basement Tapes*. Edited by Harry Smith and released on Smithsonian Folkways Records, *The Anthology of American Folk Music* only sold fifty copies in its first year, yet it influenced key figures in the folk revival to such a degree that it can be considered the folk revival's catalyst.[3] The *Anthology* is a six-LP collection of eighty-four songs recorded between 1926 and 1932, though the songs themselves are even older. Smith packaged the songs with cryptic, often fantastical liner notes and collages, and his idiosyncratic process of selection and sequencing quietly revolutionized music by disregarding standard industry methods of categorization such as race, region, and genre, instead dividing the songs into "Ballads," "Social Music," and "Songs," a move whose impact on music is difficult to understate. Traditional Child ballads such as "Fatal Flower Garden" appeared alongside Delta Blues tracks such as "Spike Driver Blues" and Appalachian songs such as "The Coo Coo Bird." The music contained here, with its subjects ranging from murder to marriage and styles from Cajun dance songs to church hymns has a hypnotic power that, in the words of Greil Marcus, "made the familiar strange, the never known into the forgotten, and the forgotten into a collective memory that teased any single listener's conscious mind."[4]

The Basement Tapes, on the other hand, is likely the most storied and bootlegged home recording of all time, making its way through the culture via commercially produced recordings released by other artists, a condensed (and overdubbed) 2-LP 1975 release by Columbia Records, and bootlegs of various lengths, qualities, and titles, with a remastered official release of all the recordings in 2014. The 139 (or more) songs, some well-known covers, others startling original compositions, were recorded over a nine-month period in 1967 in which Dylan, exhausted after a grueling tour and a mysterious motorcycle accident, retreated to a house in Saugerties, NY, and began jamming with members of his backing band the Hawks (later the Band). Even though none of the songs on *The Basement Tapes* appear on the *Anthology*, these "deserter's songs" are spiritual kin to the music on the *Anthology*, fellow residents of what Marcus refers to as "Smithville," which he defines as "a weird but clearly recognizable America within the America of the exercise of institutional majoritarian power" made up of "people holed up to wait out the end of the world," where "both murder and suicide are rituals, acts instantly transformed into legend, facts that in their specificity transform everyday life into myth, or reveal that at its highest pitch life is a joke."[5]

One cannot read about the *Anthology* or *The Basement Tapes* for long without running into this kind of rapturous, poetic prose that borders on the hyperbolic. Marcus's lack of critical distance can be viewed as a reflection of the central and simple grandeur of these songs: their concrete, direct simplicity achieves an ineffability that one cannot approach without falling back on the language of myth. Dylan himself described the music of the *Anthology* in similar terms in 1965:

> Traditional music is based on hexagrams. It comes about from legends, Bibles, plagues, and it revolves around vegetables and death. There's

nobody that's going to kill traditional music. All these songs about roses growing out of people's brains and lovers who are really geese and swans that turn into angels—they're not going to die. [...] I mean, you'd think that the traditional music people would gather from their songs that mystery is a fact, a traditional fact [...] traditional music is too unreal to die.[6]

One could easily add "older men riding lawnmowers on the highway" to Dylan's list without raising any eyebrows. Of course, *The Straight Story* is not a literal example of the traditional music that makes up the American folk revival that Dylan talks about, but its premise, style, and themes bear an uncanny resemblance to the music of the folk revival in that both adopt antiquated, anachronistic forms and styles to access and celebrate what Marcus has alternately called an "invisible republic," and "the old, weird America."[7] And in doing so, they fashion new democratic communities that understand mystery to be one of the most traditional and essential facts of life.

The Straight Story easily ranks as one of the most overlooked and underexamined features film in Lynch's filmography. When it is discussed at all, it is often treated as an outlier in Lynch's oeuvre due to its G-rating, traditional narrative structure, earnest sensibility, and lack of shocking scenes of sex and violence. But, as Justus Nieland observes, there is nothing simple about *The Straight Story*'s simplicity.[8] The film's straightforwardness, for lack of a better word, is more sophisticated than it seems. Like folk music, it is through its apparent simplicity that it gains access to not only the profound, but the weird. When it comes to identifying the weird in *The Straight Story*, many critics single out the particularly Lynchian scene of the woman who has hit her thirteenth deer in seven weeks as a visit from Lynchland in an otherwise non-Lynchian story; however, closer attention to the film's visuals reveals that Lynchian elements abound, such as the family sitting in lawn chairs and sipping beers as they watch a building burn down, the bickering brothers in matching clothes, and, most obviously, "an old geezer who's traveling on a lawnmower."

But these traditionally Lynchian elements of weirdness pale in comparison to the pervading sense of the weird that permeates every scene of the film. In his book *The Weird and the Eerie*, Mark Fisher defines weirdness as "a sensation of *wrongness*," a situation in which something exists at a time or place when it should not, creating a paradox so intense it cannot be explained away. Instead, its presence renders invalid "the categories which we have up until now used to make sense of the world." In other words, circumstances do not prove that the weird thing is wrong, but the weird thing makes plain that our conception of normality is faulty.[9] Although Lynch has certainly trafficked in this type of weirdness throughout his career, his distinct use of it in *The Straight Story* demonstrates how a sense of wrongness—the wrongness of a lawnmower on the highway, the wrongness of old-fashioned music in a world of mass media—can be a vehicle through which one can access the transcendent.

Alvin Straight, the "old geezer" on that lawnmower, is a weird figure who seems out of place in the late twentieth century. However, he would be right at home in a folk song on the *Anthology*. His strange quest certainly associates him with the cobbler in "Peg and Awl" and various ballads about John Henry such as "Gonna Die with My Hammer in My Hand" in the sense that he too is defying time and his own obsolescence through a battle with a machine. Alvin rejects most forms of modernity, most notably medical tests, eyeglasses, and a walker, in favor of the "good machine" of a 1966 John Deere tractor. However, his very demeanor as a commoner who carries nobility within him captures what Cantwell defines as the idea of folk: "independent, virtuous, honorable, but at the same time plain, modest, humble, serf as knight and knight as serf."[10] I would add a sense of guilt or regret to Cantwell's optimistic list because the qualities listed above and found in Alvin and the great folk songs are not innate characteristics that one is born with; they are earned through pain. We do not learn a great deal about Alvin's life before the events of the film, but nearly all of what we do learn is tragic: he is a widower and person in recovery from alcohol disorder who has lost half of his children in infancy, he no longer speaks to his brother (who has just suffered a stroke), and his daughter has an intellectual disability and has had her children (his grandchildren) unjustly taken away from her by the state. As if this were not enough misery, before any of these events occurred, Alvin served as a sniper in the Second World War and killed one of his fellow soldiers by accident. This information demonstrates that Alvin's monologues throughout the film about the importance of family only sound like Disneyfied reactionary pablum; his folk wisdom derives from pain and regret, not sanctimony or sentiment. In fact, it is in speaking to this pain, acknowledging it, that permits Alvin to bond with the people he meets. Likewise, the folk song gains its power and connects with audiences by giving them a glimpse into other people's pain, which gives them the courage and support to share their own and, in doing so, lay their burden down.

Exploring the affiliating identifications between the folk revival and *The Straight Story* might appear an odd fit for a film whose soundtrack is almost entirely an original score by Angelo Badalamenti, a score that itself operates quite heavily with assimilating identifications, which place viewers into less familiar territory in a gentle way that ensures a more homogenized experience.[11] The score itself certainly conjures identifications with a folk sensibility, especially when placed underneath the film's many aerial shots of corn and wheat fields; however, I want to look beyond the film score to see how placing this film's narrative, style, and thematic concerns in conversation with this moment in popular music allows for a better understanding of both, and one that a focus on Badalamenti's score alone does not provide.

The Straight Story is not discussed in terms of its relationship to popular culture, especially popular music culture, because it lacks many of the stylistic tropes and cultural touchstones. Martha Nochimson characterizes Lynch's films as being "built on the inevitability of [the viewer's] subconscious connection [...] with the materials of mass media," a statement that makes *The Straight Story* stick out as different.[12] After all, even *The Elephant Man* and *Dune* have the media of the circus and the theater in the film or rock artists such as Toto and Brian Eno on the soundtrack. It is true that *The Straight Story* lacks references to "the materials of mass media," especially Lynch's usual rockabilly inflected signature references such as mid-century pop numbers or iconography such as classic cars, poodle skirts, or snakeskin jackets; however, I agree with Devin Orgeron that their absence does not necessarily mean that the narrative is not responding to or infused with them in some way.[13] The real iconic material at the heart of *The Straight Story* is the same as the one at the heart of the folk revival, though in both cases, it is repressed: the Second World War. Watching *The Straight Story* and reading into the origins of the folk revival reveal that the trauma surrounding the so-called good war is the engine driving most of the conflict.

Like the folk revival, Lynch mounts his critique of the postwar era through the absence of such familiar iconography. As he does in *Wild at Heart* and *Lost Highway*, Lynch "draw[s] upon discourses around" the folk revival to transfer its "semiotic and dramatic power" to *The Straight Story*'s tale of repair and redemption in a manner that stretches beyond the confines of the soundtrack to permeate every aspect of the film.[14] In doing so, Lynch's work in *The Straight Story* fulfills Kassabian's criterion of affiliating identifications in that it "evokes an accumulation of meanings" from a viewer's engagement with the folk revival.[15] Lynch's film depicts the same overlooked citizenry on display in the music of the folk revival: people whose lives are marked by trauma and who pursue recognition and redemption through a kind of musical testimony or participatory performance. Lynch uses the form and substance of this musical tradition to plumb the same traumatic depths of experience as folk music and profess an old, weird America of his own.

Placing these works in conversation with each other reveals how their simple, old-fashioned structures and unassuming styles create a profound space for communal explorations of trauma in which singers/speakers and audiences testify to their honest experience through authentic performance and engaged listening. These works cling to anachronistic methods to sow tales of redemption and liberation that bring people together to heal the wounds that prevent people from engaging in the present. Critics of both Lynch and the folk revival may view the quaint anachronisms of each as empty retreats into nostalgia, especially when one considers the predominant whiteness of both the film and the 1960s folk revival;[16] however, both show how the return to the past is not a vehicle of avoidance but rather an engine for the communal engagement necessary to process both personal trauma and the trauma of the twentieth century in a way that allows a more meaningful and authentic future to exist.

Subterranean Homesick Alchemy

Even though he covered Dylan's 1964 folk classic "The Ballad of Hollis Brown" on his 2013 album *The Big Dream*, it may be a stretch for many to accept a description of Lynch as a folkie, but Cantwell's description of the energies of the folk revival also feels like a decent definition of that elusive term "Lynchian":

> [H]istory has a kind of conscious life in the institutions, ideologies, movements, and forces that seem to constitute the daylight workings of society; but it has a kind of nocturnal life as well—a dream world ruled by the various alchemies of metaphor and symbol, where the boundaries between one institution and another with which is it is constantly at war, between an idea and its contrary, swim about in a kind of cultural ectoplasm where forms change places with one another.[17]

"Alchemies of metaphor and symbol" are of great importance to David Lynch's film style. Kevin M. Moist defines alchemy as a belief that spirit and matter are ultimately "the same basic material arranged on different levels of being," and the practice of alchemy involves rearranging or breaking down baser, lower-level materials and transmuting and reconstituting them into higher, more perfect levels of being.[18] Lynch's work can be understood as alchemical in nature because it continually blurs the line between "an idea and its contrary" such as reality and dream, good and evil, sincerity and irony, frightening and funny. The tension between these forces (and his frequent refusal to distinguish between them or offer a clear statement on which of the binary he prefers) grants his films a large portion of their thematic and emotional power, blurring these lines for the viewer as well in a way that "allow[s] for a fair bit of mobility" in interpretation that can be transformative, making the familiar forever strange and the strange forever familiar.[19] In this way, one could characterize his films as a form of alchemy. *The Straight Story* may be Lynch's most alchemical work because it eschews the most up-to-date techniques available (both in the narrative and in terms of production) in favor of working with the simplest base materials. Alvin uses the "base materials" of a 1966 John Deere lawnmower to inaugurate a new age of greater, more harmonious being not just for Alvin but for everyone who comes into contact with this "good machine."[20] Further, Lynch strips down (and slows down) his own film style to something more akin to the invisible style of classical Hollywood—linear story, unobtrusive camera movement, conventional coverage and shot composition, traditional film score, etc.—to transform it into something that accesses the transcendent and the ineffable.

The kind of alchemy on display in *The Straight Story* can also be found in the folk revival: at a time when popular music was electrifying and becoming more produced and packaged for mass consumption, folk revivalists leaned into a sense of *wrongness* brought on by anachronistic songs and styles and stripped music down to its most essential elements—a string instrument (guitar, fiddle, or banjo) and the human voice—to create weird music that inspires a sense of awe and wonder in listeners and sends them on a quest for transcendence as well. The *Anthology* is an alchemical work as well. Harry Smith's rearrangement of previously released folk songs and obscure, defamiliarizing liner notes is an assemblage that performs a kind of alchemy on the music. The *Anthology* is, of course, a collection of many individual works of art; however, as Moist argues, the *Anthology* as whole—its music, its sequencing, its packaging materials—should be considered an alchemical work of art in its own right, "an artistic collage" that "transmut[es] fragmentary pieces of culture to higher levels of conceptual meaning."[21] The songs are standalone statements that were recorded at an earlier time and released on their own, but Harry Smith's arrangement and juxtaposition of these songs with each other makes them something more: individual works of art that also serve as tiles in a larger mosaic that speaks to the power of the song and that the song contributes power and meaning to. A motion picture functions in a similar way, with each scene acting as an individual unit that serves both its own purpose and a larger one. The episodic structure of *The Straight Story* communicates this sense even more strongly, making it feel even more like an anthology of scenes, discrete monologues that act in a similar way to songs performed around a campfire or at a hootenanny. Marcus also describes *The Basement Tapes* as a work of alchemy, with the basement in Big Pink acting as a "laboratory where [...] certain bedrock strains of American cultural language were retrieved and reinvented" by Dylan and the Band into new, original compositions that usher in a new state of being for American music in the form of Americana and alt-country.[22] In fact, Dylan's songwriting during this period was so alchemically attuned to the style and themes of traditional American music that even his bandmates "didn't know if he wrote them or if he remembered them."[23]

The goal of performance in a folk song is transformation. The song is not there so much to be sung; rather, Marcus, echoing Carl Sandburg, argues that it is "the song that sings the singer," to the extent that the transformation the song performs on the singer becomes an aesthetic object. The song gives the singer the opportunity, "to be transfigured" into someone new.[24] The idea of personal transformation was imperative to the folk song: the music's purpose is to perform a kind of alchemy that merges the "public persona projected in the performance and the psychological subject making the projection."[25] The alchemy of the folk revival and *The Straight Story* takes place via performance, public testimonies of grief, regret, and trauma.

Although most critics can easily accept the idea of many of David Lynch's films as being about trauma, perhaps even the trauma of the twentieth century, fewer would readily rank *The Straight Story* high on a list of Lynch's films that have personal or national trauma as their subject. In his book *The Architecture of David Lynch*, Richard Martin expresses disappointment in the lack of trauma and menace on display the film, calling it "a cinematic dead end" that lacks "spatial tension," so much so that "one longs for [*Blue Velvet*'s] Frank Booth, [*Lost Highway*'s] Mr. Eddy, or a Reindeer-led conspiracy [*á la Wild at Heart*] to inject some life into these gentle events" that, like the carefully mapped-out boundaries between road and field, "peacefully exist without threat of disturbance."[26] Nochimson agrees with Martin that "things are generally exactly where they appear to be" in the film, but she also points out that "loose ends abound" in Alvin's stories and sees "something discomforting" in his monologues that suggests "something underneath that we can't see and are being blocked from seeing."[27] Indeed, there is much more to *The Straight Story* than tranquil scenes and hokey sentimentality if one is willing to look. Like the picture-perfect montage of a typical American neighborhood at the start of *Blue Velvet*, darker things lurk beneath the amber waves of grain in *The Straight Story* that become readily visible when one avoids reflexively dismissing Alvin's monologues as "banal homilies."[28] The film is marked by trauma at every level; it simply has been, as Justus Nieland describes it, normalized, "domesticate[d]," kept at bay by a repression as rigid and orderly as the rows of corn.[29] The camera may not plunge into the ground to dredge up the trauma in *The Straight Story* as it does in *Blue Velvet*. It does not have to: these emotions well up to the surface and burst through on their own.

FIGURE 8.1 Alvin's first hootenanny. *The Straight Story* directed by David Lynch © The Walt Disney Company 1999. All rights reserved.

The Straight Story's structure revolves around the revelation of this repressed and normalized trauma through transformative public performances. After Alvin begins his journey, the film becomes episodic in nature, featuring traveling montages followed by longer scenes in which Alvin encounters a series of strangers when he stops to sleep or has mechanical trouble. These interactions build toward a moment when Alvin reflects on the traumatic events of his life in a monologue addressed to someone who is experiencing a problem similar to the one that caused Alvin some pain in the past: a pregnant teen running away from home matches Alvin's and Rose's woes as parents, the two bickering brothers relates to Alvin's rift with Lyle, and an emotionally repressed vet stirs up Alvin's memories of his alcohol use disorder and shooting a fellow soldier. Each of these monologues acts as a kind of purifying transformation for Alvin, peeling back another layer of scarring to prepare him to reconcile with Lyle. Each encounter removes another mask from Alvin until, by the time he approaches Lyle's porch, he is stripped down to his most naked self.

I refer to Alvin's monologues as testimony because they are an act of witnessing and sharing conveyed through speech. The music of the *Anthology* functions as testimony as well because of its close connections to speech and language and its preference for "the aural, the improvisatory, the formulaic, the agonistic, and the *participatory*."[30] It is in this spirit that I would like to characterize Alvin's monologues as songs and his interactions with strangers as hootenannies. For one, the subjects of his monologues are strikingly similar in content to the types of stories found in the music of the *Anthology* or *The Basement Tapes*. His story of his daughter Rose losing her children could easily fit alongside many of the ballads on the *Anthology* such as "Henry Lee" and "Sugar Baby," while Alvin's tales of abandonment and guilt have a confessional, yearning quality that echoes the most powerful songs on *The Basement Tapes* such as "Tears of Rage" and "I'm Not There" in the sense that both are fueled by "the burning sensation produced when an individual attempts to resolve the circumstance of [their] life."[31] Alvin, like the speakers of "Tears of Rage," feels condemned to "carry on the grind" as "thie[ves]" as all love "goes from bad to worse." Ernest Phipps and His Holiness Singers' song from the *Anthology* "Shine on Me" captures the way in which Alvin does not run from consequences in search of a "flowery bed of ease" but rather asks for divine assistance in giving him the courage to "bear the toil [and] endure the pain" of the circumstances of his life.

These interactions are not only transformative for Alvin, however; their impact spreads to his audiences as well. In fact, the audience's role is essential to the alchemical work being done in *The Straight Story* and the folk revival. Folk performance calls upon the audience to respond and participate in what becomes a communal performance known as a hootenanny. Defined most basically as a "community sing-along," a hootenanny is distinguished by its spontaneity and the expectation that audience members would become participants in the music.[32] These performances create what Cantwell calls "a new sense of access" for the audience to the extent that a hootenanny or similar folk performance reconceives performance spaces altogether from a place in which the many gather to hear the few perform, to one where the few and the many come together in a manner that facilitates everyone's participation. This "festive mutuality" creates a "symbolic social leveling" of high and low that sets the table for personal and communal transformations.[33] All of Alvin's interactions start from a position of difference and separation, of weirdness: the opening line in most of these scenes is always a variation of "why are you doing something as weird as riding a lawnmower?" Through spontaneous and interactive conversation and his testimony, these initially weird encounters end in a space of community in which any distance or difference that once existed has vanished and his audience is sharing details of their life with him and incorporating his thoughts into their own worldview. In short, Alvin's weirdness becomes familiar as the people he meets adjust their way of understanding the world to account for people like Alvin.

It is easy to see the transformative impact of Alvin's first hoot with the pregnant girl. She may not participate much as he, but his story does lead her to engage in creative work symbolic of repair: she leaves a bundle of sticks to symbolize the reparative work she is going to do by returning to her family instead of, like Alvin, spending years living with regret. The most transformative of Alvin's hootenannies, in which Alvin accompanies an older man to a bar, turns into a dialogue, a kind of call and response performance of grief and regret that performs a kind of alchemy on the characters in the scene as well as the soundtrack. As they talk, Alvin mentions that he turned to alcohol to stop him from "seeing all them things here that I'd seen over there" in the war and that he can "see [the war] in a man a mile away."

FIGURE 8.2 Testifying to trauma. *The Straight Story* directed by David Lynch © The Walt Disney Company 1999. All rights reserved.

Alvin's statement leads the other man to tell a story of a bomb landing in the mess tent and killing everyone in it but him. The veteran relates his story through stifled tears as the 1940s pop vocal on the jukebox fades away and sounds of mortar shells appear on the soundtrack. Next, Alvin shares his story of the time he shot a scout in his unit by mistake, and again the sounds of battle appear on the soundtrack before fading into an original composition that mixes acoustic guitar with Badalamenti's signature organ tones. While this technique may be a pretty basic use of nondiegetic sound, it has tremendous importance to the ideas of the film: the scene captures a moment where Alvin's testimony becomes participatory and alchemical, transforming the film's method of representation and fashioning a space where people reveal the ways that trauma has marked their lives so that they can be released from it through sharing and becoming part of a small community.

Lynch's alchemical work on the soundtrack demonstrates how doing so summons the past into the present for the purpose of reunion and repair. As Cantwell says of the songs on the *Anthology*, "the drive towards liberation" in these scenes "comes in the face of an unabridged awareness of an intimate confrontation with suffering."[34] Like the *Anthology*, *The Straight Story* moves through testimonies of pain and alienation to arrive at its true destination: transcendence.[35] These alchemical processes all involve complex interactions with time, a reaching across a temporal rift into an earlier period of time to bring an outmoded, antiquated, and weird conveyance (traditional music, a lawnmower, etc.) into the present with the intention of restoring the connection between the present and the past in a way that guarantees a more unified future no longer limited by trauma.

The David Lynch Memory Theater

The Anthology of American Folk Music, *The Basement Tapes*, and *The Straight Story* are about movement through time and are animated in part by the fear of immobility. Cantwell argues that the arrival of television represented a kind of "confinement" as much as it did an opening up of a global village by standardizing certain American norms of language and ethnicity. Immobilized and confined within their homes watching the same banal programming created "a deep moral hunger for real experience" that could best be fed by a reacquaintance with the weird and rough edges of folk songs that the mass-produced world of television was attempting to smooth out.[36] *The Basement Tapes* were also catalyzed by a kind of immobility in the form of Dylan's motorcycle accident. Regardless of the level of severity of the accident, which remains uncertain, Dylan's crash created a symbolic kind of immobility that sent Dylan to search out of time for something to satisfy a hunger brought on by dissatisfaction with protest music and the demands of his fanbase. Although *The Straight Story*'s entire plot is based upon (albeit slow) motion, it is important to recall that it begins with two different forms of immobility: Alvin begins the film flat on the ground after a fall, and the plot is set in motion by the stroke that immobilizes Lyle. Orgeron goes even further by describing the film in terms of emotional immobility: Alvin is a "once free-roaming man" who has been immobilized by trauma.[37] It is not until Alvin gets moving through physical space that he is able to move through emotional space. The feeling of being trapped in an inauthentic present sends these figures on a search through time. Similarly, Kassabian uses terms associated with movement—"mobility," "terrains," "field," etc.—to describe affiliating identifications. Indeed, viewers move psychically through space and time as they interact with "an accumulation of meaning from [their own] previous film experiences" and travel "over the boundaries between unconscious and conscious processes."[38] All of these types of mobility involve movements through the spatial and physical as well as the temporal and spiritual, and the merging of the two produces a transformation constitutes a form of alchemy.

Like Alvin's monologues that reach into the past or the folk revivalists' that rummage through old songs and styles, affiliating identifications engage with time through their reliance on the audience's memory. Cantwell describes how Smith's alchemical practice in the *Anthology* has a temporal dimension by associating it with the concept of the "memory theater." A "memory theater" is a kind of "thinking machine" or "mnemonic library" modeled on the *ars memoria* that seeks to "organize and present the entire cosmos of knowledge" in a theatrical space one could physically inhabit and rummage through. In the memory theater, topics would be presented via memorable images shown in sequence in "a familiar piece of architecture," permitting one to "retain all knowledge and retrieve it by systematic recall."[39] Here we have the linearity of form assisting in the circular and recursive practice of memory. Dylan's work on *The Basement Tapes* takes the memory theater a step further by demonstrating how the process of rummaging through "the entire cosmos of knowledge" leads to the creation of a new and more dynamic future (in this case in the form of alt-country Americana) marked by a renewed commitment to the authenticity of the world before mass media. *The Straight Story*, with its road movie narrative serving as "a familiar piece of architecture" and the spatial progression of memorable images and sounds triggering personal recollections, utilizes the purposes of the memory and acts as "a sacred narrative" based in ritualized performance.[40]

The memory theater represented by the *Anthology*, *The Basement Tapes*, and *The Straight Story* appeals to aural and literary imaginations that operate on a temporal dimension resembling Kassabian's affiliating identifications. Where the aural imagination "shrinks the shell of time" to pull the past into the present, the literary imagination is an expansive one that "locat[es] the anachronism on the scale of history."[41] Cantwell describes the affiliating identifications found within the *Anthology* itself as creating "an aural universe" in which the songs are occurring simultaneously, causing the psychic field of the music to flow "into the landscape and history of the country," creating "disturbances in the medium of our own being."[42] These disturbances come in the form of regional, racial, and temporal paradoxes, of a sense of wrongness. Smith's grouping of the *Anthology*'s songs into Ballads, Social Music, and Songs "detextualiz[es] folk music" by erasing the spatial and temporal boundaries that previously isolated these songs from each other, an act representing nothing short of "the complete breakdown of the old cultural geography."[43] Cantwell's language sounds remarkably like Kassabian's description of affiliating identifications that broaden the psychic field by placing viewers on the "unconscious terrains" of their "memories of emotions and subject positions."[44]

In fact, the *Anthology* and *The Basement Tapes* are full of weird temporal paradoxes. Smith's journalistic design in the *Anthology* packaging suggests the linear and orderly presentation of news on material that actively works to disrupt any sense of linearity in favor of "a wider field of dis-integrated time."[45] The complete *Basement Tapes* puts American music in shuffle mode, perhaps in a blender, juxtaposing Carter Family standards with songs by Curtis Mayfield, Johnny Cash, and Dylan originals, a kind of musical free-association that destabilizes a listener's sense of chronological continuity and places every song on a plane that is both now and eternal. Likewise, Orgeron reads the road in Lynch's work as a symbol of reunion, community, and connection.[46] *The Straight Story* has a structure and a genre—the road movie—that appears to be rigorously linear in spatial and temporal terms when those markers are but masks for its true temporal structure, which is circular. The film, like the folk revival, is really about a return, a quest to makes something whole, a circle which seeks to become unbroken. Nieland argues that time in the film is "distended experientially," spurred by "the presence of another, large vital context": another person who has experienced similar trauma.[47] Nieland describes Alvin's trip as a harvest, with Alvin and the lawnmower acting like a combine reaping traumatic memories from each person, who cannot help having these memories bloom before Alvin and his mower.[48] The bar scene discussed earlier is a perfect example of this as the sound of the battle intrudes upon the soundtrack, the past coming back to us as an aural experience in the same way that folk songs usher in the world of the past.

The folk revival and *The Straight Story* constitute a deliberate effort "to reach into the past and retrieve it" to fashion a future that is not ignorant of the past but deeply indebted to it not in a nostalgic or traditionalist way but in a manner that recognizes the past's reparative potential.[49] This continual reaching into the past and to memory to aid in creating the present creates a sense of always becoming, of the self and the country being unfinished, still full of creative and redemptive potential.[50] In this sense, the *Anthology* acts as a memory theater, "a reservoir of the various tributaries and currents of history" that itself "draw[s] upon the reservoir of public culture" to form "a new kind of history."[51] The entire project of this music, aesthetically and politically, Cantwell argues, was a reclamation, "picking up the threads of a forgotten legacy to reweave them into history."[52] Linking the present and the past through song or, in Alvin's case, testimony, involves confronting and processing the trauma that created the separation in the first place so that, through bearing witness, the rift gets mended.

Strumming the Celestial Monochord

Harry Smith saw folk music as the essential ingredient necessary to produce this kind of alchemical transformation. Although the edition of the *Anthology* reissued after the folk revival was underway featured a Depression-era farmer on its cover, Smith's original cover art features a device essential to understanding this concept. The 1952 edition of the *Anthology*, as well as the 1997 CD reissue, features a reproduction of God's hand tuning a "celestial monochord," "a primitive one-stringed instrument" that "encompasses the entire universe" and harmonically unifies "the alchemical base elements of earth, air, fire, and water."[53] For Smith, these songs stand as "a sequence of performances which could be taken as rituals whose repetition might reunite [...] a starving and spectre-like imagination with the primordial sources of its own life."[54] *The Straight Story* builds to this kind of rapture in its final scene as all of its various strands and themes come together through the careful arrangement and repetition of incredibly base cinematic elements.

FIGURE 8.3 The circle will be unbroken. *The Straight Story* directed by David Lynch © The Walt Disney Company 1999. All rights reserved.

The final scene of the film, in which Alvin reaches his destination and comes face to face with his brother Lyle, is of course overflowing with tension that has been building for over ninety minutes, but Lynch's mise-en-scene elevates this tension and brings the film to a kind of stylistic and thematic resolution that, through its bare-bones simplicity, carries the film to a more mystical, transcendent level that reaches somewhere beyond language. Alvin's entire journey and testimony has been a quest to get to this point in more than one sense, and his arrival carries with it a sense of fulfillment that each of his testimonies has been working toward. This sense of fulfillment has echoes of Marcus's definition of the freedom expressed in the *Anthology*: "the freedom of knowing exactly who you are and why you are here."[55] Lynch and cinematographer Freddie Francis cover the scene in the simplest of ways: a master shot followed by a series of mostly static, mostly wordless shot/reverse-shots from Alvin to Lyle to the lawnmower and back again, ending with a tilt up that follows Alvin's look up to the sky that then dissolves to a shot of the stars that echoes the first shot of the film and Alvin's line that he "want[s] to sit with [Lyle] and look up at the stars like we used to do so long ago." This series of looks brings the brothers together but also creates a unity within the structure of the film between the heavens and the earth, and the third item in these shots, the lawnmower, is the device that makes it all possible. This machine concerned wholly with soil and the material serves as the alchemical conduit for a journey that connects two people to the infinite cosmos in harmony.

While many songs on the *Anthology* could serve as examples of this process, two by the Alabama Sacred Harp Singers, "Rocky Road" and "Present Joys" show how the music of the folk revival and the style of *The Straight Story* approach an ineffable that "encompasses the entire universe" through the artful and repetitive arrangement of simple materials. Both are basic praise songs, with "Present Joys" thanking God "for present joys, for blessings past / and for the hope of heav'n at last" and "Rocky Road" expressing relief that, though life has been "a mighty rocky road," the speaker's "soul shall ascend to where Jesus is / and be there forever blest." These lyrics are plain and direct, relying on familiar sentiments of hope and praise; however, the layered vocal arrangements repeat, rise, and return in a way that makes the individual words of the song nearly indecipherable. Instead, what the listener hears is a hypnotic, surreal quality perpetually rising and encircling somewhere beyond language, as though the singers and the song have achieved a oneness in which all speech, all voices become a pure harmonious sound, a strumming of the celestial monochord.

Nieland reads the lawnmower (and Alvin's evaluation of it as a "good machine") as a vehicle of community, showing how "machines and humans live together in time and sustain each other in an ongoing network of attention, kindness, and generosity."[56] While Nieland focuses on the relationship between humans and machines here, we can also see how this lawnmower fosters a sense of community between people through its strangeness, its out-of-place-ness. The mower obviously serves as the conduit for repairing Alvin's relationship with Lyle, but it also creates relationships with everyone Alvin comes into contact with, each of whom leaves the interaction transformed in small or more profound ways. Alvin's travels create a "network" of "do-overs and second chances" that reanimate broken things.[57] The music of the folk revival also works as "an intermediate agency, a channel, to other living beings" through "good machines" such as record players.[58] In their weirdness, these works have a cumulative effect in which the gallery of weirdos and oddballs become a "living communit[y]."[59]

Alvin's travels and the music of the folk revival send people backward to reconnect with a past they have lost that will make their future fuller. The weirdness of the songs and the weirdness of *The Straight Story* illustrate "the path which our own traditions have taken" and locate "our own voices in relation to sounds lost, abandoned, or forgotten."[60] These sentiments resonate with Raymond Williams's work in *The Country and the City*, in which he argues that, when faced with uncertainty, "we can retreat [...] into a deep subjectivity, or we can look around us for social pictures, social signs, social messages [...] so as to discover, in some form, community" so that one can enter into a world where a person can become "a member, a discoverer, in a shared source of life."[61]

The strangeness of the *Anthology*, *The Basement Tapes*, and *The Straight Story* reanimates our aesthetic sensibilities by testing their limits. This process reaffirms the promise of art: we continue to engage, to seek out connection with it and with others through it because one day, in the words of Cantwell, "we will ultimately be satisfied: that the universe of the folk song opened up to us will ultimately deliver, somehow, the promised completion of itself."[62] Like the speaker of "I Shall Be Released," perhaps the most famous *Basement Tapes* recording, the residents of this "old, weird America" may live lives marked by regret and shame, but, through this music, they also believe that they will experience redemption. The song acts as testimony, as a plea, a reaching out in search of a true community within "this lonely crowd." *The Straight Story* and the music of the folk revival depict just this kind of reach outward, a search to forge a community as a bulwark against the uncertainty and strangeness of the world. *The Basement Tapes* are often discussed in terms of seclusion and retreat, but it is important to recall that these recordings capture the formation of a community, a small one for sure, but a community nonetheless founded on a shared appreciation for traditional music that itself spawned more community among musicians, folkheads, Dylanologists, and tape traders who yearned to listen in.

The folk song's weird power comes from a form of time travel. As music, it is both summoned from a distant past and, through the immediacy of performance and the timelessness of its themes, wholly immersed in the present, and entirely concerned with the way things will (or ought) to be, creating a sound and an effect that sounds familiar but also strange and novel, paradoxically "historical and sui generis."[63] Disillusioned by a postwar present that "organized its peace as if it were still at war" under the shadow of the atomic bomb and "a total environment of institutional power," the folk revivalists sought to "reimagine the lost America that lay in the historical hinterlands behind the great wall of World War II."[64] The *Anthology* served as a road map for this project, Moist argues, because its eighty-four songs constitute "statement[s] about the past and a suggestion about how to remake the present in the interests of the future."[65] *The Basement Tapes* and *The Straight Story* chart the same course as the *Anthology* in their form and content: each depicts what Orgeron calls "a return to the premodern" that "attempts to correct what precedes it."[66] Overwhelmed by the harsh light of rock stardom and the pressures of a political movement that asked the world of him, Dylan also retreats from the Summer of Love into the sequestered and anachronistic world of Smithville to host a private hoot with some of the greatest musicians of his time, only to emerge born again with new energy and music that remakes American music all over again. Thirty-two years later, on the precipice of a new millennium fascinated by and anxious of a brave new world of hyperlinked virtual existence, Lynch tells an old-fashioned story in a classical style that mimics the folk revival's reach to the "primitive-modernist music" of the prewar past.[67] They all see the world speeding up and look to the past and old modes of conveyance—the folk song, the lawnmower—to find meaningful and authentic experience. This journey requires an alchemy that is temporal as much as it is physical in that it is a melding of time periods. Such a melding is not an exercise in comfortable nostalgic reminiscence but an uneasy confrontation with the pain that created the gulf between the present and the recent past. Bridging this gap necessitates a sharing of grief and regret, a truth and reconciliation with one's own past.

While the America of *The Anthology of American Folk Music*, *The Basement Tapes*, and *The Straight Story* may not be the one valorized in history textbooks and campaign speeches, it might be more democratic than its more mainstream counterpart. It is in the weirdness, or the welcoming, normalizing approach to weirdness in its most unvarnished forms that makes the music of the folk revival and the films of David Lynch the clearest and most democratic and authentic portrayal of America's most idealistic values: good and bad, dark and light, sacred and profane, and, above all, a weirdness seeking to become familiar.

9

Love Is a Mixtape

The Ethics of Artistic Exchange in *Inland Empire*

Billed as a return to the experimentation of *Eraserhead* and his early short films as well as a companion piece to his previous film *Mulholland Drive*, Lynch's 2006 feature *Inland Empire* provides critics with a myriad of critical entry points over its ample running time;[1] however, it, along with *The Straight Story*, has the unfortunate distinction of being Lynch's least-discussed feature film. *The Straight Story*'s G-rating and Disney-financing certainly go a long way toward explaining its odd-film-out status in Lynch's filmography. But *Inland Empire*'s three-hour *mélange* of *doppelgängers*, time loops, sinister strangers, and familiar faces from other Lynch films such as Laura Dern, Harry Dean Stanton, and Grace Zabriskie makes it as Lynchian a film as any reasonable person could ask for, making its relative neglect surprising. When the film is discussed, the analysis frequently gravitates to topics outside the film, such as its unique production, distribution, and awards campaign and less the inner workings of its narrative and themes.

Such a focus makes perfect sense: unlike any of Lynch's previous nine features, *Inland Empire* was shot on digital video and served as his announcement that he was ending his relationship with celluloid and, perhaps, feature filmmaking altogether. These new developments in Lynch's career indeed call for new ways of talking about his work. Critics take Lynch's switch to digital as an opportunity to employ digital metaphors to describe *Inland Empire*. Steven Shaviro believes the film constitutes a "newer media form,"[2] Anthony Paraskeva defines it as a work of "digital modernism,"[3] and Kristen Daly categorizes it as a work of "database cinema," a key text in what she calls "Cinema 3.0."[4] Dennis Lim asserts the film arises "from deep within the bowels of YouTube" and "progresses with the darting, associative logic of hyperlinks,"[5] while Amy Taubin quips that instead of being governed by narrative and spatial logic, scenes and spaces in *Inland Empire* are connected "simply because they reside in the selects bin on Lynch's Avid hard drive."[6] These digital metaphors address the aspects of *Inland Empire* that make it singular in Lynch's filmography and thoughtfully position it as a landmark work of twenty-first-century cinema, but they risk keeping the film's impenetrable and not-always-coherent narrative at arm's length. While I do not claim to have worked out a grand theory about what each moment of *Inland Empire* means, I do argue that heavily favoring the digital aspects of the film's production in discussions about it overlooks the deeper relationship between *Inland Empire*'s fragmented form and confounding content. Despite the apparent randomness of the film, form, and content are as intimately linked in *Inland Empire* as they are in any other David Lynch film, though the form that most informs its content may not be digital in nature.

Inland Empire may be set in the twenty-first century, but the technology and behavior on display in it remain rooted in the twentieth. For all of Lynch's stated fascination with digital technology, he remains an artist with an analog aesthetic sensibility; phonographs and tube TVs easily outnumber cellphones and laptops in the film. Although one cannot deny *Inland Empire*'s status as a digital film, Lynch's digital turn differs from most filmmakers in that his use of digital technology, both in the film's look and its production style, enlists affiliating identifications with a distinctly analog practice: mixtape creation. Lynch's affiliating identifications with the aesthetics and ethos of mixtapes not only imbue *Inland Empire* with a warmth and a presence many early digital films lack, but these affiliating identifications also enhance, clarify, and shape the film's scattered narrative to create "emotional coherence" out of "a form of total rupture."[7]

Inland Empire would not be the first film to be compared to a mixtape. J. M. Tyree and Ben Walters dub the Coen Brothers' 1998 film *The Big Lebowski* a "Mix-Tape Movie" in the sense that its "glorious hotch-potch" of random plots, characters, and styles "revels in wanton, riotous variety, apparently for its own sake," to the extent that one could claim the disparate parts fail to add up to a coherent whole, reducing the film to "a party with a great soundtrack but no host."[8] Although these two films could not appear less similar, the same logic that governs *The Big Lebowski* governs *Inland Empire*. Both manically dart from character to character, subplot to subplot, aesthetic to aesthetic without offering much assurance along the way that a grand design exists, only "a warren of wormholes" that grows deeper and wider with each scene.[9] For one, *Inland Empire*'s detractors lob similar criticisms at the film as those flung at *Lebowski*, calling it "a miasma" of "nonexistent narrative rhythms" that "lacks concentration."[10] However, as Tyree and Walters argue about *Lebowski*, the seemingly random assemblage of both films can obscure their deeper, more humanistic projects, requiring more work on the part of the viewer to "acclimatize to [the film's] oddness and pay attention" in order to connect the disparate dots.[11] Trying to make sense of mixtape movies, both in form and content, enlists the viewer in a quest for a deeper, more relevant purpose to not only the film but to the viewer's own life, a search that Tyree and Walters claim results in "not just the solution to a mystery, but an ethos by which to navigate a jumbled place in jumbled times."[12] Where some critics see, to use a digital metaphor, a bug in these mixtape movies, Tyree, Walters, and I see a feature, an aesthetic approach that accumulates in meaning and feeling until it becomes more like an ethos. In this regard, the mixtape aesthetic instructs and guides the viewer by having the interpretive work they perform in the film mirror the work required to live meaningfully. By channeling the process and ethics of mixtaping, Lynch delivers in *Inland Empire* his most intimate and personal testament on art's ability to establish an ethical way of being in an increasingly chaotic, fragmented, and yes, digital century.

Mixing a W-H-O-L-E Out of H-O-L-E-S

For readers of a certain age, mixtapes evoke a visceral nostalgia and thus need no further definition, but since the word has taken on different meanings in the twenty-first century, especially in hip-hop, it is worth defining what I mean in brief. A mixtape is, in essence, a compilation of previously recorded and released music curated, arranged, and produced by a listener on amateur, consumer-grade equipment for personal and private use. Mixtapes enjoyed popularity in the 1980s and 1990s, a time largely post-CD but pre-CD-R and definitely pre-MP3, in the heyday of the cassette tape, the boombox, the Walkman. Listeners would gather music from a variety of sources—radio broadcasts, CDs, LPs, other cassette tapes—and transfer them to blank cassette tapes to create their own album-length compilations of music, either for the purpose of personal consumption or to gift to someone else. Blank cassette tapes were available for purchase at sites as varied as electronics stores, groceries, gas stations, drug stores, and music shops in lengths ranging from thirty to sixty minutes per side.[13]

The appeal of the mixtapes for their creators and their audiences was their personal, individualized nature. Users could become producers, creating entire fantasy albums comprised of the songs *they* wanted to hear in the order *they* wanted to hear them. In the case where someone was the recipient of a mixtape, the appeal was that these were songs chosen *for you and you alone* by someone else for the purpose of ... well, that part was not always stated, which made listening to a mixtape an act of interpretation as much as an act of entertainment. The mix presented the listener with a mystery to explore by listening to the mixtape: why these songs, why in this order? How does this song relate to the ones before and after it, and what does it all mean? Is there a grand design behind it all, or is the assemblage truly random? While the purpose of such mixtapes could be as generic as introducing the listener to songs the mixer thinks they might (or should) like or commemorating a shared experience by creating the soundtrack that accompanied it, the more common purpose of a mixtape—at least in popular conceptions of it—was to express some of the creator's romantic feelings toward its recipient, sentiments that they were not fully comfortable saying out loud but also not comfortable keeping to themselves.[14] Regardless of whether or not the impulses behind the creation of a mixtape are romantic in nature, a mixtape is always an act of love, a gift that is the product of time and labor undertaken by one person to communicate something important to someone else. Simply put, a mixtape provides one person with a window into the mind (and heart) of another, what Bas Jansen calls "a musical 'common ground'" that, through the making of and listening to the tape, becomes an experience "that is appreciated by both and therefore truly shared."[15]

No matter their purpose or the circumstances of their creation, mixtapes have a common criterion best described as "cohesion" or "flow."[16] Even though a mixtape is made entirely of preexisting elements, the bricolage of the mix must stand on its own merit. This is far more challenging than it may sound because a mixtape by the nature of its creation disrupts cohesion: it "strip[s] those original pieces of their initial meaning" and context and attempts to construct a new unity and meaning out of the rubble.[17] Each song has to adhere to the theme of the tape, maintain the flow of the tape, be authentic to the taper and considerate of the tape's recipient, and, lest we forget, fit within the time constraints of the side.[18] The connections and transitions between the collected songs have to make aesthetic sense, to the extent that the addition, deletion, or substitution of a song would disrupt the tape's coherence. Without this level of unity, the mix runs the risk of feeling like a nonsensical grab bag of material less than the sum of its parts. Jansen argues that this conflict between the mixtape's need for unity and the unity of the preexisting work each song included on the mixtape comes from proves aesthetically productive, generating new and previously unimaginable meanings and connections from both the new contexts created by the taper's juxtapositions and the listener's interpretations of those contexts.[19]

Readers familiar with *Inland Empire*'s production history may have already detected similarities between the film and this practice of making mixtapes. First, like a mixtape, *Inland Empire* is, at least in part, "a recombination of existing elements" rather than a film comprised of completely new material made specifically for that film within a set, continuous production period.[20] Several pieces in the film had been released already, most notably the short film *Rabbits*, which Lynch created in the early days of his website davidlynch.com. Other pieces, such as the lengthy monologue Nikki Grace (Laura Dern) delivers near the middle of the film, originated as standalone pieces shot without any intention of being part of a larger whole. What eventually became the entire film was shot over a three-year period without anything resembling a shooting script, with Lynch shooting ideas as he had them, even if their place in (or suitability for) a larger project was uncertain. (The eighty minutes of outtakes included on the various DVD releases of the film also testify to the unplanned nature of the production.) As Lynch himself tells it, "I never saw any whole, W-H-O-L-E. I saw plenty of holes, H-O-L-E-S."[21] It was not until Lynch was deep into this process that he approached financier Le Studio Canal with the possibility of it becoming a feature film. Thus, *Inland Empire*'s production history illustrates the mixtape process at its most basic. Scenes and stories were produced at different points in time, each with their own internal integrity, and then gradually assembled into a separate context from the one at the time of their creation to produce a new work with a new unity created through the juxtaposition of these preexisting elements.

Lynch's spontaneous acquisition of material may appear to resemble the open-ended streaming playlist more closely since this lack of pre-planning could be seen as disregarding the previously described careful planning required of the mixtape to fit the envisioned material into each side's finite running time. However, there are multiple methods of mixtape creation, and *Inland Empire* indulges in several. Not all mixtapers approach mixes as timetables. Some mixtapers prefer to craft a more freewheeling mixtape that captures their mood as they are in the process of creating it, with each song's runtime allowing the mixtaper to be fully present in the experience of hearing the tape and giving them the "room to dream" of where it could go next. As one mixtaper proudly declares, "I don't put a lot of forethought into what it will sound like to somebody else later. I put onto it whatever *I* want to listen to *right now*."[22] This free-associative process sounds akin to Lynch's description of making *Inland Empire*: "I would get an idea for a scene and shoot it, get another idea and shoot that. I didn't know how they would relate."[23] This method certainly contributes to *Inland Empire*'s fragmented feel and would threaten the overall sense of flow sought in the previously described method of mixtape creation. But *Inland Empire* is not a presentation of scenes in the order they were produced. It is a carefully edited piece of work that takes the spontaneously shot footage and constructs a narrative that makes these disruptions part of a larger whole. The editing of *Inland Empire* positions the material in a manner where the viewer can find cinematic "common ground" to construct a sense of meaning upon it that is both highly personal and "truly shared." Therefore, as a work both created in the moment and constructed in the editing room, *Inland Empire* rests between these two practices: its loose, less planned shoot aligns it with the mixtape practice described above, while the edit finds a more deliberate

Lynch attempting to make these instinctively captured bits cohere into an idea broader than how he felt at the moment of creation. This combination of styles aligns with Elizabeth Alsop's description of Lynch as an oneiric auteur, one who both instinctively receives ideas from the broader culture and then deliberately filters them through their own aesthetic sensibility.

The visual aesthetics of *Inland Empire* also match the sonic aesthetics of the mixtape in that both represent a technical downgrade from the professional level to the consumer level. As a result, the sound and images produced by these formats are rougher and contain more noise than their professional-grade counterparts. Like mixtapers take audio produced with and recorded to high-quality equipment and transfer it to consumer-grade material, so Lynch assembles the standard industry apparatus—movie stars, soundstages, etc.—and transfers it to consumer-grade equipment such as MiniDV tape. Many bemoaned the downgrade in visual quality found in *Inland Empire*, wondering why one of cinema's greatest image makers would opt to make a film on equipment that produces such ugly images.[24] However, the downgrade in quality bolsters *Inland Empire*'s mixtape aesthetic and overall thematic purpose. As Martha Nochimson adroitly notes, the Sony MiniDV PD150 gives *Inland Empire* a look and feel less like the crisp, noise-free image promised by digital advocates than "the grainy images of underground film."[25] These rough edges give *Inland Empire* more than underground cache: they give the film a handmade quality that, when combined with the star power of Laura Dern or Jeremy Irons, creates a productive tension between the artifice of Hollywood and the immediacy of underground or homemade art that can make the film more emotionally and psychologically affecting. Lim notes how Lynch's choice of capture format here actually increases the film's sense of intimacy rather than producing greater estrangement. Because MiniDV is a consumer-grade format, its images are the sort that audiences are quite comfortable with because it is "the medium of home movies, viral videos, and pornography."[26] As a result, Lim speculates that *Inland Empire* may have a greater emotional impact on viewers when they watch it in a more intimate setting, such as alone at home, rather than in a movie theater. As we will see, the film itself seems to favor such a private viewing experience by locating emotional and ethical core of the film in the character of the Lost Girl (Carolina Gruszka) and her emotional response to watching the film alone on her hotel room television.

Haunted Media

But the film, like a mixtape, is about much more than its production methods. Or, perhaps more accurately, those methods reinforce and are reinforced by the narrative, working together to accumulate in meaning. When critics dare to offer a broad interpretation of what *Inland Empire* is about, they settle on reading the film as a commentary on creating art. The horror of the film, as many have noted, derives from the assertion that art can be menacing.[27] Art haunts, art pursues, art is a place where people lose themselves. In the film, we see how Nikki Grace has blurred the lines between art and life for so long that she has lost the ability to distinguish the real from the fake or one role from another, and the film depicts her harrowing descent into a state where once clearly defined boundaries no longer hold. As her psyche grows more fragmented, she finds herself abruptly thrust into different personas and roles, as well as different countries and contexts, without warning and with no roadmap. In one scene, she literally finds herself trapped on the other side of a movie set, unable to establish contact even with the artificial world of the Hollywood soundstage, let alone the real world.

These events appear to suggest that a preponderance of artifice can lead to the dissolution of the real; however, this is only half of *Inland Empire*'s story. The tension between these boundaries, both within the film's story and within its production methods, gives *Inland Empire* its power and constructs an ethical approach to art and the world. Like Nikki Grace, the viewer of *Inland Empire* is overwhelmed by multiple incompatible characters, storylines, and contexts competing for prominence in their minds. As Richard Martin observes, "*Inland Empire* is inhabited," perhaps even haunted "by competing media."[28] First of all, the characters immersed in the making of the film-within-the-film *On High in Blue Tomorrows* are competing with another version of it, the unfinished Polish ghost production *47*. The viewer must grapple with those two projects and situate them within the context of the film *Inland Empire* that contains them both. Next, the abrupt narrative jumps thrust Nikki and viewers into a wide, sometimes incompatible range of situations and contexts, to the extent that each scene feels like an entirely different film, as though someone had edited together scenes from multiple Laura Dern films and played them as one film. The scope of the film grows so vast—crossing genres, continents, and timelines—that it feels like the film contains "a whole geography of cinema under one roof," transforming a single soundstage into a "hulking heterotopia" populated with "multiple, endlessly changing worlds."[29]

But those are not the only forms of media that appear to be competing. The film also features multiple different forms of media onscreen: 78rpm records, broadcast television, VHS videocassettes, 35mm Panavision film cameras, all of which have bearing on the story and vie for authority over the viewer, or at the very least display multiple claims to authority, making the film a contested space. In addition to those pieces of media, the viewer must juggle the different "pieces" of media that comprise the film, those pieces that were shot separately, edited together and, if one saw the film in its theatrical release, transferred to 35mm film. This collision of disparate media forms, some analog, some digital, all must then be received and processed through the same channel, the viewer, making the process of interpreting *Inland Empire* exhausting, even terrifying, to the extent that Nikki's descent into madness stands in for the viewer's maddening descent into *Inland Empire* as they attempt to pull the different pieces of the film together. In this regard, *Inland Empire* does more than simply mimic the heterogeneity of mixtapes: it serves as a fitting analogue (no pun intended) to the experience of living in the first half of the twenty-first century as the world undergoes dramatic shifts in ways of relating to and communicating through this media.

This interpretation may not be surprising at first glance—the story does concern the making of a film, after all. However, Lynch's treatment of this story goes further than most films of this sort, somewhere much more personal than what J. Hoberman calls "a meditation on the power of recording."[30] More than a meditation, the film uses these collisions of different media into one space to depict the urgency and necessity of sharing those recordings with someone else. This distinguishes *Inland Empire* from other works of metacinema such as Fellini's *8 ½* or Jonze's *Adaptation* because it is more outward-looking than mere autobiography or industry satire. Instead, as Taubin notes, *Inland Empire* is more interested in the "processes of consciousness involved in making a work of art."[31] Shooting on miniDV without a finished script or a predetermined idea of what the film is to be makes *Inland Empire* "as personal as a diary film" and watching it the closest viewers can get to knowing what it is like to be inside David Lynch's head.[32] Lynch's handling of this material goes beyond the mere navel-gazing of dramatizing "the experience [he] undergoes as a creator" in the sense that it models a participatory ethic of creation that is equally concerned with the consciousness that receives a work of art as it is with the consciousness that made it.[33] In fact, it seems to argue that one is worthless without the other because it is in the participatory exchange, the interaction between one consciousness and another, that the work is made. Without this intimate exchange of consciousnesses, the creator and the viewer will be unable to escape the kind of loneliness and solipsism that can lead to such navel gazing so often found in metacinematic works.

Becoming Media

The mixtape aesthetics in the film constitute a crucial part of depicting this exchange of consciousness. Like a mixtape, *Inland Empire* is comprised of unified material removed from its unified context and juxtaposed with other unified material to create a new work that, if successful, creates a unity of its own by being shared. This unity cannot be created without an audience because a mixtape depends upon a shared experience that establishes an aesthetic common ground. Nochimson argues that, both in its form and its content, *Inland Empire* demonstrates that "true information is gained in the upheavals of experience" that occur when a film is made or "actively watched."[34] It is crucial to note how Nochimson places the filmmaker and the film viewer on equal footing linguistically. *Inland Empire* positions their roles as mutually dependent and equally important. Even though all works of art require the audience to complete them, *Inland Empire*, like a mixtape, takes this notion a step further, eschewing self-contained internal coherence for connection with an active viewer: by interacting with "the bits of information and the void between the bits," the viewer builds "an aggregate of what is known" and thus maps the vast territory of *Inland Empire* for themselves.[35]

Lynch dramatizes these ideas through the character of the Lost Girl. Importantly, she is the first character to appear in the film, and one who appears at most of the film's major points of transition. We learn very little about the Lost Girl except what we gather in the opening scene: she is a sex worker who has some kind of dissociative episode during sex with a coarse man. She remains in the room afterward and weeps as she watches television, making her the first troubled woman to appear in a film described by Lynch as being about "a woman in trouble." The material she watches on the television starts off as static, then features sped-up footage of material we see later in the film: first *Rabbits*, then Grace Zabriskie's character walking to Nikki Grace's house, then back to *Rabbits*, which comes to fill the frame as the film gets underway. The next time the Lost Girl appears in the film is when Nikki's story reaches its first breaking point. Nikki has

FIGURE 9.1 The Lost Girl watches TV. *Inland Empire* directed by David Lynch © StudioCanal 2006. All rights reserved.

lost her grip on the boundaries between the role she is playing in *On High in Blue Tomorrows* and her personal life and starts experiencing hallucinatory episodes where she suddenly finds herself in unfamiliar locations surrounded by strangers.

The first location is a hotel room in which a group of women lounge on the floor and share stories about their bodies and experiences with men. This scene abruptly cuts to a snowy Polish street, where two of the women accompany Nikki. The film returns to a shot of the phonograph from the opening sequence, only now with Nikki's face superimposed over the phonograph. Next the film cuts to the Lost Girl watching television and crying, then back to the phonograph, only now with the Lost Girl's face superimposed over it and the Lost Girl begins to speak to Nikki, asking her "Do you want to see?" She then proceeds to instruct Nikki on how to make a device for seeing other layers of reality by burning a hole in silk with a cigarette, a kind of primitive camera. Later in the film, Nikki takes this advice and her inland empire expands exponentially as a result. The physics of how this interaction takes place are far less important than their suggested method of communication: they "speak" through the phonograph about making a kind of camera. Justus Nieland notes how this scene depicts the Lost Girl and Nikki "becoming media for and to each other."[36] Media connects their consciousnesses and allows them to communicate across space and time. As mystical and strange as this may seem, this is merely a visual literalization of what happens when one person shares a work of art with someone else, be it something they have made from scratch, like a film, or something they have compiled from previously existing materials, like a mixtape.

FIGURE 9.2 The Lost Girl appears to Nikki. *Inland Empire* directed by David Lynch © StudioCanal 2006. All rights reserved.

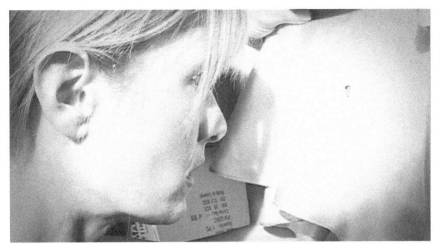

FIGURE 9.3 Nikki's *camera obscura*. *Inland Empire* directed by David Lynch © StudioCanal 2006.

The placement of the Lost Girl's first return in the film seems significant as well because it suggests an ethical relationship developing. It follows the first time Nikki breaks out of the Hollywood apparatus and finds herself in a room full of women instead of men, listening instead of talking, audience rather than performer. After she begins listening to these stories, she can detect other voices calling out to her through media. As Nikki forms "networks of relationships with others," she begins to form a different view of herself, her work, and its relation to the rest of the world. This sequence in the film introduces the notion that through media, one can see how they are part of a larger "community of mediated recognition," one that requires their participation, presence, and care.[37]

This idea comes to fruition in the climax of the film, where Nikki and the Lost Girl have their most profound interaction. After Nikki "dies" on the Walk of Fame on Hollywood Blvd., the camera tracks back to reveal that this scene is not real but the final shot of a film Nikki is acting in. As the director declares a wrap for Nikki on the shoot, the crew applauds and she leaves the set. As she passes through the soundstage, she senses something and turns to look at it. Here, Lynch cuts to another closeup of the Lost Girl watching television. Her eyeline matches Nikki's. The next shot cuts to Nikki on the Lost Girl's television, looking directly into camera, seemingly at the Lost Girl. However, this moment of recognition through media goes beyond their earlier interaction via phonograph. Nikki spends the next sequence traveling through a series of bizarre portholes in time and space—including the *Rabbits* set and an empty movie theater playing her lengthy monologue on screen—until she shoots a villainous man in a hotel room.

FIGURE 9.4 Audience and artist embrace. *Inland Empire* directed by David Lynch
© StudioCanal 2006. All rights reserved.

After the shooting, she wanders the hallways of the hotel until she winds
up in the Lost Girl's room. Once in the room, Nikki approaches the Lost
Girl, kisses her, and then disappears. For the first time in the film, the Lost
Girl smiles and races out of the hotel room to reunite with her husband and
child.

As bizarre and layered as it may seem, this sequence is but a representation
of a commonplace but nevertheless profound experience that people have
when they interact with art and are deeply moved. This reading would
summarize her storyline as follows: Distraught, the Lost Girl turns to art,
where she sees her experience reflected to her so accurately that it feels
as though the person she identified with (Nikki) came into her room and
embraced her, helping her to understand and make sense of her life in a way
that allows her to keep going. As the film has depicted several times already,
art serves as a conduit—a medium—for two consciousnesses to interact and
ease each other's pain. The only change Lynch makes is in literalizing the
encounter between the artist and audience in order to suggest the intense
power of one consciousness encountering and understanding another fully
so that viewers can, like the Lost Girl, adopt this ethos to their experiences.
This change may seem like the natural choice for a medium as concrete as
film, but it articulates the ethos of *Inland Empire* and Lynch's view of the
relationship between art and consciousness. The film may argue, as Lim
and Martin claim, that art can haunt, but it argues much more passionately
and persuasively in these scenes that art can heal. This dynamic, this tension
renders art equal parts risk and gift. The film does depict art as a place where
people can lose themselves, but the climax of the film illustrates that art is

also a place where people can find themselves or, more importantly, be or feel found by others. The title of Lynch's film proves unbelievably apt here: the story, both in its form and content, depicts the inland empire of the self, a territory both unfathomably vast and rigidly constrained by seemingly unbreachable borders, reaching outward through media to invade the inland empire of another self in the hope that doing so will ease the trauma of loneliness, of being stuck within that inland empire of one. This claim forms the affirmative core of not just *Inland Empire* but of Lynch's entire body of work, and one can detect instances of such affirmations in the radiator of *Eraserhead*, John Merrick's bedside painting in *The Elephant Man*, music in *Wild at Heart*, Laura's encounter with the Log Lady in *Fire Walk with Me*, Rebekah Del Rio's performance in *Mulholland Drive*, as well as the many Roadhouse performances throughout every iteration of *Twin Peaks*.

A New Kind of Aura

The fragmented, handmade, and amateurish qualities of the mixtape only enhance the power of this ethos because mixtapes possess a quality that many other mechanically produced forms of art lack: a sense of presence. Contrary to how it may seem since they are comprised of various pieces of mechanically produced art, mixtapes have an aura and a sense of authenticity about them that stems from this "unique arrangement of elements."[38] Where the original recording may lose the aura of a live musical performance during playback, the mixtape acquires a new kind of aura, one that the original music never had: the presence of the person who made the tape before passing it along to someone else. Thus, mixtapes use the tools of mechanical reproduction to create something that retains the intimacy of the handmade, a trace of the ritual "infused with energy imparted from the interactions of human personalities, embodied now in the form of an artifact with powers of its own."[39] (This is especially true if the taper goes into any detail with decorating the case or track listing.) It is a different presence for sure, but everything about mixtapes differs from its source materials. *Inland Empire* dramatizes this process in its content involving Nikki and the Lost Girl and in its handmade form that makes present "processes of consciousness involved in making a work of art" to argue that it is possible—and necessary—for one person to communicate and commune with another through the exchange of significant artworks.

Watching *Inland Empire*, then, is more than just watching the film get made and take shape as it goes; watching it is also watching David Lynch's consciousness, his understanding of the film he is making as well as his understanding of himself, take shape. Even though mixtapes are composed,

FIGURE 9.5 Lynch's triumphant ending. *Inland Empire* directed by David Lynch
© StudioCanal 2006. All rights reserved.

like *Inland Empire*, of previously created material, they also construct the
identity of their creator in real time. In many ways, this is the purpose of
the mixtape. Whether the tape is made for someone else or for the creator's
own enjoyment, the tape becomes an expression of self, of "what it is like to
be this person and to exist in connection to [this] music, technology, people,
and ideas in a certain place and time."[40] And this is where the ethic of the
film materializes: like the Lost Girl, the viewer receives this constructed
self and engages with it. If they engage openly and sincerely, the ecstatic
credits sequence of *Inland Empire* becomes possible. This scene, in which
a host of characters gather and dance to Nina Simone's song "Sinnerman,"
almost constitutes a David Lynch mixtape in itself as actors and tropes
from other Lynch films congregate in a jubilant celebration of release
and accomplishment. Where it could seem like, as J. Hoberman suggests,
Lynch includes the scene to reward the viewer for enduring the film, it
serves as a demonstration of the kind of transcendence possible when two
consciousnesses share an aesthetic experience.[41]

   The true feat that *Inland Empire* performs is that it takes "a form of total
rupture" to produce a work of "emotional coherence."[42] Despite the lack of
traditional continuity, context, and transition, *Inland Empire*'s assemblage
of previously produced material has an emotional continuity of its own that
invites the viewer into a more active, participatory role in constructing the
film's meaning, asking them to find the logic at work behind the juxtaposition
as they experience it. It is important to note how this work in *Inland Empire*
differs from the "solve-for-x" approach of puzzle films, in which there is
one "correct" solution to the mystery. *Inland Empire* does not dictate to the

audience in this manner; rather, its mixtape aesthetic creates space for the viewer to find what the collection of scenes means *to them*. This invitation to collaborate, while it may prove alienating for many accustomed to a more predetermined, directed cinematic experience as defined by Kassabian's assimilating identifications, facilitates the emotional impact on those moved by the film and resembles something a lot like love because it uses media to "collapse distances between bodies and minds" to create a shared experience founded upon a desire for mutual understanding.[43]

With *Inland Empire*, Lynch does in a way come full circle to the handmade feel of *Eraserhead* and his early short films, although now this work is made by hand for a less internal purpose. Even though both titles—*Eraserhead* and *Inland Empire*—are thoroughly insular, their trajectories could not be more opposed. Instead of being terrified of the world outside one's head, as *Eraserhead* is, *Inland Empire* comes to see reaching outside of oneself as a necessity. Lynch's artistic approach in *Inland Empire* captures much about his thematic process and the core ideas of this book: through juxtaposition and affiliation, the viewer has more—and more powerful—ways to connect with Lynch's work. Lynch understands how the collision of different media artifacts and references stokes ideas and associations within the viewer that make their experience of his films more complex and more personal. By tapping into our cultural memory and experience, our subconscious affiliations with music and literature, Lynch accesses more of our consciousness and attention over the course of his film. We bring our entire media experience to Lynch's films, and Lynch meets us where we are, revealing our collective dreams and nightmares as citizens of the dreamscape that is the hypermediated United States.

Conclusion

"You're Like Me": Affiliating Identifications after Lynch

This book has explored some of the literary and musical affiliating identifications that make David Lynch's filmography an uncanny dreamscape of the postwar American zeitgeist. These texts may not be direct influences on Lynch's work in the ways that influence is traditionally discussed, yet their resonance with Lynch's work demonstrates their continued impact on the American imagination. Like radio signals running through the culture, these ideas broadcast through the American subconscious, and as we have seen, Lynch's work has continually been tuned to these frequencies, receiving and transmitting them to the mainstream. When examined in this way, we can see how Lynch has synthesized the various American traditions discussed in this book into a vision of America all his own: a nation buckling under the pressure of a failing nostalgic fantasy and the horrifying reality the fantasy has been attempting to obscure. Lynch's films clearly depict the choice facing America: cling more desperately to the fantasy and watch reality unravel like Henry in *Eraserhead*, Fred in *Lost Highway*, Diane in *Mulholland Drive*, or the entire world of *Twin Peaks*; or forge a new community through a shared confrontation with the trauma of the past like Sailor and Lula in *Wild at Heart*, Alvin and Lyle in *The Straight Story*, or Nikki and the Lost Girl in *Inland Empire*. David Lynch's American Dreamscape offers a panoramic

---

Portions of this chapter appeared, in different form, in *Literature/Film Quarterly*: Mike Miley, "'This Muddy *Both*ness': The Absorbed Adaptation of David Lynch by David Foster Wallace," *Literature/Film Quarterly* 48, no. 1 (2020), accessed January 20, 2024.

view of where America has been since July 16, 1945, and guidance on where it can go from here.

But this work would be too limited if it were to stop with Lynch. It is necessary to consider how his affiliative method of working extends beyond him and impacts the work of subsequent artists. Lynch's work has certainly inspired many imitators, most of whom attempt to mimic his American twist on surrealism to varying degrees of success; however, other artists have adopted his affiliative process, only now they use his films as the intertexts. In doing so, they not only broaden his thematic concerns to other media and audiences, but also develop their own distinct style and voice. Since this book has studied Lynch's literary and musical affiliating identifications, this final chapter will focus on a writer and a musician who have respectively incorporated Lynch's work into their network of affiliating identifications: David Foster Wallace and Lana Del Rey. Rather than making their work derivative, their discovery of Lynch has proven generative, helping to develop the signature aesthetics that established them as unique generational talents. By looking at their work, we can see how Lynch functions as a medium for strong currents in American culture, one that takes in a wide swath of American iconography, filters it through his aesthetic sensibility, and beams it out into the culture for others such as Del Rey and Wallace to receive and process into work of their own.

Few have examined how deeply Del Rey and Wallace's aesthetic relationship with Lynch runs beyond the occasional name-check in an interview or profile, even though both Del Rey and Wallace have expressed their admiration for Lynch and his work. Their similarities are more than the industry standard professions of respect: they engage with Lynch on a dialogic, generative level that runs deeper than mere inspiration. Jonathan Rosenbaum offers a useful term for Del Rey and Wallace's relationship to Lynch's work: absorption. In his article on David Cronenberg's *Naked Lunch*, Rosenbaum compares Cronenberg's work adapting William S. Burroughs's novel to that of the Method actor. Rather than adapting the surface elements of the novel—plot, character, etc.—Cronenberg adopts the Method actor's "manner of working inside rather than outside" of their source text to create a work that incorporates "certain principles and texts from Burroughs into [his] particular cosmology and style."[1] The final product contains elements "recognizable" as Burroughs's that have been "fully transformed" by Cronenberg into a work that is simultaneously an adaptation and a wholly original entity brought about by "an overlap and/or interface of these two personalities."[2] Rosenbaum's one-word distillation of this process—absorption—captures Wallace and Del Rey's affiliative relationship with David Lynch's work. They are not adapting any of his films into literature or music; instead, they have gone Method and absorbed "certain principles and texts" of Lynch into their "cosmology and style." We can simultaneously identify the Lynchian elements of their work and acknowledge them as singular artists following a unique personal vision borne out of the "interface" of their aesthetic sensibility with Lynch's. Through their process of absorption, Wallace and Del Rey reinterpret Lynch's work into their own, "percolating [its] meaning through a personal filter" in the same manner that Lynch filters teen tragedy ballads or Nathanael West's fictional project into his cinematic one.[3] By not adapting Lynch directly, Wallace and Del Rey's work surpasses Cronenberg's absorption of Burroughs in its originality and autonomy and exemplifies how one can create personal, evocative art in an age dominated by postmodern allusion.

Examining the Lynchian affiliating identifications that run throughout their work shows how many of their signature concerns and stylistic tropes originate with Lynch. The grotesque figures, hideous men, and cycles of abuse and trauma intruding upon mundane slices of white-bread Americana that define Wallace's works can be found in *Blue Velvet*, *Twin Peaks*, *Lost Highway*, and *Mulholland Drive*. Del Rey's trademark fascination with a sordid-but-romantic Hollywood topography populated by glamorous-but-doomed ingenues and dangerous-but-alluring men also follows a Lynchian template that blends the women of Lynch's work—Dorothy Valens, Lula Fortune, and Laura Palmer—into a singularly potent persona. Further, Lynch's career as a commercial artist guides Wallace and Del Rey through their own industries, allowing them to persevere as artists in a commercial market. For Wallace, this would be in the masterful ways Lynch smuggles avant-garde, experimental material into commercial entertainment in a manner that does not compromise the experimentation but rather enhances it. For Del Rey, Lynch's career provides a picture of longevity that instructs her on the ways to move past mere ephemeral pop iconography based in provocation toward an art that uses the glamorously grotesque to critique postwar American culture.

Laura Palmer becomes the Lynchian archetype that inspires Wallace and Del Rey's most compelling work. They populate their work with beautiful, affluent figures who are, like Laura Palmer, "radiant on the surface but dying inside."[4] Wallace turns to Laura Palmer to explore the double-binds of consciousness in American society through characters who are tormented by the fear that their beauty and achievement only confirm their inherent, inescapable fraudulence. Del Rey, on the other hand, creates work that plays like an extended remix of *Fire Walk with Me* in the ways that it enacts an objectified cultural fantasy to rebuke the culture responsible for objectification. *Fire Walk with Me* gives this clichéd character an interiority that other works typically deny this figure, which Del Rey and Wallace take as a *starting* point for their work, allowing them to work with clichés in a manner that imbues them with meaning while implicitly taking to task the forces that have reduced objectification and trauma to the level of clichéd sentimentality.

Although both stand out as singular, once-in-a-generation voices in their respective fields, Wallace's and Del Rey's fanbases and the discourses around their work rarely cross-pollinate. There are several possible explanations for this that are worth exploring at greater length elsewhere (e.g., gender bias and anti-pop snobbery); however, it is useful to consider this lack of interaction between their work, their critics, and their fans to be a benefit rather than a drawback when tracking affiliating identifications with Lynch's work. The fact that their work and their audiences can be so different and distinct from each other yet still derive strongly from Lynch's work testifies to the enduring resonance of Lynch's work and his affiliative methods. His signals come from everywhere and go out everywhere, taking on a wide array of forms, connecting with diverse audiences, and reshaping the direction of literature and music in the process.

Laura Palmer Pop

Lynch's juxtaposition of sincere pop ballads with horrific, surreal violence extends beyond merely making Quentin Tarantino or horror movie trailers possible: this approach has changed pop music as well. Frank Guan argues that "Lynch is as essential to music as music is essential to his films," and he is not talking about *Crazy Clown Time*.[5] Lynch's films and his use of music within them demonstrate how one can create powerful work from the resonance of the affiliating identifications and signifiers of America, using commercial clichés and well-worn tropes to reach for something transcendent that wrests the authentic out of the artificial. While some areas of pop music look at Lynch's template and run screaming toward brighter, unironic landscapes, others have sought a plot of their own within it, and no pop artist has settled into Lynch's sensibility quite like Lana Del Rey.

Critics have been drawing comparisons between Lynch and Del Rey since before *Born to Die* was even released, and her 2012 cover of "Blue Velvet" ensured that those comparisons would never stop. With a few notable exceptions, these comparisons remain superficial, using Lynch's name and aesthetic as a shorthand for dark and weird applications of American iconography. Descriptions of Del Rey's work could be swapped into articles about Lynch's films and escape detection: Nitsuh Abebe sees her work expressing "the whole faded cheer of a mid-century nation,"[6] Claire Shaffer describes her songs as "soundtracks [of] the death of the American dream right from the heart of Hollywood,"[7] while Brian Hiatt calls her music videos "id-infested pageants of creepy-nostalgic Americana."[8] But not only critics have detected the similarities between Lynch's and Del Rey's artistic projects. One YouTube creator with over 1800 subscribers, girlfrmars, has made over thirty videos of clips from *Twin Peaks* set to Del

Rey's songs.[9] Each video features a different Del Rey song and focuses on a particular theme of the series. Many of the videos use Del Rey's music to capture the spirit of a particular couple's relationship, such as Sherry and Bobby or Dale and Annie, whereas others limit their scope to a single female character. Some of the videos are quite poignant, such as footage of Big Ed and Norma Jennings set to "Young and Beautiful" or an Annie Blackburn montage set to "Hope is a dangerous thing for a woman like me to have—but I have it," while others can be lacking in subtlety, such as the video editing clips of Josie Packard to "Fucked My Way to the Top." No matter how on the nose many of the edits can be, each video (and the sheer number of them) demonstrates how critics and fans such as girlfrmars can see that the aesthetic and emotional registers of *Twin Peaks* and Lana Del Rey's music are clearly in alignment. The works are powerful and unique enough to stand on their own while still resonating with each other and the host of affiliating identifications that they traffic in.[10]

Lana Del Rey's music inaugurates a subgenre that I would like to call Laura Palmer Pop, which I am defining succinctly as pop from the point of view of, to borrow a phrase of Lynch's, "a woman in trouble." Laura Palmer Pop songs adopt the persona of the doomed femme fatale, a Lolita-esque "harlot starlet" with a "tar black soul" who sings a siren song to a predatory patriarchy as she falls through space and bursts into beautiful fire.[11] Laura Palmer Pop songs feature soaring, ethereal Badalamenti melodies fit for a Julee Cruise-esque torch chanteuse with lyrics written by Frank Booth. This clash of styles and sensibilities creates a sound that is both brutal and tender, dramatic and trivial, tragic and comic, sincere and ironic. With their numerous references to decades worth of popular culture, these songs and their speakers are fully aware of their status as constructed artifacts in an image-based environment and the ways that artificiality is simultaneously liberating and imprisoning. These varying degrees of awareness create a troubling-but-productive tension within the songs in the sense that one cannot always determine the speaker's attitude toward the trouble she is in. Sometimes she appears to like it, others to dread it, others to believe it is her damnation, others to fear it holds the key to her salvation. The ambiguity alternates between immature provocation and incisive cultural critique, often within the same song. Laura Palmer Pop is, simply put, the latest form of the teen tragedy ballad, updated for an era in which one not only knows that the innocence of those songs is long gone, but that it never existed in the first place. It is an awareness of a loss that the speaker clings to with an anger and longing stronger than any reality check ever could. While Del Rey originates this style, many have followed her lead to commercial and critical success, from Lorde and Billie Eilish to Sky Ferreria and Phoebe Bridgers. Even Taylor Swift has emulated Del Rey at times on *folklore* and *evermore* (not to mention including her, however inaudibly, on *Midnights*), while Olivia Rodrigo has adapted Del Rey's sensibility for a younger audience and

Mitski has engaged in Laura Palmer Pop to interrogate its racial politics. These artists all demonstrate that Laura Palmer Pop is a phenomenon that extends far beyond Lynch and Del Rey and, as each of these artists garners sales and acclaim, shows little sign of running out of steam.

While there is no shortage of Lana Del Rey songs that adhere to this template, the leadoff track to her sophomore LP *Ultraviolence*, "Cruel World," serves as the quintessential Laura Palmer Pop track. The slow, spacious, echoey production by Dan Auerbach acts like the theme from *Twin Peaks*. The guitar and drums slide like a weight drawing the listener deep into the sordid world of the song. The lyrics twist and turn through breakup and party song clichés until the listener cannot determine whether the song is an anthem of dejection, empowerment, or negation. The speaker claims "you're dancing circles around me," when the opposite is the case: Del Rey's deft navigation of pop tropes and transgressive positions swirls around the listener until the most familiar cultural object of the postwar era—the pop song—becomes strange and, well, cruel. Lynch achieves similar levels of pop defamiliarization through his juxtaposition of soothing, dreamy early 1960s pop classics with disturbing situations such as the appearance of "In Dreams" in *Blue Velvet*, and in Laura Palmer Pop songs such as "Cruel World," Del Rey absorbs these techniques to deliver songs that provoke the same levels of estrangement without the aid of an image to employ for juxtaposition.

Lana's Dream Dump

Although her debut album *Born to Die* has its share of cultural references, her play with American signifiers truly goes off to the races on her 2012 EP *Paradise*. With songs bearing titles such as "Lolita," "American," "Cola," "Body Electric," "Bel Air," and, of course, "Blue Velvet," one can appreciate Mina Tavakoli's characterization of Del Rey as "an exceptional hunter-gatherer of white American arcana [...] an aesthetic howitzer, exploding a broad but deeply personal index of iconography into her own nation of death-driven kitsch."[12] These song titles, as well as their lyrics, use these American signifiers to mix the wholesome and the depraved, the innocent and the tainted in the same way that *Twin Peaks* filled viewers' living rooms with images of saddle oxfords and cocaine, cherry pie and dead girls, all wrapped in a plastic American flag.

The iconography on display in Del Rey's music "build[s] atmospheric ballads out of dead-stock pop tropes," sprinkling snippets of other pop standards throughout her lyrics in a manner that can seem at once empty and full.[13] "Tomorrow Never Came," a track off her 2017 LP *Lust for Life*, offers a distilled example of the range and depth of her allusive lyrics.

In the space of four lines, Del Rey pulls Bob Dylan's "Lay, Lady, Lay," F. Scott Fitzgerald's *This Side of Paradise*, Henry Miller's *Tropic of Cancer* and Elton John's "Tiny Dancer" into her musical orbit. Each reference goes beyond the simple name-drop or collection of signifiers of cool she parodies in a song like "Brooklyn Baby." Rather, each relates to Del Rey's Laura Palmer Pop persona and constructs a vision of America that her torch songs celebrate one last time before burning them to the ground. First, the references to Bob Dylan's 1969 track and Elton John's 1971 track capture the alluring submission of the groupies, side pieces, and kept women of Del Rey's songs who cling to controlling men who regard them as sexual objects or dolls. Second, the literary references align with Del Rey's portrayal of decadent, affluent relationships based upon transgression and transaction where women abject themselves for access to the trappings of high society and materialistic transcendence. Taken together, these references trace a line through twentieth-century musical and literary representation of exotic, turbulent women before Del Rey places herself as this motif's final destination, putting the glamour and desire of this vision on display in all its vacuous glory.

We can certainly see such complex resonances in Lynch's later work. Films such as *Lost Highway* and *Mulholland Drive* offer a cornucopia of cinematic, musical, literary, and cultural references, from *Sunset Blvd.* and *Vertigo* to *The Day of the Locust* and *The Postman Always Rings Twice*, Roy Orbison and O. J. Simpson to Marilyns Monroe and Manson. This process of affiliating identifications prompts the same question from her critics that Lynch receives from his: do these references amount to something greater than the sum or their parts, or are they merely "a litter of quotation marks" concealing a dearth of ideas?[14] The dizzying array of affiliating identifications exceeds an individual viewer's ability to trace them individually and instead requires that they take in the work as a whole to appreciate what Del Rey and Lynch are doing with them. Del Rey's work often gets described as "cinematic" in its scope and grand sense of drama, but Tavakoli identifies the centrality of affiliating identifications to Del Rey's cinematic industrial symphonies: "she offered us a canon of heritage markers recast in '10s-era drama and became the rare sort of talent that was able to congeal past and present into seductively conceptual cinema."[15] Even though Tavakoli does not use the term "affiliating identifications," her description captures the cumulative effect of such work: it collapses past and present to show the American imagination's resistance to time. This working through of the beautiful and damned in American culture captures on a micro level what *Blue Velvet* and *Twin Peaks* achieve at the macro level. The power of *Blue Velvet* or *Twin Peaks* derives in part from this congealing of past and present to create a landscape that is less the America of the 1980s (or the 1950s for that matter) but rather a dreamscape in which the entire postwar American fantasy becomes a photorealistic environment. Once the work reifies that dream world, it seeks to unravel it to show the nightmare reality lurking beneath like the beetles in the opening to *Blue Velvet*. By the end of *Twin Peaks* (2017), if not sooner, one can see how Lynch reveals every quaint delight of the sleepy town of Twin Peaks—every glazed donut, every snappy jazz shuffle, every poodle skirt—to be an illusion constructed to conceal the horrors of the American century, both foreign and domestic.

Both Lynch and Del Rey understand the hypnotic power these images have on the American imagination, and they present their critique of it sympathetically from the point of view of the dreamers to demonstrate their appeal. While Del Rey's music does not have the benefit of concrete images, it still takes her audience into the heart of fantasy and presents it as real. This presentation so often gets mistaken as endorsement, but Chris Richards sees it as "a spiritual exercise" that espouses "a belief in the eternal return."[16] Del Rey may have titled her first album *Born to Die*, but her music continually testifies to the immortality of American dreams. As much as Laura Palmer Pop may show these dreams to be empty and damaging, Del Rey also acknowledges that it will take much more than a pop song or a film for these dreams to die. They will always continue to haunt the American imagination, and to listen to a Lana Del Rey song is to hear her go diving through the same Dream Dump Nathanael West writes about and resurrect the dreams of a culture that refuses to wake up.

But of course, the best descriptor of Lynch's and Del Rey's shared aesthetic and affiliative sensibility hides in plain sight in the title of Del Rey's fifth album: *Norman Fucking Rockwell*. In three words, we see quaint, tranquil Americana interrupted by the obscene. It is a juxtaposition that, once the initial shock wears off, reveals the sickness at the heart of the placid fantasy that the placid fantasy attempts to obscure. If one wishes to see Norman Fucking Rockwell distilled to a single image, one need look no further than the wide shot of Jeffrey's dad collapsed on the lawn from the opening to

FIGURE 10.1 Norman Fucking Rockwell. *Blue Velvet* directed by David Lynch © De Laurentiis Entertainment Group 1986. All rights reserved.

Blue Velvet. The surroundings are picture-perfect small-town America: the cute toddler wobbles down a smooth driveway as he licks a colorful lollipop, while a dog snaps at the hose as it sprays across the well-tended garden. The image is the stuff of cutesy postcards and cheap paintings, until one looks at the center of the image to see a man splayed out in distress on the lawn. With one detail, the sentimental image of innocence becomes a disturbing image of horror and dread. In songs such as "Body Electric," Del Rey's music likewise pursues the paradoxes that capture "America at its most mythic: purple mountains' majesty, rockets' red gleaming, Monroe, Manson."[17] She takes listeners to the zenith and nadir of American culture, presenting it as a landscape as flat as the Great Plains, accompanied by a slumping, swooning pop rhythm that is equal parts anthem and dirge. The number of signifiers is bountiful and eclectic, presenting the myth and the anti-myth as one, without any context or comment in favor of one or the other. That is Lana Del Rey. That is David Lynch. That is Norman Fucking Rockwell.

Sincerity-in-Irony Post-Lynch

A phrase such as Norman Fucking Rockwell, let alone the concept it represents, cannot pass through the culture without invoking a fair amount of pearl-clutching and misinterpretation. As a statement, it demands to be received outrageously, inviting the question of how seriously one should take it. This question perpetually nags Lynch's, Wallace's, and Del Rey's works: Are they being sincere or ironic? The simple truth is that they are both at the same time, which makes them more difficult to interpret. The divisive reactions to Lynch's films, Wallace's fiction, and Del Rey's music demonstrate their complex understanding of irony. Stephen Burn describes Wallace's prose as "double-voiced" in that it is imbued with "the quality of '*both*ness,'" and Paolo Pitari cites this "*both*ness" as representative of the "divided consciousnesses that Wallace sees in Lynch's work" and absorbs into his own fiction.[18] Del Rey's music is equally "double-voiced," with speakers who are as defined by "*both*ness" as Lynch's and Wallace's protagonists. Bothness is integral to all of their work, and, as Wallace writes about the critical response to *Fire Walk with Me*, "we hate this '*both*' shit because it requires the audience to inhabit conflicting perspectives and critical positions simultaneously without any additional guidance or handholding."[19]

Some critics handle this *both*ness by critiquing the work until it sits on one side of the fence, sincere or ironic, but, as we have seen in this book, the "sincerity-in-irony" approach as defined by Nicholas Rombes offers more productive interpretive possibilities by taking this *both*ness head-on. Rombes effectively pushes back against claims that Lynch's films act as reactionary "send-up[s] of misplaced innocence" or "subversive expose[s] of a kind of sham past," arguing for viewing Lynch's sensibility as "sincerity-in-irony": "Lynch's films fully enact, rather than reflect, the postmodern [...] but with none of the high seriousness of modernism, nor the ironic, 'in-crowd' detachment of postmodernism."[20] The Club Silencio scene in *Mulholland Drive* discussed in Chapter 3 stands as the most clear-cut example of this. Lynch foregrounds cinema's artifice to grant viewers permission to be affected by Del Rio's performance openly and unironically. It is entirely artificial, but the audience's awareness of that artifice enables outpourings of genuine emotion on both sides of the screen. Lynch's ironic overtures disarm cynical viewers, luring them into the very emotional engagement that they thought they were too sophisticated to succumb to. Thus, the most intense conflict in Lynch's films occurs between the audience and the film because audiences must acknowledge how culture has conditioned them to interpret intense outpourings of sincere emotion, such as Sandy's dream of robins or Sarah Palmer's reaction to Laura's death in *Twin Peaks*, as ironic, phony, or sentimental.[21] Del Rey and Wallace's complex use of irony stems from their understanding of Lynch's sincerity-in-irony, and they use it in similar ways and for similar creative purposes.

In addition to her talents as a singer-songwriter, Lana Del Rey shares Lynch's talent for generating strong opinions about the sincerity of her work and her persona. Before her first record, *Born to Die*, was even released, music critics worked themselves into a frenzy either to hail her as the Next Big Thing in Pop or denounce her as an industry plant crafted in a poptimist lab to appeal to jaded millennials. Maura Johnston questions the sincerity of Del Rey's "bummer quotient," asking whether it is intended to be "self-serious like *Valley of the Dolls*" or whether it has the "camp impulse" of *Beyond Valley of the Dolls*.[22] Others, such as Mark Richardson, do not know whether to laugh at the hipster accessorizing-as-personality on display in songs like the hilarious, infectious "Brooklyn Baby" or to read them as a celebration of "the colorful tapestry that is American popular culture."[23] Del Rey's treatment of these details and her critics' baffled reactions to it exemplify the "sincerity-in-irony" Rombes sees in Lynch. It would be overly simplistic to write her work off as jaded kitsch, yet we are too knowing to embrace it as wholly serious. Like Lynch, Del Rey can be heartbreaking, disturbing, and ridiculous all at the same moment, and American culture has an increasingly hard time parsing work that has such a wide tonal range and refuses to tell its audience how to interpret it. Like Lynch, Del Rey litters her work with potentially ironic kitschy signifiers that stroke the egos of her knowing, post-everything audience, but she does so to disarm, not entertain. This process leads listeners toward "a less self-conscious emotional involvement" that accrues sentiment and meaning as each layer is presented and deconstructed until listeners are faced with a body of work in which the sincere and ironic are inextricably linked and mutually dependent.[24]

Though her artistry has grown since *Born to Die*, the bridge to "National Anthem" presents everything that will come afterward and captures her brand of sincerity-in-irony: the themes, the values, the persona, and the critique of all three. The lyrics present a picture of excess and abandon that pushes knowing ironic detachment to the edge of nihilism as Del Rey appears to stare into the abyss and says "Let's rock." The speaker gleefully plunges into a "sick rampage" of artifice and excess because the possibility of meaning has been exhausted. Although there is plenty in the song and throughout Del Rey's work that appears to be enamored with this abandon, the critique of that abandon and the circumstances which make it so appealing in the first place follows closely. Juxtaposing "excessive buying" with "overdose and dying" and fantasy with anger characterizes this era as one in which more is being blurred than "the lines between the real and the fake." Add to that the fact that the name of the song is "National Anthem," and we can see more at play than simple ironic posturing: Del Rey is updating this Lynchian dyad between sincerity and irony, darkness and light, the real and the fake to the cynical post-truth era, turning her work into a cracked coke mirror reflecting a culture conspicuously consumed by artifice. In this regard, Lana Del Rey has stretched Betty's audition scene from *Mulholland Drive* from two minutes to over a decade, taking a clichéd script too vapid to be believed and, at a moment's notice, imbuing it with a sensuality and menace so believable as to make everyone's head spin when all she has truly done is immersed her audience in the artifice of their own desires.

Lana Is the One

In his 2014 exposé "Vamp of Constant Sorrow," Brian Hiatt calls Del Rey "a baffling bundle of contradictory signifiers, a mystery 10,000 tortured think-pieces have failed to solve."[25] While the question of Del Rey's sincerity and authenticity certainly plays a role, Hiatt's statement homes in on contradiction as the main factor making her persona eternally perplexing and in need of "solving." Del Rey's persona appears to encompass everything and nothing at the same time, switching identities and poses from track to track: "she is innocent, and she is a whore; she is a homecoming queen, and she is addicted to cocaine; she is a loving maternal figure, and she is a cold-blooded manipulator."[26] That last quote may appear to capture Del Rey so accurately as to come from Hiatt's profile or any of the other 9,999 "tortured think-pieces" about Del Rey, but the quote actually comes from Todd McGowan's analysis of *Fire Walk with Me*. McGowan's reading of Laura Palmer demonstrates the real thematic and political potential of Lana Del Rey's artistic project as well as Laura Palmer Pop as a whole.

Where others may hear echoes of Lula Fortune or Dorothy Valens in Del Rey's music, Laura Palmer remains a stronger force in her music because Laura is both Lula and Dorothy at the same time—she is the carnal, effervescent ingenue and the mysterious, tormented woman. The complexity of Del Rey's music stems from the fact that her persona houses so many different attitudes and poses, just as Laura Palmer seems to be a different person to everyone who encounters her. McGowan's analysis of *Fire Walk with Me* shows us that, like Laura Palmer, Lana Del Rey "embodies in one person all the contradictory male fantasies about women," and as such, both Laura Palmer and Lana Del Rey become "screen[s] onto which we project our desire and/or our loathing."[27] The desire to "unmask" or expose Del Rey as a fraud represents a cultural attempt to control and dismiss aspects of a patriarchal culture that audiences find discomforting. By projecting contradictory desires and roles onto a figure such as Del Rey and then attacking her, these desires and roles can be controlled and potentially neutralized. This process resembles the desire of characters and viewers of *Twin Peaks* to "solve" the mystery of Laura Palmer: by getting to the bottom of who she was and what happened to her, they can maintain the illusion of innocence and wholesomeness that her death threatens to destroy. Simply put, in revealing who these women "really" are, the investigators can dismiss what the "mysteries" attending their lives reveal about the obsessive investigators. What Lynch achieves in *Fire Walk with Me* and *Lost Highway* and Del Rey achieves in her music—especially *Ultraviolence*—is granting the objectified female a subject position that reveals the male fantasy as the impossible, empty construction that it is. This revelation has the effect of troubling the audience who constructed that image and comforting women who feel trapped by it.

Such an assertion may be surprising given the amount of criticism surrounding Del Rey's portrayals of women in her music. When critics are not taking her to task for perceived insincerity, they are condemning her work as a (sincere) toxic retrograde sensibility that glamorizes abuse, vacuous materialism, and patriarchy. However, these critiques—most of which persist to this day—overlook a complexity to her persona that is easier to see when one looks at her work as Laura Palmer Pop. Del Rey's songs undeniably enact toxic clichés, but, like Lynch's work, the way in which she depicts them reflects dark currents in American culture so openly, honestly, and accurately that many mistake it for endorsement. Her songs offer up a view of cultural archetypes and the cultural subconscious—what McGowan calls "the invisible forces that create a hostile social reality"— that makes people very uncomfortable when it is exposed to the light.[28]

Del Rey's persona traffics in emptiness and negation, and the closer one investigates the persona, the more one sees, as McGowan says about Laura Palmer, the centrality of negation to it. From the start, Del Rey's "drowsy and distant" persona and music "exuded a half-glamorous aura of pure nothingness" that has only grown in resonance over the last ten years.[29]

Like Laura Palmer, there is a "structuring absence" to the persona portrayed in Del Rey's music, making her "the impossible object" that "organizes the desire" of her audience. McGowan argues that *Fire Walk with Me's* radical maneuver involves playing the embodied "predominant fantasy of femininity," Laura Palmer, as the central point of view of the film. By making Laura Palmer not only the protagonist but the central consciousness of *Fire Walk with Me*, Lynch not only brings the dead homecoming queen to life but reveals the "fundamental emptiness" at the core of the fantasy she represents.[30] Del Rey also places this figure at the forefront of her music by making her not only the central point of view but the only point of view; no other voice exists in her music. Lindsay Zoladz describes the impact of this quality in Del Rey's second studio album *Ultraviolence* when she argues it "seems to suggest how unfulfilling it is to embody a male fantasy. *I have become the perfect American girl just like you wanted me to*, Del Rey seems to be saying, *and I'm so lonesome I could die*."[31] Lynch and Del Rey allow the dead girl to speak, to return the gaze, and her reciprocal stare has the power to trouble the entire worldview.[32]

One song by Del Rey depicts these forces at play and encapsulates the way that she absorbs the Laura Palmer persona to make grand aesthetic statements of her own. 2023's "A & W" is an atmospheric piano ballad that sounds like a home demo backed by an ambitious sound collage on par with her 2019 song "Venice Bitch." As the title indicates, juxtaposed dualities dominate every aspect of the song. Musically, the song has two distinct halves. In the first half, her frequently multi-tracked vocals cartwheel around her range, mixing together pouty-lipped confessions, sultry whispers, and ethereal falsettos as echoey piano and acoustic bass create a vast and empty sonic space. A drum machine signals the arrival of the second half and a promise of an increase in energy that is undercut by Del Rey's vocals, which are an enervated druggy droll as emotionally vacant as they are repetitive. The lyrics follow the pattern established by the music, with the first half instantly announcing itself as a soul-bearing confession and the second retreating from such vulnerability toward the repetition of nonsense lyrics that would be more at home in a schoolyard hand-slapping rhyme or breakfast cereal jingle. Del Rey crafts a harrowing first half in which the speaker's revelations of sexual assault, animosity toward her body, and the existential crisis of feeling like a ghost are dismissed, only to shift the focus of the second half to a male partner even though he shows affection only "when he wanna get high." Musically and lyrically, "A & W" sounds like two songs with opposing subjects and viewpoints sutured together; however, Del Rey unifies these halves conceptually in the chorus, which appears in both parts and clarifies Del Rey's artistic project: "This is the experience of being an American whore." In this line, the A and the W are united, now and forever. In a single song, Del Rey captures the irreconcilable expectations of femininity—to be both emotionally available and remote, in possession of an inner life and lacking all interiority, subject and object—in a manner so sonically cavernous to suggest that none of these figures are actually present, that absence is all that can be displayed.

This point is where the title becomes subversively clever. The ampersand in the title may appear to suggest that these two identities, American and whore, are separate and mutually exclusive, thus ratifying the virgin/whore dichotomy that governs a large part of patriarchal fantasies and views about women. However, before examining the lyrics to the song, one is likely to assume that the title refers to a popular brand of root beer. While this might just feel like a cheeky callback to Del Rey's 2012 song "Cola" and its notorious opening lyric "my pussy tastes like Pepsi-Cola," the association of the song title with A&W Root Beer merges this alleged dichotomy into one container: like A&W Root Beer, the American whore is a product, a commodity produced, promoted, and purchased by a culture that views her and her trauma as something that "doesn't really matter" or something that, in her attempts to conform to societal expectations, she asked for.

As McGowan says about Laura Palmer, the characters in Lana Del Rey's music meet the criteria for every fantasy there is about American femininity but do not and cannot experience any pleasure or fulfillment from meeting that impossible criteria because being both the wholesome American homecoming queen and the depraved American whore blends pure and impure, sacred and profane, until they are revealed to be always already indistinguishable, part of the same depraved imagination.[33] This revelation elicits resentment, disdain, and abuse from those invested in this impossible fantasy because her achievement of it places the fantasy's empty, fabricated nature—and their total dependence upon it—on display.[34] By "reveal[ing] … that she has nothing to reveal," Del Rey and David Lynch do not celebrate the Sad Girl Nihilism of Laura Palmer so much as treat her persona as a reflection of decades of postwar American cultural tropes.[35] From what we can see of the cultural reaction to Del Rey, many do not like what they see and pin the blame on her for calling their attention to it. Del Rey's comments about no longer waving an American flag during her performances post-2016 highlights this conflict further. "It's certainly uncomfortable," she says. "It's not going to happen. […] it would feel weird to me now. […] I'd rather have static."[36] Regardless of whether she displays the flag or the static, Del Rey's sincerity-in-irony, like Lynch's, presents both simultaneously. One would be hard-pressed to find a more sincere and authentic way to talk about twenty-first-century America.

The Avant-Garde Ghost in the Commercial Machine

David Foster Wallace's professional writing career essentially begins with him fending off comparisons to other writers, most notably Thomas Pynchon.

Since then, critics (and Wallace himself) have been too busy situating his work alongside his literary and philosophical ancestors such as John Barth, Don DeLillo, and Ludwig Wittgenstein to explore the degree to which this *writer* might have absorbed the work of a *filmmaker* into his fiction. Even though Wallace wrote a lengthy essay about Lynch and the making of *Lost Highway* for *Premiere*, entitled "David Lynch Keeps His Head," discussions of the relationship between Wallace and Lynch focus more on what Wallace has to say about Lynch when the obverse might be the more fruitful investigation.[37] The significance of Lynch's influence on Wallace is so plainly stated as to be easily underestimated and overlooked: Wallace says that Lynch's films "affected the way [he] see[s] and organize[s] the world."[38] He even recalls the day saw *Blue Velvet*: March 30, 1986.[39] At the time, Wallace was an MFA student in Arizona, where he and his peers were engaged in an aesthetic battle pitting their own "experimental" writing against the stodgy realism of their professors. According to Wallace, *Blue Velvet* demonstrated to him how flawed he was to believe realist and experimental work were mutually exclusive. As avant-garde and weird as Lynch's style is, *Blue Velvet* remains grounded in realism and well-rounded characters, which allows Lynch to employ avant-garde techniques without seeming "solipsistic and pretentious and self-conscious and masturbatory and bad" but authentic to "the way the U.S. present acted on our nerve endings."[40] The film for Wallace was "something crucial that couldn't be analyzed or reduced to a system of codes or aesthetic principles or workshop techniques."[41] *Blue Velvet* ended the battle between Wallace and his teachers by synthesizing their positions, showing that neither held the secret to effective aesthetic representation. Seeing differently led to Wallace creating differently, and Wallace composes most of his literary work after this epiphanic encounter with *Blue Velvet*.

What is perhaps most revelatory for Wallace here is that this epiphany comes in the package of a relatively mainstream film. *Blue Velvet* may have been an independent production, but it was financed by megaproducer Dino DeLaurentis and went on to receive multiple Oscar nominations in an era where indie films rarely received Academy recognition. From *Blue Velvet* onward, Lynch has worked with one foot in the Hollywood system but makes films that continually disrupt conventional narrative cinema by smuggling avant-garde experimentation into traditional Hollywood structures, and his success in doing this has largely served as the model followed by filmmakers of the independent cinema boom of the 1980s and 1990s.[42] Despite his admiration of the experimental and avant-garde, Wallace sought mainstream success and viewed Lynch as the artist capable of "broker[ing] a new marriage between art and commerce in U.S. movies, opening formula-frozen Hollywood to some of the eccentricity and vigor of art film."[43] Lana Del Rey too had to walk this tightrope between art and commerce from the moment "Video Games" took the pop press by surprise and critics debated whether she was a bona-fide artist or an industry concoction designed to rake in as much money as possible, as though a female artist could not be successful artistically and commercially. All three achieve this balance in their best work: their art is fragmented but features three-dimensional characters, experimental but "in the service of human emotion, and with the same motives."[44]

Artifice's Sincere Core

One of the most prominent lines of inquiry into Wallace's work examines how his fiction rejects ironic postmodern gamesmanship in favor of a more sincere engagement with the reader. These readings of Wallace take as their starting point what Adam Kelly has called the "essay-interview nexus": Wallace's essay "*E Unibus Pluram*: Television and U.S. Fiction" and his interview with Larry McCaffery, both originally published in *The Review of Contemporary Fiction* in 1993.[45] Wallace closes "*E Unibus*" with an oft-quoted paragraph that many interpret as Wallace's manifesto for a new kind of fiction in which "the next real literary 'rebels'" will "back away from ironic watching," "eschew self-consciousness and hip fatigue," and "have the childish gall actually to endorse and instantiate single-entendre principles" and "risk accusations of sentimentality."[46] By freeing themselves from irony-laden image fiction, Wallace's literary rebels will gain greater access to the kind of genuine feeling that slick commercial postmodernism has used irony to shield itself from and, in doing so, liberate readers to rediscover the value of living with affect rather than ironic detachment.

Critics generally accept this rejection of postmodern irony in "*E Unibus*" as Wallace's unique contribution to American fiction, but this reading overlooks how much his postironic project is indebted to Lynch. *Blue Velvet* provides Wallace with the roadmap for "how to recover sincerity without losing the critical edge that irony provides."[47] A scene such as the "Robins of

FIGURE 10.2 Lynch's sincere dream. *Blue Velvet* directed by David Lynch © De Laurentiis Entertainment Group 1986. All rights reserved.

Love" scene in *Blue Velvet* may appear ridiculous to a knowing viewer, but Lynch's film implies that such hopeful earnestness may be the only defense against the vile and sadistic cynicism of Frank Booth. Scenes like this bravely "risk the yawn, the rolled eyes" from critics and audience members who view "ironic self-consciousness [as] the one and only universally recognized badge of sophistication."[48] This knowing earnestness makes Lynch's work both more formally accomplished and emotionally engaging than its hiply jaded ironic counterparts.

One can see where Wallace absorbs Lynch's sincerity-in-irony most prominently in his later story collections, *Brief Interviews with Hideous Men* and *Oblivion*. Like Lynch, the self-reflexive narratives that shape many of these stories become gateways to finding genuinely felt emotion in an artificial world, not defenses against it.[49] Halfway through Wallace's 1999 story "Octet," the "pseudopomo" gimmick of a pop quiz structure that has organized the first half of the story gives way to a more urgent interrogation of the purpose of postmodern trickery, authorial interpolations, and self-awareness of postmodern fiction when the narrative voice of the story addresses the reader directly and asks the reader to imagine themselves as a Fiction-Writer attempting to write a story comprised of a series of pop quizzes that is not turning out the way they wanted it to. This interrogation builds in intensity (and recursivity) until the narrator places the reader and writer in the same position, both "quivering in the mud of the trench," both "fundamentally lost and confused and frightened and unsure about whether to trust even your most fundamental intuitions about urgency and sameness and whether other people deep inside experience things in anything like the same way you do."[50] In *Oblivion*'s "The Soul Is Not a Smithy," a traumatized elementary school student constructs a narrative to mentally escape the fact that his substitute teacher has taken his class hostage, only to have details from the terror unfolding around him seep into these fantasies. The story's ending masterfully applies the folly of such narrative repression to the entire nation via an American history pageant in which America's violent past gets glamorized through a sugarcoated lens of "aluminum foil bayonets" and "papier mâché bulwarks" that is eerily reminiscent of Lynch's celebrated opening to *Blue Velvet*.[51] In both instances, fiction becomes both an escape from a horrifying reality and a manifestation of that reality. Like *Blue Velvet*'s opening sequence, the pageant in "Smithy" reveals how these repressive tendencies are not just the habits of one schoolboy or town but of an entire country, thus alerting the reader to how they have been conditioned to repress horrors around them by masking these events in collective national narratives of violence.

What stands out about Lynch's and Wallace's sincerity-in-irony in comparison to Lana Del Rey's is their relative naiveté. This difference boils down to a matter of point of view. Wallace's male narrators align more closely with the Jeffrey Beaumonts and Dale Coopers in Lynch's work, men whose privileged daily experience still allows them to willfully pretend some innocence lingers in the world, despite the horrors they have witnessed. Del Rey's Laura Palmer Pop cannot afford such luxurious willful ignorance because the speakers of her songs are often the victims of the horrors the men in Wallace's and Lynch's works have witnessed or perpetrated. Pretending that the world is a good place in light of their experience of it would constitute the height of insincerity. As she sings in 2023's "Fingertips," the "exotic places and people" that populate her musical universe "don't take the place" of a stable life. The song also contains her most direct rebuke to her critics when she sings "They say there's irony in the music, it's a tragedy, I / See nothing Greek in it." This line may go a long way toward explaining why critics have a hard time parsing Del Rey's sincerity: from her point of view, the sincerity reads even darker than the irony, which plays less as a hip post-everything pose to avoid awkward feelings of vulnerability than as a genuine defense mechanism to ward off trauma. While her post-*Norman Fucking Rockwell* albums do wear earnestness on their sleeve and yearn for transcendence more than her earlier albums, they do so with a mature awareness that such contentment is incredibly difficult to achieve and even harder to hold onto. Where Lynch and Wallace follow the horrors they depict with a reassurance that the robins will come, Del Rey's music favors a resigned-but-genuine acceptance of what little light remains.

The Uncomfortable Mirror

By acknowledging and foregrounding their work's artifice, Lynch, Wallace, and Del Rey alert the audience to the presence of a creative consciousness controlling the text. They then use that awareness to deconstruct the audience's critical defenses and make them uncomfortably aware of their own position as spectators and subjects for the purpose of steering them to a more mindful and attentive state of awareness in their own lives. For Wallace, this process is in many ways as confrontational as it is confessional: Lynch, he claims, "get[s] inside your head" by offering an unobstructed view inside his own, which gives viewers a glimpse at "some of the very parts of [themselves they've] gone to the movies to try to forget about."[52]

The scene in *Blue Velvet* where Frank forces Jeffrey to watch him abuse Dorothy Valens serves as a perfect example. In the scene, the camera occupies Jeffrey's position in the back seat of Frank's car looking at Frank in the front, aligning the audience's point of view with Jeffrey's. The audience has been encouraged to identify with Jeffrey throughout the film, and now, like Jeffrey, they look on in fear and disgust, eager to escape, to look away. However, they cannot: the camera's gaze, like Jeffery's, remains fixed on Frank in perverse fascination and terror. Suddenly, Frank turns to Jeffrey,

FIGURE 10.3 The audience looks in the mirror. *Blue Velvet* directed by David Lynch © De Laurentiis Entertainment Group 1986.

stares into the camera with wild eyes, and lustfully proclaims "You're like me." In the reverse shot, Jeffrey immediately looks down and away in shame. Lynch's camera placement, editing, and subtle rupture of the fourth wall fill an already dreadful scene with a shock of recognition because the camera forces the captive audience to accept that Frank's statement applies as much to themselves as it does to Jeffrey Beaumont, perhaps even more so. After all, their watching is voluntary; no one is pinning them to their seat. This moment typifies the emotional impact of self-reflexive sincerity-in-irony in Lynch's films that Wallace adapts most directly in *Infinite Jest*'s critiques of passive entertainment consumption and *Brief Interviews with Hideous Men*'s extended dissections of misogyny and rape culture.

According to Wallace's reading of Lynch and his own absorption of Lynch's work, this effect cannot be achieved without immersing the audience in the mind of the creator. Wallace's self-reflexive fiction continually pushes out from the page to address, confront, and connect with the reader in the hopes of achieving literature's transformative potential. Inhabiting someone else's consciousness is more than an authoritarian demonstration of control that seeks to "vulnerabilize" and "dominate"; rather, it forces audiences to peer out "through the tiny little keyhole" of themselves and confront that other people do in fact experience things in the same way that they do, even if they were not aware of it beforehand and would prefer not to acknowledge it upon discovery.[53] The most sustained, effective, and traumatic of Lynch's mirrors to reappear in Wallace's fiction is also one of Lynch's most archetypal characters: *Twin Peaks*' Laura Palmer. These characters first appear after Wallace's transformative encounter with Lynch in early stories such as "My Appearance." After Lynch introduces the world to Laura Palmer, versions of this character occur with increasing frequency in Wallace in the form of high-achieving characters who, despite their beauty and intellect, feel hollow

FIGURE 10.4 The audience is ashamed. *Blue Velvet* directed by David Lynch © De
Laurentiis Entertainment Group 1986.

inside, in works such as *Infinite Jest* (Hal Incandenza, the other students at
Enfield Tennis Academy, Prettiest Girl of All Time Joelle van Dyne), *Brief
Interviews with Hideous Men* ("The Depressed Person," "The Devil is a
Busy Man," "Octet"), on to *Oblivion* and his posthumous novel *The Pale
King*, both of which feature Wallace adapting the Laura Palmer character to
his own authorial persona.

Laura Palmer serves as the source for many of Wallace's most engaging
split protagonists because she perfectly embodies this split consciousness.
As the *Twin Peaks* saga goes on, audiences see how Laura Palmer's
status as "the cultural image of desire" alienates her from herself and
the world.[54] Embodying an abstract, depersonalized cultural ideal—the
blonde, high-achieving, self-sacrificing homecoming queen—creates "a
fundamental emptiness" at the center of Laura Palmer where the culture
has fantasized a fullness beyond measure.[55] Wallace posits that this bothness
in Lynch's work makes viewers reject it because "it require[s] of us an
empathetic confrontation with the exact same muddy *both*ness in ourselves
and our intimates that makes the real world of moral selves so tense
and uncomfortable."[56] From *Twin Peaks* onward, Lynch's work investigates
the cascade of contradictions that constitute selfhood, and Wallace adapts
and extends Lynch's exploration of contradictory selfhood in *Oblivion* to
show how *both*ness becomes the human condition.[57] George Toles notes
that Lynch inflicts the "greatest torments [on] those most deeply enfolded in
artifice," proving that "the fact of a character's conspicuous fabrication is no
safeguard against real hurt."[58]

Wallace dramatizes this jarring dynamic best in his story "Good Old
Neon," adapting the relationship the viewer has with Laura Palmer to the one
David Wallace has with Neal, the story's apparent narrator, who, like Laura,
has a "neon aura around him all the time."[59] Despite all his accolades, Neal
defines himself as a fraud with "no true inner self," who is "trapped in a false
way of being," surrounded by other people too "pliable and credulous" to

detect his emptiness and pain.[60] Like Laura Palmer, the reader's identification with Neal comes from confronting his emptiness, and Wallace, like Lynch, allows readers to inhabit "the impossible perspective of the absent object."[61] Neal is, as yoga instructor Master Gurpreet calls him, "the statue": a monument to some higher ideal, but as lifeless, inert, and impenetrable as Laura Palmer's body wrapped in plastic.[62] Like Laura, Neal cannot even experience his suffering as real because being "a fair-haired boy [...] on the fast track" who is also deeply unhappy despite his accomplishments is "such a cliché."[63] In fact, Neal decides to end his life after seeing his pain reduced to a punchline on a sitcom: his turmoil is so commonplace as to be "the butt of a joke" for a mass audience.[64] As it does to Laura, the culture alienates Neal from his own alienation, and their mutual tragedy is the inability of the people around them to comprehend that one can be both "impressive and authentically at ease in the world" and a "dithering, pathetically self-conscious outline or ghost of a person."[65] Characters like Laura and Neal allow Wallace and Lynch to sincerely demonstrate both the reality within the fake and the fakery within the real, allowing these characters to testify to the authenticity of feelings of artifice and fraudulence, asserting that feeling like a fake in a materialistic culture consumed by the appearance of achievement is perhaps the most real feeling of all.

"Good Old Neon" ends with Wallace pushing Laura Palmer's split consciousness beyond a single character when the story shifts its point of view to reveal that Neal's entire monologue may in fact be entirely in the mind of David Wallace, a high school classmate of Neal's who peers "through the tiny little keyhole of himself, to imagine what all must have happened to lead up to [Neal's] death" by suicide.[66] This point-of-view shift resembles the final act of *Mulholland Drive*, which reveals Betty to be as much a projection of Diane's fragmented psyche as Neal is a projection of David Wallace's thoughts about himself; however, Wallace's absorption of Lynch broadens the effect of this split from the characters in the work outward to the author and, by extension, the reader, thus dissolving all remaining boundaries to create a space of intense identification born out of the conflict between one's outer "neon aura" and one's inner turmoil. *Oblivion, Fire Walk with Me, Lost Highway, Mulholland Drive,* and *Inland Empire* depict tortured souls who "[suffer] personhood *as* tragedy"; their becoming aware of themselves and their realities becomes a nightmare from which they cannot awaken.[67] Wallace shares Lynch's increasing concern with trauma's effect on consciousness, suggesting in *Oblivion* that consciousness is trauma and that "language is the vortex of the clash between culture and the subconscious."[68] "Inside and outside are distinctions that no longer hold" in Lynch and Wallace; Lynch externalizes the pressures normality imposes on a person as forces abusing a body and as spaces opening up to allow those forces in, while Wallace in *Oblivion* depicts these pressures as being so all-consuming internally as to prevent characters from ever seeing through "the tiny little keyhole" of themselves.[69]

Filling the Hole of Language

The differences between Lynch's and Wallace's chosen media can be most felt in the main point of thematic divergence between the two artists: Wallace is far less optimistic. Lynch's characters frequently achieve a kind of victory or transcendence, however measured, over the forces that torment them. The endings to *Eraserhead, Blue Velvet, Wild at Heart, Fire Walk with Me, The Straight Story*, and *Inland Empire* each offer "tiny instant[s]" where their protagonists "feel suddenly connected to something larger and much more of the complete picture."[70] In Wallace's fiction, characters frequently wind up trapped within their own heads, unable to communicate or be understood. Neal may speak at great length in "Good Old Neon," both to the reader and to various therapists, holy men, and life coaches in the story, but he uses language to construct barriers between himself and others, to the extent that every utterance moves him further away from connection. This failure to communicate stems from Neal's fundamental distrust of language: he claims:

> [T]ry[ing] to convey to other people what we're thinking and to find out what they're thinking [is] a charade [...] What goes on inside is just too fast and huge and all interconnected for words to do more than barely sketch the outlines of at most one tiny little part of it at any given instant.[71]

Wallace does not locate a clear "exit from the linguistic labyrinth"; if one does exist, it does not present itself as "richly available to us" in his fiction.[72]

In this regard, Lynch parts ways with his ironic postmodern counterparts such as Quentin Tarantino or the Coen Brothers and rejects the notion of "culture as a kind of solipsism, language as a kind of chimera, and meaning as a phantom."[73] Instead, his self-reflexive sincerity-in-irony envisions a transcendent, enlightened state that exists beyond language but is accessible through cinema. Lynch can present a more optimistic view of communication than Wallace because, as a filmmaker, he has more languages at his disposal than Wallace does as a fiction writer. Martha Nochimson describes Lynch's cinematic language in incredibly open, fluid terms, showing how a language like cinema can generate genuine, sustained moments of empathy and transcendence:

> [E]ye and picture *are in each other*, as they move together. Lynch has internalized [...] a sense of narrative image that holds the possibility, not of the doomed quest for an illusory holy grail, but of empathy—among people, and between people and the universe. His belief in the image as a possible bridge to the real does not depend on any abstract framework but rather on a visceral sense of the essential truth of an empathetic—not solipsistic—relationship with art.[74]

FIGURE 10.5 "Not another word." *Mulholland Drive* directed by David Lynch ©
Universal Pictures 2001. All rights reserved.

Wallace's fiction can imagine and gesture toward but never realize such
a dynamic, whereas Lynch's cinema succeeds because it is "not English
anymore, it's not getting squeezed through any hole."[75] The final lines
of "Good Old Neon" and *Mulholland Drive*, "Not another word" and
"Silencio" respectively, may appear to be literal copies of each other;
however, while "not another word" signals the termination of fiction's ability
to communicate, "Silencio" does not "silence" cinema's communicative
potential. Lynch's belief in the real possibility of transcendence follows from
the fact that cinema is not dependent upon the verbal; if anything, especially
in Lynch's cinema, its origins are pre-verbal and can continue to peer out
through the "tiny little keyhole" of the camera without having to worry
about "squeezing" what it sees through the hole of language.

David Lynch's Unified States of America

I want to return to the ending of Lynch's last film because it exuberantly
illustrates the affiliative process that this book has dedicated itself to
exploring. After a grueling three-hour-long descent into darkness, chaos,
and madness, *Inland Empire* jolts back to life with a credits sequence that
is perhaps the most celebratory, joyous moment in Lynch's filmography.
Set to Nina Simone's "Sinnerman," the credits sequence of *Inland Empire*
stages a bizarre, raucous Lynchian party in which Laura Dern's Nikki Grace
mingles with figures from what one might jokingly refer to as the Lynchian
Cinematic Universe. We see not only Dern but *Mulholland Drive*'s Laura

Elena Harring, a *Twin Peaks*-esque lumberjack, a capuchin monkey from *Fire Walk with Me* and *What Did Jack Do?*, to name just a few references to Lynch's other works. This triumphant ending, which can almost have the look of a wrap party for a film shoot, feels like more than the culmination of just one film and more like what Dennis Lim calls "a state of grace."[76] In an interview with Lynch, Richard A. Barney describes the credits sequence of *Inland Empire* as a "unification" of Lynch's body of work that celebrates "the crew and the pleasure of the film as a film." In response, Lynch, ever the revealing interview subject, says "Let's just say that's a good way to think."[77]

It has become clear to me over the course of writing this book that unification has been a major theme in Lynch's work all along. His affiliative, both/and approach to binary distinctions such as sincerity and irony or reality and fantasy can be understood as him viewing them not as distinct opposites but rather part of a unified whole, a single entity. Although such a view threatens to be so broad as to eliminate all distinctions whatsoever, it proves instead to be amazingly pliable and liberating, allowing each viewer to pick up the signals and trace a path through these distinctions toward an understanding of the paradoxical nature of the world that rigidly demarcated and enforced boundaries preclude. These different readings do not seem to cancel each other out like binary distinctions but rather coexist in his work, sitting together like the group at the end of *Inland Empire*. This is David Lynch's American Dreamscape, a place where the dark and the light, the dream and the reality coexist and resonate with each other, producing creative energy that generates more art. Different and distinct, but unified.

Unification is also the end result of the affiliating identifications tracked in this book. Looking at Lynch's films in this way reveals how his work represents a pulling together of postwar American popular culture into a unified whole, a single dreamscape. The 1950s and the 1990s coincide in Lynch's films because that not-so-distant past has never left our imagination; it has instead sat beside our present and struck up a conversation like two party guests. And as we continue to add more to the body politic, the work grows even more unified, not into one entity but rather a group gathered under one roof, a truly big tent.

However far reaching this book may seem, it provides but a small glimpse of that cultural well Lynch draws from. The readings and intertexts offered here are hardly exhaustive or definitive. Making such a totalizing claim would not only be inaccurate and impossible but foolish because it runs counter to Lynch's kind of unification. There are more guests at this large party, and more will continue to arrive. This work is neither an end nor a beginning but a continuation, another reading of his work spawned by the work and other scholars' engagements with it that seeks to offer and generate more ways to read his work. It is a body of work that resonates and radiates outward while continuously drawing us back to it for more. *It's happening again.*

NOTES

Introduction

1 This material is adapted from my article "'This Muddy *Both*ness': The Absorbed Adaptation of David Lynch by David Foster Wallace," *Literature/ Film Quarterly* 48, no. 1 (2020), accessed January 20, 2024.

2 This notion derives from Thomas Leitch's tenth fallacy in adaptation theory: "Adaptations Are Adapting Exactly One Text Apiece." From "Twelve Fallacies in Contemporary Adaptation Theory," *Criticism* 45, no. 2 (Spring 2003): 164.

3 David Lynch and Chris Rodley, *Lynch on Lynch* (London: Faber and Faber, 1997), 56.

4 Dave Kehr, "The Plot's Thinning," in *Chicago Tribune* (Chicago, IL: Tribune Publishing, November 23, 1986), accessed January 5, 2024.

5 Hossein Eidizadeh, "When You See Me Again It Won't Be Me: The Metamorphosis, Franz Kafka and David Lynch's Life-Long Obsession," *Senses of Cinema*, no. 88 (October 2018), accessed May 21, 2021.

6 Mark Mazullo, "Remembering Pop: David Lynch and the Sound of the '60s," *American Music* 23, no. 4 (2005): 494–5.

7 Nicholas Rombes, "Blue Velvet Underground: David Lynch's Post-Punk Poetics," in *The Cinema of David Lynch: American Dreams, Nightmare Visions*, ed. Erica Sheen and Annette Davison (London: Wallflower Press, 2005), 63, 70, 75.

8 Julia Kristeva, *Desire in Language: A Semiotic Approach to Literature and Art*, ed. and trans. Leon S. Roudiez (New York: Columbia University Press, 1980), 65, 66.

9 Graham Allen, *Intertextuality*, 2nd ed. (London: Routledge, 2011), 64; Kristeva, *Desire in Language*, 66.

10 Roland Barthes, "From Work to Text," in *Image, Music, Text* (New York: Hill and Wang, 1977), 157.

11 Barthes, "From Work to Text," 159, 161, 159, 160.

12 Barthes, "From Work to Text," 163.

13 Barthes, "From Work to Text," 164.

14 Michael Riffaterre, "Syllepsis," *Critical Inquiry* 6, no. 4 (1980): 626, 628, http://www.jstor.org/stable/1343223.

15 Jay Clayton and Eric Rothstein, "Figures in the Corpus: Theories of Influence and Intertextuality," in *Influence and Intertextuality in Literary History* (Madison, WI: University of Wisconsin Press, 1991), 22; Barthes, "From Work to Text," 160.

16 Riffaterre, "Syllepsis," 628. Riffaterre argues that there is such a thing as a "correct" or "proper" intertextual interpretation, an assertion I am less comfortable with; however, his observation that the level of a reader's cultural awareness has a proportional impact on their ability to engage with a work intertextually serves as a strong foundation for the kind of intertextual analysis attempted in this book.

17 Allen, *Intertextuality*, 2.

18 Anahid Kassabian, *Hearing Film: Tracking Identifications in Contemporary Hollywood Film Music* (New York: Routledge, 2001), 2.

19 Kassabian, *Hearing Film*, 3.

20 Riffaterre, "Syllepsis," 628.

21 Kassabian, *Hearing Film*, 3, 88, 3.

22 For this conception of Lynch, I am indebted to David Cowart. David Cowart, *Don DeLillo: The Physics of Language*, rev. ed. (Athens, GA: University of Georgia Press, 2007), 1–2.

23 Kristeva, *Desire in Language*, 83, 87.

24 Barthes, "From Work to Text," 160; Roland Barthes, *S/Z: An Essay*, trans. Richard Miller and Richard Howard (New York: Hill and Wang, 1974), 10.

25 Elizabeth Alsop, "'It's No Longer Your Film': Fictions of Authorship in Lynch's *Mulholland Drive*," *Journal of Film and Video* 71, no. 3 (2019): 52, Research Library Prep (2323121050).

26 Alsop, "It's No Longer Your Film," 52–3.

27 Alsop, "It's No Longer Your Film," 54.

28 Alsop, "It's No Longer Your Film," 58.

29 Alsop, "It's No Longer Your Film," 57–8.

30 Roland Barthes, "The Death of the Author," in *Image, Music, Text* (New York: Hill and Wang, 1977), 146; Kristeva, *Desire in Language*, 83.

31 Alsop, "It's No Longer Your Film," 52.

32 Karyn Kusama, *Lynch/Oz*, directed by Alexandre O. Philippe, New York: Janus Films, 2022.

33 Justin Benson and Aaron Moorhead, *Lynch/Oz*.

34 Lynch and Rodley, *Lynch on Lynch*, 48.

35 Steven Mackenzie, "David Lynch: 'Home Is a Beautiful Word,'" *Big Issue*, last modified July 8, 2019, accessed January 5, 2024.

36 Barthes, "Death of the Author," 147.

37 Lynch and Rodley, *Lynch on Lynch*, 54.

38 Alsop, "It's No Longer Your Film," 53.

39 David Lynch, "Harold Lloyd Masters Seminar" (lecture, American Film Institute, Los Angeles, CA, October 10, 2001).

40 Rombes, "Blue Velvet Underground," 75.

41 Rombes, "Blue Velvet Underground," 70–1.

42 Clayton and Rothstein, "Figures in the Corpus," 23.

43 Mazullo, "Remembering Pop," 495, 496.

44 Louise O'Riordan, "The Popular Song Performs," in *Cinemusic?: Constructing the Film Score*, ed. David Cooper, Christopher Fox and Ian Sapiro (Newcastle: Cambridge Scholars Publishing, 2008), 85.

45 O'Riordan, "The Popular Song Performs," 87, 88.

46 O'Riordan, "The Popular Song Performs," 88.

47 Michael Rings, "Doing It Their Way: Rock Covers, Genre, and Appreciation," *The Journal of Aesthetics and Art Criticism* 71, no. 1 (Winter 2013): 58, accessed August 23, 2018.

48 Spotify user Chris Markwardt has kept a running playlist of the songs Lynch mentions. Chris Markwardt, "David Lynch's Weather Report—Musical Musings," Spotify, accessed January 20, 2024.

49 Lynch and Rodley, *Lynch on Lynch*, 223.

Chapter 1

1 "David Lynch: David Lean Lecture," video, 32:09, YouTube, posted by BAFTA Guru, May 26, 2017, accessed January 8, 2024.

2 Kenneth C. Kaleta, *David Lynch* (New York: Twayne, 1995), 11.

3 Nathan Lee, "David Lynch Made a Man out of Me," in *The Village Voice* (New York: Village Voice Media, 2007), Research Library Prep (232267941).

4 Kaleta, *David Lynch*, 30.

5 Michael Wilmington, "Lynch's *Mulholland Drive* Takes Us to a Hair-raising Alternate World," in *Chicago Tribune* (Chicago, IL: Tribune Publishing, 2001), Research Library Prep (419472768).

6 Kaleta, *David Lynch*, 14.

7 Todd B. Gruel, "The Darkness Within: 13 Films That Burrow into Our Psyches," *PopMatters*, October 29, 2018, Research Library Prep (2126702212), accessed August 20, 2024.

8 Wilmington, "Lynch's *Mulholland Drive*."

9 Kaleta, *David Lynch*, 11.

10 Jonathan Rosenbaum, "The Lynch-Pin Fallacy," JonathanRosenbaum.net, last modified January 29, 2022, accessed January 27, 2024.

11 Elaine Showalter, "On Hysterical Narrative," *Narrative* 1, no. 1 (1993): 26, 24, JSTOR.

12 Paula A. Treichler, "Escaping the Sentence: Diagnosis and Discourse in 'The Yellow Wallpaper,'" *Tulsa Studies in Women's Literature* 3, no. 1/2 (1984): 61, 62.

13 Charlotte Perkins Gilman, "The Yellow Wallpaper," in *The Yellow Wallpaper, Herland, and Selected Writings* (New York: Penguin Books, 2019), 179; Diane Price Herndl, "The Writing Cure: Charlotte Perkins Gilman, Anna O., and 'Hysterical' Writing," *NWSA Journal* 1, no. 1 (1988): 53, JSTOR.

14 Todd McGowan, *The Impossible David Lynch* (New York: Columbia University Press, 2007), 141.

15 Justus Nieland, *David Lynch* (Urbana: University of Illinois Press, 2012), 10.

16 Sandra M. Gilbert and Susan Gubar, *The Madwoman in the Attic: The Woman Writer and the Nineteenth-century Literary Imagination*, 2nd ed. (New Haven: Yale University Press, 2000), 88.

17 Carmen Bonasera, "Of Mirrors and Bell Jars: Heterotopia and Liminal Spaces as Reconfigurations of Female Identity in Sylvia Plath," *Humanities* 8, no. 1 (2019): 2.

18 Bonasera, "Of Mirrors and Bell Jars," 3, 8.

19 Bonasera, "Of Mirrors and Bell Jars," 4.

20 Showalter, "On Hysterical Narrative," 31.

21 Sylvia Plath, *The Bell Jar*, ed. Bantam Windstone (Toronto: Bantam Books, 1981), 69.

22 Gilman, "The Yellow Wallpaper," 179.

23 Gilman, "The Yellow Wallpaper," 179.

24 Gilman, "The Yellow Wallpaper," 179, 181.

25 Gilman, "The Yellow Wallpaper," 180.

26 Gilman, "The Yellow Wallpaper," 181.

27 Gilman, "The Yellow Wallpaper," 179.

28 Gilman, "The Yellow Wallpaper," 181.

29 Gilman, "The Yellow Wallpaper," 185, 186.

30 Elizabeth Boa, "Creepy-crawlies: Gilman's 'The Yellow Wallpaper' and Kafka's *The Metamorphosis*," *Paragraph* 13, no. 1 (1990): 22, JSTOR.

31 Plath, *The Bell Jar*, 115.

32 Plath, *The Bell Jar*, 115, 116.

33 Plath, *The Bell Jar*, 116.

34 Plath, *The Bell Jar*, 116.

35 Richard Martin, *The Architecture of David Lynch* (London, England: Bloomsbury Academic, 2020), 26.

36 Martin, *The Architecture of David Lynch*, 26; Nieland, *David Lynch*, 14.

37 Plath, *The Bell Jar*, 129, 152.

38 Gilman, "The Yellow Wallpaper," 188.

39 Gilman, "The Yellow Wallpaper," 187; emphasis added.

40 Plath, *The Bell Jar*, 70, 193.

41 Bonasera, "Of Mirrors and Bell Jars," 11.

42 Bonasera, "Of Mirrors and Bell Jars," 4.

43 Treichler, "Escaping the Sentence," 66.

44 Gilman, "The Yellow Wallpaper," 186, 185, 186.

45 Gilman, "The Yellow Wallpaper," 187.

46 Gilman, "The Yellow Wallpaper," 188, 189; emphasis added.

47 Gilman, "The Yellow Wallpaper," 190.

48 Gilman, "The Yellow Wallpaper," 194.

49 Gilman, "The Yellow Wallpaper," 194.

50 Plath, *The Bell Jar*, 76.

51 Plath, *The Bell Jar*, 104–5.

52 Plath, *The Bell Jar*, 117–18.

53 Plath, *The Bell Jar*, 193, 194.

54 Plath, *The Bell Jar*, 195.

55 Plath, *The Bell Jar*, 200.

56 Gilman, "The Yellow Wallpaper," 187.

57 Martha P. Nochimson, *The Passion of David Lynch: Wild at Heart in Hollywood* (Austin: University of Texas Press, 1997), 155.

58 McGowan, *The Impossible David Lynch*, 45.

59 McGowan, *The Impossible David Lynch*, 47–8.

60 Boa, "Creepy-crawlies," 22.

61 Boa, "Creepy-crawlies," 21.

62 Martin, *The Architecture of David Lynch*, 26.

63 Aaron Taylor, "Rough Beasts Slouch toward Bethlehem to Be Born: *Eraserhead* and the Grotesque Infant (Whose Hour Has Come round at Last)," *Revue Canadienne d'Études Cinématographiques / Canadian Journal of Film Studies* 9, no. 2 (2000): 63–4, JSTOR.

64 Showalter, "On Hysterical Narrative," 32.

65 Dennis Lim, *David Lynch: The Man from Another Place* (New York: Amazon Publishing, 2017), 31.

66 Lynch has described his motivation in going back to *Twin Peaks* as follows: "I couldn't get myself to leave the world of Twin Peaks. I was in love with the character of Laura Palmer and her contradictions: radiant on the surface but dying inside. I wanted to see her live, move, and talk. I was in love with that world and I hadn't finished with it" (Lynch and Rodley, *Lynch on Lynch*, 184).

67 Michel Chion, *David Lynch*, 2nd ed. (London: BFI, 2006), 44.

68 McGowan, *The Impossible David Lynch*, 135.

69 McGowan, *The Impossible David Lynch*, 134.

70 McGowan, *The Impossible David Lynch*, 135.

71 Nochimson, *The Passion of David Lynch*, 186.

72 Nochimson, *The Passion of David Lynch*, 177.

73 Nochimson, *The Passion of David Lynch*, 174; McGowan, *The Impossible David Lynch*, 153.

74 Nochimson, *The Passion of David Lynch*, 185.

75 Boa, "Creepy-crawlies," 26.

76 Treichler, "Escaping the Sentence," 73.

77 Vivian Delchamps, "'A Slight Hysterical Tendency': Performing Diagnosis in Charlotte Perkins Gilman's 'The Yellow Wallpaper,'" in *Performing Hysteria: Images and Imaginations of Hysteria*, by Johanna Braun (Leuven: Leuven University Press, 2020), 119.

78 Delchamps, "A Slight Hysterical Tendency," 106.

79 Treichler, "Escaping the Sentence," 75.

80 Nochimson, *The Passion of David Lynch*, 197.

81 Showalter, "On Hysterical Narrative," 32.

Chapter 2

1 For an overview of this debate, see Gubar and Kimberley Reynolds, *Children's Literature: A Very Short Introduction* (Oxford: Oxford University Press, 2011).

2 Marah Gubar, "On Not Defining Children's Literature," *PMLA* 126, no. 1 (2011): 214, JSTOR.

3 Gubar, "On Not Defining Children's Literature," 212, 213.

4 Jack Halberstam, *Wild Things: The Disorder of Desire* (Durham: Duke University Press, 2020), 132.

For a fuller discussion of these aspects of Lynch's work, see McGowan, Sam Ishii-Gonzales's "Mysteries of Love: Lynch's *Blue Velvet*/Freud's Wolf-Man," Lynne Layton's "*Blue Velvet*: A Parable of Male Development," James Lindroth's, "Down the Yellow Brick Road: Two Dorothys and the Journey of Initiation in Dream and Nightmare," or Mulvey's *Fetishism and Curiosity*.

5 Paul Coughlin, "*Blue Velvet*: Postmodern Parody and the Subversion of Conservative Frameworks," *Literature/Film Quarterly* 31, no. 4 (2003): 304, JSTOR.

6 A few scholars have already begun this work, such as Janet L. Preston's analysis of the film alongside Dante, Michael Moon's discussion of how the Sandman informs *Blue Velvet*, or Laura Mulvey's explorations of the Gothic in the film, though these too limit the film to a more mature frame of reference when its perspective is much more childlike.

7 Golan Moskowitz, *Wild Visionary: Maurice Sendak in Queer Jewish Context* (Stanford, CA: Stanford University Press, 2020), 2. Kaleta argues that "Lynch is also in the romantic tradition. He glorifies nature. He courts the supernatural. He is flamboyant. Romantic, in this sense, is not only a descriptor—it is a philosophy. Lynch employs the romantic code" (180–1).

8 Sarah Gilead, "Magic Abjured: Closure in Children's Fantasy Fiction," *PMLA* 106, no. 2 (1991): 277, 278.

9   Philip Nel, "Wild Things, Children and Art: The Life and Work of Maurice Sendak," *The Comics Journal*, no. 302 (2013): 21.

10 Moskowitz, *Wild Visionary*, 7.

11 Moskowitz, *Wild Visionary*, 19.

12 John Clement Ball, "Max's Colonial Fantasy: Rereading Sendak's *Where the Wild Things Are*," *Ariel: A Review of International English Literature* 28, no. 1 (1997): 167.

13 Maurice Sendak, *Where the Wild Things Are* (New York: Harper Collins Publishers, 1988).

14 A closer examination of the early pages of *Where the Wild Things Are* shows how the wild things permeate the order of the real world. The first image of the book depicts Max building the tent he will later occupy as king in the land of the wild things, and the stuffed animal dangling from a coat hanger prefigures him swinging from branches during the wild rumpus. The second image features a drawing of a monster on the wall that later greets Max on the shore of the land of the wild things. Lastly, Max's wolf suit, especially its color and clawed feet, matches the color and feet of a goat-like monster who appears to be king and who disappears after Max's coronation. While many of these details can be explained as bits of foreshadowing that manifest themselves in fantasy, they suggest worlds with more porous boundaries than the layout of the book would suggest. Further, the fact that Max's drawing hangs in a prominent place in the home signals that some aspects of fantasy are welcomed and encouraged rather than forcibly repressed. Suffice it to say, the difference between these worlds has been greatly exaggerated, so much so that one could suggest that the idea these two worlds are separate is itself a fantasy.

15 Sendak, *Where the Wild Things Are*.

16 Sendak, *Where the Wild Things Are*.

17 Sendak, *Where the Wild Things Are*.

18 Sendak, *Where the Wild Things Are*.

19 McGowan, *The Impossible David Lynch*, 90; Betsy Berry, "Forever, in My Dreams: Generic Conventions and the Subversive Imagination in *Blue Velvet*," *Literature/Film Quarterly* 16, no. 2 (1988): 82, Research Library Prep (226990228).

20 Howard Hampton, "David Lynch's Secret History of the United States," *Film Comment* 29, no. 3 (1993): 38, JSTOR.

21 Lim, *The Man from Another Place*, 66.

22 Irena Makarushka, "Subverting Eden: Ambiguity of Evil and the American Dream in *Blue Velvet*," *Religion and American Culture: A Journal of Interpretation* 1, no. 1 (1991): 33.

23 Makarushka, "Subverting Eden," 33.

24 Sendak, *Where the Wild Things Are*.

25 McGowan, *The Impossible David Lynch*, 91.

26 Gilead, "Magic Abjured," 282.

27 The geography of Lumberton makes this dynamic clear. It is not a geography
    of real social space but a geography of the mind. As McGowan notes, the
    evils of Lumberton cannot conceivably occur in a town so small. It is highly
    unlikely that the big-city style drug deals and kidnapping schemes performed
    by Frank Booth and his crime syndicate would exist within walking distance
    of carefully manicured small-town lawns. But there is one place where they do
    reside so closely: the fearful minds of suburbanites eager to protect an idealized
    American innocence at all costs. Lynch places these locales in close physical
    proximity to illustrate the way they butt up against each other in psychological
    space (92).

28 Ball, "Max's Colonial Fantasy," 168.

29 McGowan, *The Impossible David Lynch*, 91.

30 Berry, "Forever, in My Dreams," 83–4.

31 McGowan, *The Impossible David Lynch*, 92–3.

32 McGowan, *The Impossible David Lynch*, 93.

33 Lim, *David Lynch*, 80, 81.

34 Halberstam, *Wild Things*, 3.

35 Halberstam, *Wild Things*, 31.

36 Moskowitz, *Wild Visionary*, 26–7, 42, 44–5.

37 Halberstam, *Wild Things*, 3.

38 Sendak, *Where the Wild Things Are*.

39 McGowan, *The Impossible David Lynch*, 101. I am not convinced that
    the problem of the film is as much "a failure of representation" within the
    character of Jeffrey Beaumont or within the film but more a failure of the male
    director's imagination to conceive of female subjectivity outside the confines of
    male definitions of femininity. Lynch's post-*Fire Walk with Me* career largely
    rectifies this shortcoming in his work (103).

40 McGowan, *The Impossible David Lynch*, 102.

41 Halberstam, *Wild Things*, 5.

42 Halberstam, *Wild Things*, 5.

43 Halberstam, *Wild Things*, 134.

44 Sendak, *Where the Wild Things Are*.

45 Moskowitz, *Wild Visionary*, 56.

46 Halberstam, *Wild Things*, 131, 145.

47 Halberstam, *Wild Things*, 5.

48 Halberstam, *Wild Things*, 5–6.

49 Halberstam, *Wild Things*, 134.

50 Gilead, "Magic Abjured," 280–1.

51 Gilead, "Magic Abjured," 282; emphasis original.

52 Gilead, "Magic Abjured," 278, 285.

53 Gilead, "Magic Abjured," 285.

54 Gilead, "Magic Abjured," 278.

55 Moskowitz, *Wild Visionary*, 56.

56 James Lindroth, "Down the Yellow Brick Road: Two Dorothys and the Journey of Initiation in Dream and Nightmare," *Literature/Film Quarterly* 18, no. 3 (1990): 166, JSTOR.

57 McGowan, *The Impossible David Lynch*, 108.

58 Coughlin, "Postmodern Parody," 306, 309.

59 Janet L. Preston, "Dantean Imagery in *Blue Velvet*," *Literature/Film Quarterly* 18, no. 3 (1990): 172, JSTOR.

60 Berry, "Forever, In My Dreams," 89.

61 Coughlin, "Postmodern Parody," 307.

62 Chion, *David Lynch*, 87.

63 Lynch and Rodley, *Lynch on Lynch*, 22.

64 Makarushska, "Subverting Eden," 38.

65 Gilead, "Magic Abjured," 288.

66 McGowan, *The Impossible David Lynch*, 108.

67 Lim, *David Lynch*, 66–7.

68 Lim, *David Lynch*, 76.

Chapter 3

1 For instances of critics mentioning West, see Manohla Dargis, "The Trippy Dream Factory of David Lynch: [Review]," *New York Times* (New York, NY), 2006. Stephen Holden, "Hollywood, a Funhouse of Fantasy: [Review]," *New York Times* (New York, NY), 2001, late edition (East Coast) edition. Wilmington, "Lynch's *Mulholland Drive*." For Lynch saying he likes the book, see "David Lynch in Competition for 4th Time: A Smooth Exterior but Wild at Heart," Research Library Prep, last modified 2001.

2 Holden, "Hollywood, a Funhouse of Fantasy."

3 Jonathan Veitch, "Reading Hollywood," *Salmagundi*, no. 126/127 (2000): 210.

4 Rita Barnard, "'When you wish upon a star': Fantasy, Experience, and Mass Culture in Nathanael West," *American Literature* 66, no. 2 (1994): 328.

5 Mathew Roberts, "Bonfire of the Avant-garde: Cultural Rage and Readerly Complicity in *The Day of the Locust*," *Modern Fiction Studies* 42, no. 1 (1996): 62, JSTOR.

6 Nathanael West, *Miss Lonelyhearts* and *The Day of the Locust*, 35th ed. (New York: New Directions, 2007), 39.

7 John Springer, "'This Is a Riot You're In': Hollywood and American Mass Culture in Nathanael West's *The Day of the Locust*," *Literature/Film Quarterly* 24, no. 4 (1996): 439, JSTOR.

8   Springer, "This Is a Riot," 441.

9   Nathanael West, *A Cool Million* and *The Dream Life of Balso Snell: Two Novels* (New York: Farrar, Straus and Giroux, 2006), 5.

10 Lim, *David Lynch*, 142.

11 Erik D. Curren, "Noir or Gothic: Visions of Apocalypse in the Depression-era L.A. Novel," *Southern California Quarterly* 78, no. 1 (1996): 14.

12 West, *Day of the Locust*, 134.

13 Lim, *David Lynch*, 153.

14 West, *Day of the Locust*, 62, 68.

15 West, *Day of the Locust*, 80–1.

16 West, *Day of the Locust*, 80, 81.

17 West, *Miss Lonelyhearts*, 1.

18 West, *Miss Lonelyhearts*, 49.

19 West, *A Cool Million*, 98.

20 Lim, *David Lynch*, 141.

21 David D. Galloway, "A Picaresque Apprenticeship: Nathanael West's *The Dream Life of Balso Snell* and *A Cool Million*," *Wisconsin Studies in Contemporary Literature* 5, no. 2 (1964): 124.

22 West, *A Cool Million*, 74.

23 West, *A Cool Million*, 74–5.

24 West, *A Cool Million*, 138.

25 West, *A Cool Million*, 178.

26 West, *A Cool Million*, 179.

27 Will Scheibel, "A Fallen Star over *Mulholland Drive*: Representation of the Actress," *Film Criticism* 42, no. 1 (2018).

28 Martha P. Nochimson, "'All I Need Is the Girl': The Life and Death of Creativity in *Mulholland Drive*," in *The Cinema of David Lynch: American Dreams, Nightmare Visions*, reprinted ed., ed. Erica Sheen and Annette Davison (London: Wallflower Press, 2004), 166.

29 Nochimson, "All I Need Is the Girl," 179.

30 M. A. Klug, "Nathanael West: Prophet of Failure," *College Literature* 14, no. 1 (1987): 18.

31 Todd McGowan, "Accumulation and Enjoyment," *The Comparatist* 39 (2015): 102.

32 Deborah Wyrick, "Dadaist Collage Structure and Nathanael West's *Dream Life of Balso Snell*," *Studies in the Novel* 11, no. 3 (1979): 350, JSTOR.

33 Nochimson, "All I Need Is the Girl," 170.

34 West, *The Dream Life of Balso Snell*, 8.

35 West, *Day of the Locust*, 132.

36 West, *Day of the Locust*, 132.

37 Veitch, "Reading Hollywood," 215, 217.

38 McGowan, "Accumulation and Enjoyment," 103.

39 McGowan, "Accumulation and Enjoyment," 110.

40 Veitch, "Reading Hollywood," 216.

41 George Toles, "Auditioning Betty in *Mulholland Drive*," *Film Quarterly* 58, no. 1 (2004): 11, Research Library Prep (212275837).

42 Toles, "Auditioning Betty," 8–9.

43 Thomas Strychacz, "Making Sense of Hollywood: Mass Discourses and the Literary Order in Nathanael West's *The Day of the Locust*," *Western American Literature* 22, no. 2 (1987): 150.

44 West, *Day of the Locust*, 67; Roberts, "Bonfire of the Avant-garde," 66.

45 Scheibel, "A Fallen Star."

46 Scheibel, "A Fallen Star."

47 Barnard, "When you wish upon a star," 335.

48 Springer, "This Is a Riot," 443.

49 West, *Balso Snell*, 31.

50 Curren, "Noir or Gothic," 15.

51 Roberts, "Bonfire of the Avant-garde," 84.

52 Roberts, "Bonfire of the Avant-garde," 64.

53 *The Cheated* was West's original title for *The Day of the Locust*.

54 Roberts, "Bonfire of the Avant-garde."

55 West, *Balso Snell*, 51.

56 West, *Balso Snell*, 37.

57 Wyrick, "Dadaist Collage Structure," 355.

58 Wyrick, "Dadaist Collage Structure," 355, 356.

59 Lim, *David Lynch*, 157.

60 Doug Haynes, "'Laughing at the Laugh': Unhappy Consciousness in Nathanael West's *The Dream Life of Balso Snell*," *The Modern Language Review* 102, no. 2 (2007): 345.

Chapter 4

1 Quoted in Jennifer Fay, *Inhospitable World: Cinema in the Time of the Anthropocene* (New York: Oxford University Press, 2018), 64.

2 Fay, *Inhospitable World*, 64.

3 Timothy Morton, *Hyperobjects: Philosophy and Ecology after the End of the World* (Minneapolis: University of Minnesota Press, 2013), 1.

4 Morton, *Hyperobjects*, 32, 49.

5 Morton, *Hyperobjects*, 15.

6 Morton, *Hyperobjects*, 37.

7 Morton, *Hyperobjects*, 180.

8 Ashlee Joyce, "The Nuclear Anxiety of *Twin Peaks: The Return*," in *The Politics of Twin Peaks*, ed. Amanda DiPaolo and Jamie Gillies (Lanham: Lexington Books, 2019), 13.

9 Fay, *Inhospitable World*, 64.

10 Fay, *Inhospitable World*, 66.

11 Jeff Wood, "Hurricane Bob: Part 2," *3:AM Magazine*, accessed February 10, 2021; emphasis original.

12 Daniel Cordle, "Cultures of Terror: Nuclear Criticism during and since the Cold War," *Literature Compass* 3, no. 6 (November 2006): 1188; emphasis original.

13 Deborah Lovatt, "A Terrible Beauty: The Nuclear Sublime in Philip Ridley's *The Reflecting Skin* (1991)," *European Journal of American Culture* 21, no. 3 (November 1, 2002): 135.

14 Cordle, "Cultures of Terror," 1188.

15 Cordle, "Cultures of Terror," 1188.

16 Cordle, "Cultures of Terror," 1193.

17 Wood, "Hurricane Bob: Part 2."

18 Wood, "Hurricane Bob: Part 2."

19 Joyce, "The Nuclear Anxiety of *Twin Peaks*," 13.

20 Cormac McCarthy, *The Crossing* (New York: Vintage International, 1995), 423–4.

21 McCarthy, *The Crossing*, 425–6.

22 McCarthy, *The Crossing*, 426.

23 McCarthy, *The Crossing*, 424.

24 McCarthy, *The Crossing*, 127.

25 McCarthy, *The Crossing*, 127; Alex Hunt, "Right and False Suns: Cormac McCarthy's *The Crossing* and the Advent of the Atomic Age," *Southwestern American Literature* 28, no. 2 (Spring, 1998): 33.

26 McCarthy, *The Crossing*, 127, 22.

27 McCarthy, *The Crossing*, 424.

28 McCarthy, *The Crossing*, 3.

29 Hunt, "Right and False Suns," 34.

30 Morton, *Hyperobjects*, 195.

31 Timothy Parrish, "History and the Problem of Evil in McCarthy's Western Novels," in *The Cambridge Companion to Cormac McCarthy*, reprinted ed., ed. Steven Frye (New York: Cambridge University Press, 2014), 76.

32 Parrish, "History and the Problem of Evil," 75, 76.

33 McCarthy and Lynch's protagonists strive to act as forces opposed to this destructive knowledge; however, their efforts either prove futile (Billy Parham in *The Crossing*) or reveal themselves to be dabbling in the same elemental properties that gave rise to something like the Bomb (Agent Dale Cooper).

34 Walter Metz, "The Atomic Gambit of *Twin Peaks: The Return*," *Film Criticism* 41, no. 3 (November 2017).

35 Pierre Lagayette, "The Border Trilogy, *The Road*, and the Cold War," in *The Cambridge Companion to Cormac McCarthy*, reprinted ed., ed. Steven Frye (New York: Cambridge University Press, 2014), 88.

36 Hunt, "Right and False Suns," 32.

37 Hunt, "Right and False Suns," 31.

38 Anthony Ballas, "'My Log Has a Message for You,' or Vibrant Matter and *Twin Peaks*: On Thing-Power and Subjectivity," in *Critical Essays on Twin Peaks: The Return*, ed. Antonio Sanna (Cham: Palgrave Macmillan, 2019), 129–30.

39 Ryan Coogan, "'Here's to the Pie That Saved Your Life, Dougie': The Weird Realism of *Twin Peaks*," in *Critical Essays on Twin Peaks: The Return*, ed. Antonio Sanna (Cham: Palgrave Macmillan, 2019), 135.

40 Morton, *Hyperobjects*, 55.

41 Morton, *Hyperobjects*, 29.

42 Morton, *Hyperobjects*, 129.

43 Andrew T. Burt, "Is It the Wind in the Tall Trees or Just the Distant Buzz of Electricity?: Sound and Music as Portent in *Twin Peaks'* Season Three," in *Critical Essays on Twin Peaks*, ed. Antonio Sanna (Cham: Palgrave Macmillan US, 2019), 265.

44 Fay, *Inhospitable World*, 78–9.

45 Joyce, "The Nuclear Anxiety of *Twin Peaks*," 24–5. This speech also calls to mind a similar scene in *Kiss Me Deadly* in which "a series of words" ("Los Alamos. Manhattan Project. Trinity.") appear both ominous and divorced from the real things they are meant to signify (Caryl Flinn, "Sound, Woman, and the Bomb: Dismembering the 'Great Whatsit' in *Kiss Me Deadly*," Screening the Past, last modified June 30, 2000, accessed June 11, 2024).

46 Metz, "The Atomic Gambit of *Twin Peaks*." One could also make the argument that Laura Palmer herself functions as a hyperobject within the world of *Twin Peaks* in the sense that she is simultaneously everywhere and absent.

47 Hunt, "Right and False Suns," 32.

48 Joyce, "The Nuclear Anxiety of *Twin Peaks*," 24.

49 Morton, *Hyperobjects*, 130.

50 Morton, *Hyperobjects*, 173.

51 Joyce, "The Nuclear Anxiety of *Twin Peaks*," 23.

52 Cormac McCarthy, *The Passenger* (New York: Alfred A. Knopf, 2022), 30.

53 Metz, "The Atomic Gambit of *Twin Peaks*"; Elizabeth Lowry, "Extraterrestrial Intelligences in the Atomic Age: Exploring the Rhetorical Function of Aliens

and the 'Alien' in the *Twin Peaks* Universe," in *Critical Essays on Twin Peaks: The Return*, ed. Antonio Sanna (Cham: Palgrave Macmillan, 2019), 41.

54 Donald McCarthy, "How Mark Frost's *Twin Peaks* Books Clarify and Confound the Nature of Reality," in *Critical Essays on Twin Peaks: The Return*, ed. Antonio Sanna (Cham: Palgrave Macmillan, 2019), 176.

55 Joyce, "The Nuclear Anxiety of *Twin Peaks*," 27.

56 Joyce, "The Nuclear Anxiety of *Twin Peaks*," 28.

57 Joyce, "The Nuclear Anxiety of *Twin Peaks*," 28.

58 Lowry, "Extraterrestrial Intelligences," 47–8.

59 Cordle, "Cultures of Terror," 1195, 1196.

60 McCarthy, *The Passenger*, 370.

61 McCarthy, *The Passenger*, 116.

62 McCarthy, *The Passenger*, 377.

63 McCarthy, *The Crossing*, 22.

64 McCarthy, *The Crossing*, 22.

65 McCarthy, *The Crossing*, 22.

66 Hunt, "Right and False Suns," 31.

67 McCarthy, *The Crossing*, 127.

68 McCarthy, *The Crossing*, 46.

69 McCarthy, *The Crossing*, 45.

70 McCarthy, *The Crossing*, 46.

71 McCarthy, *The Crossing*, 47.

72 McCarthy, *The Crossing*, 47.

73 McCarthy, *The Crossing*, 127.

74 McCarthy, *The Crossing*, 46.

75 McCarthy, *The Crossing*, 416.

76 McCarthy, *The Passenger*, 142–3.

77 Fay, *Inhospitable World*, 81.

78 Metz, "The Atomic Gambit of *Twin Peaks*."

Chapter 5

1 Lynch and Rodley, *Lynch on Lynch*, 193.

2 Kathleen Murphy, "Dead Heat on a Merry-Go-Round," *Film Comment* 26, no. 6 (1990): 59–60, JSTOR.

3 Eric Wilson, *The Strange World of David Lynch: Transcendental Irony from Eraserhead to Mulholland Drive* (New York: Continuum, 2007), 106.

4 Murphy "Dead Heat on a Merry-Go-Round," 59–60.

5   Timothy Corrigan, *A Cinema without Walls: Movies and Culture after Vietnam* (New Brunswick, NJ: Rutgers University Press, 1991), 72.

6   Cyndy Hendershot, "Postmodern Allegory and David Lynch's *Wild at Heart*," *Critical Arts* 9, no. 1 (January 1995).

7   Rombes, "Blue Velvet Underground," 63, 73.

8   Wilson, *The Strange World of David Lynch*, 106.

9   Hendershot, "Postmodern Allegory and David Lynch's *Wild at Heart*."

10 Annette Davison, "'Up in Flames': Love, Control, and Collaboration in the Soundtrack to *Wild at Heart*," in *The Cinema of David Lynch: American Dreams, Nightmare Visions*, ed. Erica Sheen and Annette Davison (London: Wallflower Press, 2005), 123–4, 130–1.

11 Davison, "Up in Flames," 122.

12 Davison, "Up in Flames," 120.

13 Greil Marcus, *Mystery Train: Images of America in Rock 'N' Roll Music*, 5th ed. (New York, NY: Plume, 2008), 29–30.

14 Marcus, *Mystery Train*, 4, 13, 21.

15 Marcus, *Mystery Train*, 30.

16 Marcus, *Mystery Train*, 27, 31.

17 Marcus, *Mystery Train*, 15.

18 Mark Mazullo, "Fans and Critics: Greil Marcus's *Mystery Train* as Rock 'N' Roll History," *The Musical Quarterly* 81, no. 2 (1997): 147, http://www.jstor.org/stable/742456.

19 Marcus, *Mystery Train*, 21, 128.

20 Marcus, *Mystery Train*, 128.

21 Mazullo, "Fans and Critics," 156, 156–7.

22 Mazullo, "Fans and Critics," 158.

23 Mazullo, "Fans and Critics," 152, 158.

24 Marcus, *Mystery Train*, 69, 70; emphasis added.

25 Marcus, *Mystery Train*, 70, 71.

26 Simon Frith, "'The Magic That Can Set You Free': The Ideology of Folk and the Myth of Rock Community," *Popular Music* 1 (1981): 168. Quoted in Mazullo.

27 Nochimson, *The Passion of David Lynch*, 51.

28 Marcus, *Mystery Train*, 5.

29 Ronald Rodman, "The Popular Song as Leitmotif in 1990s Film," *Changing Tunes: The Use of Pre-existing Music in Film*, ed. Phil Powrie and Robynn Stilwell (Aldershot: Ashgate Publishing, 2006), 120–1. Rodman shows how Tarantino associates Vincent Vega with surf rock and 1950s/1960s popular culture in *Pulp Fiction* and how Danny Boyle connects Mark Renton with musicians known for injecting drugs in the past like Iggy Pop and Lou Reed through specific song cues; however, these associations determine their

characters to a far less rigid degree than that of Sailor Ripley and add little depth to the films as a whole, making *Wild at Heart*'s use of music far more innovative.

30 Rodman, "The Popular Song as Leitmotif," 135.

31 Kassabian, *Hearing Film*, 141.

32 Kassabian, *Hearing Film*, 142–3.

33 These archetypes play out most overtly in nostalgic rock 'n' roll revival works such as *Grease* (Randal Kleiser, 1978), *Cry-Baby* (John Waters, 1990), Meat Loaf's *Bat Out of Hell* album (1977), and the tracks "Born to Run" and "Thunder Road" on Bruce Springsteen's *Born to Run* album (1975). Springsteen's affinity for Marcus's conception of rock becomes evident in his endorsement that appears on the front cover of the paperback fifth edition of *Mystery Train*: Marcus, says Springsteen, "gets as close to the heart and soul of America and American music as the best of rock 'n' roll." In some regards, these nostalgic works mentioned above synthesize the disparate rock archetypes described above into singular statements.

34 Hendershot, "Postmodern Allegory and David Lynch's *Wild at Heart*."

35 John Alexander, *The Films of David Lynch* (London: Charles Letts & Co, 1993), 116.

36 Alexander, *The Films of David Lynch*, 115–16.

37 Nochimson, *The Passion of David Lynch*, 11.

38 Kiel Hume, "Politicizing Lynch/Lynching Politics: Reification in *Blue Velvet* and *Wild at Heart*," *Quarterly Review of Film and Video* 27, no. 3 (2010): 225.

39 Marcus, *Mystery Train*, 18; emphasis original.

40 Hendershot, "Postmodern Allegory and David Lynch's *Wild at Heart*."

41 Marcus, *Mystery Train*, 30.

42 Nochimson, *The Passion of David Lynch*, 26.

43 Thanks must go to YouTube user "JS3105" for pointing this out in the comments to the "*Wild at Heart*—00 Spool" clip on YouTube, http://www.youtube.com/watch?v=XRh_vxYASZ4.

44 Christopher Smith. "Papa Legba and the Liminal Spaces of the Blues: Roots Music in Deep South Film," in *American Cinema and the Southern Imaginary*, ed. Deborah E. Barker and Kathryn McKee (Athens: University of Georgia Press, 2011), 317, 318.

45 Smith, "Papa Legba," 317, 321.

46 Samuel A. Floyd, "Ring Shout! Literary Studies, Historical Studies, and Black Music Inquiry," *Black Music Research Journal* 11, no. 2 (Autumn, 1991): 198. Quoted in Smith.

47 Smith, "Papa Legba," 320.

48 Smith, "Papa Legba," 331; emphasis added.

49 Smith, "Papa Legba," 331.

50 Marcus, *Mystery Train*, 29.

51 Marcus, *Mystery Train*, 24. "Up in Flames" and "Wicked Game," the two most despondent songs in the film, both express similar sentiments.

52 Marcus, *Mystery Train*, 21.

53 Chion, *David Lynch*, 132.

54 Marcus, *Mystery Train*, 173.

55 Davison, "Up in Flames," 123–4, 130–1.

56 See Davison, "Up in Flames," 121–2 for a careful list of all the appearances of "Slaughterhouse" in the film, time codes included.

57 McGowan, *The Impossible David Lynch*, 119–20.

58 Chion, *David Lynch*, 127.

59 Nochimson, *The Passion of David Lynch*, 10.

60 Chion, *David Lynch*, 125; Kaleta, *David Lynch*, 180–1.

61 Nochimson, *The Passion of David Lynch*, 47.

62 Nochimson, *The Passion of David Lynch*, 10, 11, 52.

63 Nochimson, *The Passion of David Lynch*, 10, 13.

64 Jeff Johnson, "Pervert in the Pulpit: The Puritanical Impulse in the Films of David Lynch," *Journal of Film and Video* 55, no. 4 (Winter, 2003): 10.

65 Wilson, *The Strange World of David Lynch*, 106.

66 Rombes, "Blue Velvet Underground," 72.

67 Nochimson, *The Passion of David Lynch*, 13.

68 McGowan, *The Impossible David Lynch*, 128; Nochimson, *The Passion of David Lynch*, 13.

69 Marcus, *Mystery Train*, 140.

70 Marcus, *Mystery Train*, 131; second emphasis added.

71 Marcus, *Mystery Train*, 173.

72 Marcus, *Mystery Train*, 5, 6.

73 Marcus, *Mystery Train*, 175.

74 O'Riordan, "The Popular Song Performs," 87, 86.

Chapter 6

1 John Richardson, "*Laura* and *Twin Peaks*: Postmodern Parody and the Musical Reconstruction of the Absent *Femme Fatale*," in *The Cinema of David Lynch: American Dreams, Nightmare Visions*, ed. Erica Sheen and Annette Davison (London: Wallflower Press, 2004), 87.

2 Mazullo, "Remembering Pop," 494.

3 Mazullo, "Remembering Pop," 504–5.

4 R. Serge Denisoff, "'Teen Angel': Resistance, Rebellion and Death—Revisited," *Journal of Popular Culture* 16, no. 4 (1983): 116. The teen tragedy ballad's history goes back even further than the American postwar era to murder ballads of the Middle Ages that have been passed down through folk traditions such as Child Ballads. Laura Plummer is one of the only critics to look back this far into the literary past for affiliating identifications to *Twin Peaks*, locating the show's origins in fairy tales such as Sleeping Beauty, where men seek to reawaken dead women with an act of love (Laura Plummer, "'I'm Not Laura Palmer': David Lynch's Fractured Fairy Tale," *Literature/Film Quarterly* 25, no. 4 [1997]: 309, JSTOR). At the heart of these tales lies what Daniel A. Cohen refers to as "the beautiful female murder victim [...] a cultural motif" that occurs across time, genre, and artistic form. In addition to being beautiful, female, and murdered, the victim of this motif is also young, single, and perceived as innocent prior to some kind of sexual transgression that results in her death at the hands of another single young man who murders her after some kind of sexual encounter or assault (Daniel A. Cohen, "The Beautiful Female Murder Victim: Literary Genres and Courtship Practices in the Origins of a Cultural Motif, 1590–1850," *Journal of Social History* 31, no. 2 [1997]: 278, JSTOR). Mark Mazullo names the motif "the drowned virgin-whore model" where a "woman meets a watery fate specifically as a result of her transformation into a sexually experienced being" (Mark Mazullo, "Revisiting the Wreck: PJ Harvey's *Dry* and the Drowned Virgin-Whore," *Popular Music* 20, no. 3 [2001]: 432). One does not have to examine *Twin Peaks* for long to see that Laura Palmer meets all these criteria save the age and marital status of the man who kills her, though her killer's identity is partially obscured by the many suspects who do meet the motif's profile exactly: Bobby Briggs, James Hurley, etc.

5 Ian Inglis, "A Brief Life: Broken Hearts and Sudden Deaths," *Popular Music and Society* 27, no. 4 (2004): 483, Research Library Prep (208069227).

6 Inglis, "A Brief Life," 482.

7 Inglis, "A Brief Life," 485.

8 David Atkinson, "Magical Corpses: Ballads, Intertextuality, and the Discovery of Murder," *Journal of Folklore Research* 36, no. 1 (1999): 19, JSTOR.

9 Lynch frequently references songs by the band in his YouTube weather reports.

10 Katherine M. Reed, "'We Cannot Content Ourselves with Remaining Spectators': Musical Performance, Audience Interaction, and Nostalgia in the Films of David Lynch," *Music and the Moving Image* 9, no. 1 (2016): 4.

11 Mazullo, "Remembering Pop," 495.

12 Reed, "We Cannot Content Ourselves," 4.

13 Mazullo, "Remembering Pop," 496.

14 Mazullo, "Remembering Pop," 497.

15 Nieland, *David Lynch*, 81.

16 Jimmy Cross's 1965 song "I Want My Baby Back," the most extreme parody of these songs, is so stuffed with effects and studio wizardry that it feels more like a radio play than a song.

17 Sheli Ayers, "*Twin Peaks*, Weak Language, and the Resurrection of Affect," in *The Cinema of David Lynch: American Dreams, Nightmare Visions*, ed. Erica Sheen and Annette Davison (London: Wallflower Press, 2004), 96.

18 Ayers, "*Twin Peaks*, Weak Language, and the Resurrection of Affect," 103, 104.

19 Atkinson, "Magical Corpses," 1. Atkinson discusses several Child Ballads where supernatural events lead to the discovery of a murder, and he even notes an instance of a talking bird in "Young Hunting," which will make *Twin Peaks* fans immediately think of Jacques Renault's talking myna bird (9).

20 Ayers, "*Twin Peaks*, Weak Language, and the Resurrection of Affect," 94.

21 Ayers, "*Twin Peaks*, Weak Language, and the Resurrection of Affect," 100.

22 Nochimson, *The Passion of David Lynch*, 81, 84.

23 Brooke McCorkle Okazaki, "Where Music Is Always in the Air: Voice and Nostalgia in *Twin Peaks*," in *Music in Twin Peaks: Listen to the Sounds* (Milton, UK: Routledge, 2021), 50–1.

24 Mazullo, "Remembering Pop," 506.

25 Chion, *David Lynch*, 109.

26 Chion, *David Lynch*, 109.

27 Chion, *David Lynch*, 111.

28 Martin, *The Architecture of David Lynch*, 92. Justus Nieland follows a similar logic when he identifies plastic as the essential substance for Lynch. As a material both artificial and extremely malleable, it serves as the perfect metaphor for the nostalgic impulse, an "alchemical substance" that makes manifest the desire to shrink-wrap "a past that never was" in protection "against the realities of the present" (Nieland, *David Lynch*, 2, 3).

29 Denisoff, "Teen Angel," 117, 118.

30 Inglis, "A Brief Life," 486, 487.

31 Atkinson, "Magical Corpses," 4.

32 Quoted in Lim, *The Man from Another Place*, 100.

33 Mazullo, "Revisiting the Wreck," 432, JSTOR.

34 Mazullo, "Revisiting the Wreck," 433, 431.

35 McGowan, *The Impossible David Lynch*, 130.

36 McGowan, *The Impossible David Lynch*, 134.

37 McGowan, *The Impossible David Lynch*, 134.

38 Joshua Jones, "'The Past Dictates the Future': Epistemic Ambivalence and the Compromised Ethics of Complicity in *Twin Peaks: The Return* and *Fire Walk with Me*," *NANO: New American Notes Online*, no. 15 (2020), Publicly Available Content Database; Research Library Prep (2356774067).

39 Amanda DiPaolo, "Is It Future or Is It Past?: The Politics and Use of Nostalgia in *Twin Peaks*," in *The Politics of Twin Peaks*, ed. Amanda DiPaolo and Jamie Gillies (Lanham: Lexington Books, 2019), 48.

40 Nieland, *David Lynch*, 84.

41 Ayers, "*Twin Peaks*, Weak Language, and the Resurrection of Affect," 95; Nochimson, *The Passion of David Lynch*, 176.

42 DiPaolo, "Is It Future or Is It Past?," 36.

43 DiPaolo, "Is It Future or Is It Past?," 38.

44 Dave Marsh, "Barbara Allen," in *The Rose and the Briar: Death, Love and Liberty in the American Ballad*, ed. Sean Wilentz and Greil Marcus (New York: W.W. Norton, 2005), 16.

Chapter 7

1 The album peaked at number seven on the Billboard charts and sold over 500,000 copies before receiving a deluxe vinyl reissue in 2017. (Katie Rife, "*Lost Highway* Put David Lynch onto America's Car Stereos," *AV Club*, last modified May 23, 2017, accessed January 20, 2024.)

2 "*Lost Highway* Press Kit," *Lynchnet.com*, accessed January 20, 2024. John Balance of the band Coil makes a similar claim, discrediting the project as Lynch simply looking for ways to cash in: "He wanted whoever he could get. He just said, 'These people are really big. I want this film to be really big.' He didn't give a fuck about the integrity" (Jon Whitney, "Jon Whitney Interview—Part I," *Brainwashed*, last modified May 5, 1997, accessed January 20, 2024). Balance's raw antipathy for the project may stem from Lynch rejecting one of their songs for inclusion on the soundtrack despite the urgings of soundtrack producer (and Nine Inch Nails frontman) Trent Reznor (Rife, "Lost Highway").

3 Mazullo, "Remembering Pop," 494.

4 Mazullo, "Remembering Pop," 494.

5 As Michel Chion notes, Lynch has been playing around with the notion of resurrected doubles (or covers) for some time, driven in large part by the influence of Hitchcock's *Vertigo*. For example, Madeline functions as a cover version of Laura Palmer in *Twin Peaks*, not to mention *Mulholland Drive*'s extended play with doubles and imagined alter-egos (Chion, *David Lynch*, 202).

6 Gabriel Solis, "I Did It My Way: Rock and the Logic of Covers," *Popular Music and Society* 33, no. 3 (2010): 298.

7 Rings, "Doing It Their Way," 56, 59.

8 Kassabian, *Hearing Film*, 85.

9 Nochimson, *The Passion of David Lynch*, 205; Greil Marcus, "New Songs in Old Skins," in *Bob Dylan: Writings 1968–2010* (New York: Public Affairs, 2010), 231.

10 Kassabian, *Hearing Film*, 3, 88.

11 Sara Cohen, "Popular Music, Gender and Sexuality," in *The Cambridge Companion to Pop and Rock*, ed. Simon Frith, Will Straw and John Street (Cambridge: Cambridge University Press, 2001), 231.

12 Nochimson, *The Passion of David Lynch*, 215.

13 Kassabian, *Hearing Film*, 138.

14 Nochimson, *The Passion of David Lynch*, 203.

15 To make matters even more complex, the song playing at the party as the Mystery Man approaches, Barry Adamson's "Something Wicked This Way Comes," contains a sample from Massive Attack's "Blue Lines," which, while not technically a cover, does make every element in the scene work to take viewers somewhere they have already been until they no longer know where they are. (Thanks to Kevin Donnelly for pointing this out during the question-and-answer session at the 2019 Music and the Moving Image Conference.)

16 Rings, "Doing It Their Way," 58.

17 Rings, "Doing It Their Way," 60.

18 Solis, "I Did It My Way," 309.

19 Greg Hainge, "Weird or Loopy? Specular Spaces, Feedback and Artifice in *Lost Highway*'s Aesthetics of Sensation," in *The Cinema of David Lynch: American Dreams, Nightmare Visions*, ed. Erica Sheen and Annette Davison (London: Wallflower Press, 2005), 141.

20 Solis, "I Did It My Way," 309.

21 Anne Jerslev, "Beyond Boundaries: David Lynch's *Lost Highway*," in *The Cinema of David Lynch: American Dreams, Nightmare Visions*, ed. Erica Sheen and Annette Davison (London: Wallflower Press, 2005), 155.

22 Kassabian, *Hearing Film*, 117.

23 Mazullo, "Remembering Pop," 495.

24 Steve Bailey, "Faithful or Foolish: The Emergence of the 'Ironic Cover Album' and Rock Culture," *Popular Music and Society* 26, no. 2 (2003): 156, accessed August 23, 2018.

25 McGowan, *The Impossible David Lynch*, 155.

26 Frida Beckman, "From Irony to Narrative Crisis: Reconsidering the Femme Fatale in the Films of David Lynch," *Cinema Journal* 52, no. 1 (Fall, 2012): 27, accessed May 21, 2018, JSTOR.

27 Beckman, "From Irony to Narrative Crisis," 28.

28 Beckman, "From Irony to Narrative Crisis," 34.

29 Beckman, "From Irony to Narrative Crisis," 34.

30 Jerslev, "Beyond Boundaries," 161.

31 Beckman, "From Irony to Narrative Crisis," 41.

32 Jerslev, "Beyond Boundaries," 160.

33 Solis, "I Did It My Way," 309.

34 This scene begins with Pete's pained reaction to a piece of music playing on the radio: Angelo Badalamenti's "Red Bats with Teeth," which is the same song Fred played on the saxophone earlier in the film. Thus, one moment of return precedes another.

35 Kassabian, *Hearing Film*, 89.

36 Mazullo, "Remembering Pop," 502.

37 George Plasketes, "Re-flections on the Cover Age: A Collage of Continuous Coverage in Popular Music," *Popular Music and Society* 28, no. 2 (May 2005): 157, accessed August 23, 2018.

38 Plasketes, "Re-flections on the Cover Age," 157.

39 Marcus, "New Songs in Old Skins," 232.

40 Alistair Mactaggart, *The Film Paintings of David Lynch: Challenging Film Theory* (London: Intellect, 2010), 81; McGowan, *The Impossible David Lynch*, 164.

41 McGowan, *The Impossible David Lynch*, 155.

42 McGowan, *The Impossible David Lynch*, 171–2.

43 Beckman, "From Irony to Narrative Crisis," 43.

44 Nochimson, *The Passion of David Lynch*, 215.

45 Jerslev, "Beyond Boundaries," 156.

46 David Lynch and Kristine McKenna, *Room to Dream* (New York: Random House, 2018), 234.

47 Chion, *David Lynch*, 203.

48 Jerslev, "Beyond Boundaries," 156.

49 Marina Warner, "Voodoo Road: *Lost Highway* by David Lynch," *Sight and Sound* 7, no. 8 (August 1997): 10. Quoted in Hainge, "Weird or Loopy?," 149.

50 Stéphane Girard, "(Un)originality, Hypertextuality, and Identity in Tiga's 'Sunglasses at Night,'" *Popular Music* 30, no. 1 (January 2011): 116–17, accessed August 24, 2018.

51 Girard, "(Un)originality, Hypertextuality, and Identity," 121.

52 Mazullo, "Remembering Pop," 510.

53 Tom O'Connor, "The Pitfalls of Media 'Representations': David Lynch's *Lost Highway*," *Journal of Film and Video* 57, no. 3 (Fall, 2005): 27, accessed May 21, 2018.

Chapter 8

1 Ron Eyerman and Scott Barretta, "From the 30s to the 60s: The Folk Music Revival in the United States," *Theory and Society* 25, no. 4 (1996): 503, JSTOR.

2 Robert Cantwell, *When We Were Good: The Folk Revival* (Cambridge, MA: Harvard University Press, 1996), 8, 2. Cantwell alternately marks Dylan's electric performance at the 1965 Newport Folk Festival as a symbolic and definitive end to the folk revival, the moment when rock 'n' roll claimed the crowned prince of the folk revival.

3 Katherine Skinner, "'Must Be Born Again': Resurrecting the *Anthology of American Folk Music*," *Popular Music* 25, no. 1 (2006): 63, JSTOR. Although

I am speaking about the *Anthology* specifically here, it is important to note, as Katherine Skinner shows, that the *Anthology* was not always the monolithic, legendary text that it is currently held up to be. Its reputation and stature as the catalyst for the folk revival are largely created in the rearview mirror. In fact, the *Anthology* sold very few copies during its initial release in 1952 in part because its 6LPs made for a hefty price tag that limited many of its purchases to libraries and collectors. Those who did encounter it, however, were impacted greatly, and the *Anthology* circulated through more intimate networks of enthusiasts sharing the records the way that a folk singer would share a song (64). When we talk about the *Anthology*, we are using at "shorthand for [the] complicated historical context" that led to the folk revival (72). Until recently, *The Basement Tapes* existed as a similar shorthand for Dylan's and popular music's fascination with the *Anthology* and what ultimately became the Americana and alt-country genres.

4   Greil Marcus, *The Old, Weird America: The World of Bob Dylan's Basement Tapes*, updated edition (New York, NY: Picador, 2011), 93.

5   Marcus, *The Old, Weird America*, xxii, 121.

6   Bob Dylan, "The *Playboy* Interview," by Nat Hentoff, Playboy Interview: Bob Dylan, accessed May 10, 2022.

7   Marcus, *The Old, Weird America*, 87.

8   Nieland, *David Lynch*, 125.

9   Mark Fisher, *The Weird and the Eerie* (London: Repeater Books, 2016), 15.

10 Cantwell, *When We Were Good*, 52. Similarly, Paul Nelson's description of the typical folk revivalist sounds like a description of David Lynch: underneath all the style and fashion, "there beat the heart [...] of a Boy Scout, one who is kind to his elders, helps old ladies across the street, walks the dog every night." Paul Nelson, "Newport: Down There on a Visit," *Little Sandy Review* 30 (1965): 53. Quoted in Cantwell, *When We Were Good*, 326.

11 Kassabian, *Hearing Film*, 2.

12 Nochimson, *The Passion of David Lynch*, 51.

13 Devin Orgeron, "Revising the Postmodern American Road Movie: David Lynch's *The Straight Story*," *Journal of Film and Video* 54, no. 4 (2002): 44, JSTOR.

14 Rodman, "The Popular Song as Leitmotif," 120–1.

15 Kassabian, *Hearing Film*, 88.

16 The association of the folk revival with whiteness can lead one to assume that folk music has always been coded as white; however, folk music's racial identity has not remained constant. What has remained constant is the act of othering involved in calling a music folk music. As William G. Roy has shown, folk is not a term its practitioners would self-apply. Rather, it is a label applied to them and their music by an outside group with a certain agenda that has shifted over time (William G. Roy, "Aesthetic Identity, Race, and American Folk Music," *Qualitative Sociology* 25, no. 3 [2002]: 467). Initially, American folk music constituted "a creolized synthesis of European and African influences" whose European aspects were later lionized by folklorists as "authentic" folk,

dividing folk music into "race" records and "hillbilly" records (462–3). Leftists later championed folk songs by Black as well as white performers in the 1920s and 1930s to celebrate it as "the people's music" and further their cause of a unified workers' revolution (464–5); however, because their project was more political than commercial in nature, their vision of folk music failed to establish a foothold in the marketplace and the public imagination (466). As a result, by the time of the 1960s folk revival, folk music's appeal was limited to white audiences who embraced folk music "because it helped them imagine themselves as someone other than who they feared they were: white middle-class consumers" (467). Even though the Civil Rights Movement and the folk revival coincided, Black audiences were less enamored of folk music because it required them to sentimentalize a marginal status that they were fighting to transcend (467). In adopting the vision of an all-white folk put forth by the folk revival, *The Straight Story* commits a similar error, preventing it from imagining a world that contains other varieties of identities and experiences, even when such perspective might support or enhance its themes.

17 Cantwell, *When We Were Good*, 18.

18 Kevin M. Moist, "Collecting, Collage, and Alchemy: The Harry Smith *Anthology of American Folk Music* as Art and Cultural Intervention," *American Studies* 48, no. 4 (2007): 117–18, JSTOR.

19 Kassabian, *Hearing Film*, 3.

20 Moist, "Collecting, Collage, and Alchemy," 117.

21 Moist, "Collecting, Collage, and Alchemy," 112.

22 Marcus, *The Old, Weird America*, xxi.

23 Marcus, *The Old, Weird America*, xxiv.

24 Marcus, *The Old, Weird America*, 27, 36.

25 Cantwell, *When We Were Good*, 120.

26 Martin, *The Architecture of David Lynch*, 132, 131, 127.

27 Martha P. Nochimson, *David Lynch Swerves: Uncertainty from Lost Highway to Inland Empire* (Austin: University of Texas Press, 2013), 60, 74.

28 Martin, *The Architecture of David Lynch*, 128.

29 Nieland, *David Lynch*, 131.

30 Robert Cantwell, "Smith's Memory Theater: The Folkways *Anthology of American Folk Music*," *New England Review* 13, no. 3/4 (1991): 395, JSTOR; emphasis added.

31 Marcus, *The Old, Weird America*, 59.

32 Eyerman and Barretta, "From the 30s to the 60s," 519.

33 Cantwell, *When We Were Good*, 142.

34 Cantwell, "Smith's Memory Theater," 391.

35 Cantwell, "Smith's Memory Theater," 394.

36 Cantwell, "Smith's Memory Theater," 370–1.

37 Orgeron, "Revising the Postmodern American Road Movie," 43.

38 Kassabian, *Hearing Film*, 88–9.

39 Cantwell, "Smith's Memory Theater," 373–4.

40 Cantwell, "Smith's Memory Theater," 374.

41 Cantwell, "Smith's Memory Theater," 370.

42 Cantwell, "Smith's Memory Theater," 381.

43 Cantwell, "Smith's Memory Theater," 366–7.

44 Kassabian, *Hearing Film*, 3, 88.

45 Cantwell, "Smith's Memory Theater," 369–70.

46 Orgeron, "Revising the Postmodern American Road Movie," 32.

47 Nieland, *David Lynch*, 133.

48 Nieland, *David Lynch*, 133.

49 Cantwell, "Smith's Memory Theater," 380.

50 Marcus, *The Old, Weird America*, 68.

51 Cantwell, "Smith's Memory Theater," 380; Eyerman and Barretta, "From the 30s to the 60s," 535.

52 Cantwell, *When We Were Good*, 325–6.

53 Moist, "Collecting, Collage, and Alchemy," 114; Cantwell, "Smith's Memory Theater," 373.

54 Cantwell, "Smith's Memory Theater," 374.

55 Marcus, *The Old, Weird America*, 105.

56 Nieland, *David Lynch*, 128.

57 Nieland, *David Lynch*, 133.

58 Nieland, *David Lynch*, 128.

59 Cantwell, "Smith's Memory Theater," 383.

60 Cantwell, "Smith's Memory Theater," 375.

61 Raymond Williams, *The Country and the City* (New York: Oxford University Press, 1973), 295, 297–8.

62 Cantwell, "Smith's Memory Theater," 377–8.

63 Marcus, *The Old, Weird America*, xxi.

64 Cantwell, *When We Were Good*, 356, 334, 186.

65 Moist, "Collecting, Collage, and Alchemy," 111.

66 Orgeron, "Revising the Postmodern American Road Movie," 31.

67 Marcus, *The Old, Weird America*, 148.

Chapter 9

1 Mactaggart, *The Film Paintings of David Lynch*, 141–2.

2 Steven Shaviro, "Southland Tales," *The Pinocchio Theory* (blog), entry posted December 10, 2007, accessed June 19, 2023.

3   Anthony Paraskeva, "Digital Modernism and the Unfinished Performance in David Lynch's *Inland Empire*," *Film Criticism* 37, no. 1 (2012): 4, JSTOR.

4   Kristen Daly, "Cinema 3.0: The Interactive-Image," *Cinema Journal* 50, no. 1 (2010): 95, JSTOR.

5   Lim, *David Lynch*, 173.

6   Amy Taubin, "The Big Rupture," *Film Comment* 43, no. 1 (2007): 56, JSTOR.

7   Martin, *The Architecture of David Lynch*, 165.

8   J. M. Tyree and Ben Walters, *The Big Lebowski* (London: Palgrave Macmillan, 2007), 13, 14.

9   Lim, *David Lynch*, 171.

10   J. Hoberman, *Film after Film: (or, What Became of 21st Century Cinema?)* (New York: Verso, 2014), 245.

11   Tyree and Walters, *The Big Lebowski*, 14.

12   Tyree and Walters, *The Big Lebowski*, 14–15.

13   Although its closest digital analogue is the playlist on a streaming service, the differences are distinct and worth noting. Mixtapes are more bound by the constraints of time and required more labor on the part of the listener/creator. A nonlinear Spotify playlist can continue for as long as the creator and the listener (if they are different people) has the stamina to add songs or continue listening, whereas mixtapes were made within a dwindling hourglass of time—the length of the side—that could not be adjusted in retrospect without performing some of the labor of recording again. Further, as playlists on streaming services are increasingly created and proliferated by the services themselves (or their algorithms), the user's level of agency and creativity in their creation has decreased in direct proportion with the labor required to produce it.

14   For the most enduring definition of the romantic stakes of the mixtape, see Rob Sheffield's memoir *Love Is a Mixtape* or this passage from Nick Hornby's *High Fidelity*: "To me, making a tape is like writing a letter—there's a lot of erasing and rethinking and starting again [...] A good compilation tape, like breaking up, is hard to do. You've got to kick it off with a corker, to hold the attention [...] and then you've got to up it a notch, or cool it a notch, and you can't have white music and black music together, unless the white music sounds like black music, and you can't have two tracks by the same artist side by side, unless you've done the whole thing in pairs, and ... oh, there are loads of rules" (Nick Hornby, *High Fidelity* [New York: Riverhead Books, 1995], 88–9).

15   Bas Jansen, "Tape Cassettes and Former Selves: How Mix Tapes Mediate Memories," in *Sound Souvenirs: Audio Technologies, Memory and Cultural Practices*, by Karin Bijsterveld and José Van dijck (Amsterdam: Amsterdam University Press, 2009), 48, JSTOR.

16   Jansen, "Tape Cassettes and Former Selves," 47.

17   Ryansenseless, *The Truth Is in the Details*, quoted in Jansen, "Tape Cassettes and Former Selves," 47.

18 Jansen, "Tape Cassettes and Former Selves," 48.

19 Jansen, "Tape Cassettes and Former Selves," 47.

20 Jansen, "Tape Cassettes and Former Selves," 46.

21 Dennis Lim, "David Lynch Returns: Expect Moody Conditions, with Surreal Gusts," *New York Times*, last modified October 1, 2006, accessed June 20, 2023.

22 Jansen, "Tape Cassettes and Former Selves," 46; emphasis original.

23 Lim, "David Lynch Returns."

24 Mactaggart, *The Film Paintings of David Lynch*, 143.

25 Martha P. Nochimson, "*Inland Empire*," *Film Quarterly* 60, no. 4 (2007): 10.

26 Lim, *David Lynch*, 173.

27 For a lengthier reading of the film in these terms, see Lim, *David Lynch*.

28 Martin, *The Architecture of David Lynch*, 177.

29 Martin, *The Architecture of David Lynch*, 150.

30 Hoberman, *Film after Film*, 243.

31 Taubin, "The Big Rupture," 56.

32 Hoberman, *Film after Film*, 243.

33 Nochimson, "*Inland Empire*," 11.

34 Nochimson, *David Lynch Swerves*, 144.

35 Nochimson, *David Lynch Swerves*, 127.

36 Nieland, *David Lynch*, 136.

37 Nieland, *David Lynch*, 138, 148.

38 Albin J. Zak, "Writing Records," in *The Poetics of Rock: Cutting Tracks, Making Records* (Berkeley: University of California Press, 2001), 19, JSTOR.

39 Zak, "Writing Records," 20.

40 Jansen, "Tape Cassettes and Former Selves," 52.

41 Hoberman, *Film after Film*, 245.

42 Martin, *The Architecture of David Lynch*, 165.

43 Nieland, *David Lynch*, 135.

Conclusion

1 Jonathan Rosenbaum, "Two Forms of Adaptation: Housekeeping and Naked Lunch," in *Film Adaptation*, ed. James Naremore (New Brunswick, NJ: Rutgers University Press, 2000), 209, 218.

2 Rosenbaum, "Two Forms of Adaptation," 217, 219.

3 Olivia Horn, "Lana Del Rey: *Did You Know There's a Tunnel under Ocean Blvd* Album Review," *Pitchfork*, last modified March 24, 2023, accessed July 13, 2023.

4   Lynch and Rodley, *Lynch on Lynch*, 184.

5   Frank Guan, "Where David Lynch and Lana Del Rey Meet," *Vulture*, last modified July 25, 2017, accessed July 13, 2023.

6   Nitsuh Abebe, "The Imagination of Lana Del Rey," *Pitchfork*, last modified September 30, 2011, accessed July 13, 2023.

7   Claire Shaffer, "Lana Del Rey's *Chemtrails over the Country Club* Is a Somber American Travelogue," *Rolling Stone*, last modified March 22, 2021, accessed July 13, 2023.

8   Brian Hiatt, "Lana Del Rey: Vamp of Constant Sorrow," *Rolling Stone*, last modified July 31, 2014, accessed July 13, 2023.

9   To watch all of their videos, visit https://www.youtube.com/@girlfrmars.

10 The resonance is not lost on Lynch and Del Rey. In 2015, Del Rey insisted she "would love to do anything with David Lynch." In addition to expressing his appreciation for Del Rey and her admiration of him, Lynch mentioned "Video Games" in his daily weather report on December 2, 2021. Luke Morgan Britton, "Lana Del Rey Open to David Lynch Collaboration: 'I Would Love to Do Anything with Him,'" *NME*, last modified December 11, 2015, accessed July 13, 2023; "David Lynch's Weather Report 12/2/21," video, 01:28, YouTube, posted by David Lynch, December 2, 2021, accessed July 13, 2023.

11 "Off to the Races," performed by Lana Del Rey, on *Born to Die*, Interscope Records, 2012, compact disc.

12 Mina Tavakoli, "Lana Del Rey: *Chemtrails over the Country Club* Album Review," Pitchfork, last modified March 19, 2021, accessed July 13, 2023.

13 Chris Richards, "Lana Del Rey Suddenly Sounds like the Poet Laureate of Post-truth: Her New Album, *Lust for Life*, Proves That Dreaming Is Free, Even When Reality Is at Risk," Research Library Prep, last modified 2017.

14 Murphy, "Dead Heat on a Merry-Go-Round," 59–60.

15 Tavakoli, "Lana Del Rey," *Pitchfork*.

16 Richards, "Lana Del Rey."

17 Meaghan Garvey, "Lana Del Rey: *Lust for Life* Album Review," *Pitchfork*, last modified July 25, 2017, accessed July 13, 2023.

18 Stephen J. Burn, "'Webs of Nerves Pulsing and Firing': *Infinite Jest* and the Science of Mind," in *A Companion to David Foster Wallace Studies*, ed. Marshall Boswell and Stephen Burn (New York, NY: Palgrave Macmillan, 2013), 61, 72; Paolo Pitari, "David Lynch's Influence on David Foster Wallace's *Infinite Jest*," *Camera Stylo* 12 (2017): 163.

19 David Foster Wallace, "David Lynch Keeps His Head," in *A Supposedly Fun Thing I'll Never Do Again: Essays and Arguments* (New York, NY: Back Bay Books, 2008), 211.

20 Rombes, "Blue Velvet Underground," 75.

21 Rombes, "Blue Velvet Underground," 65.

22 Maura Johnston, "Review: Lana Del Rey Indulges in Nostalgia, Reverb on Fourth LP," *Rolling Stone*, last modified July 25, 2017, accessed July 13, 2023.

23 Mark Richardson, "Lana Del Rey: *Ultraviolence* Album Review," *Pitchfork*, last modified June 16, 2014, accessed July 13, 2023.

24 Ayers, "*Twin Peaks*," 103.

25 Hiatt, "Lana Del Rey."

26 McGowan, *The Impossible David Lynch*, 134.

27 McGowan, *The Impossible David Lynch*, 134; Richardson, "Lana Del Rey."

28 McGowan, *The Impossible David Lynch*, 141.

29 Richards, "Lana Del Rey."

30 McGowan, *The Impossible David Lynch*, 130, 131.

31 Lindsay Zoladz, "Pretty When You Cry," *Pitchfork*, last modified June 19, 2014, accessed July 13, 2023; emphasis original.

32 Erin Kappeler and Tracy Ryan, "Editors' Introduction for NANO Special Issue 16: 'This Is What Makes Us Girls': Gender, Genre, and Popular Music," *NANO: New American Notes Online*, no. 16 (2022), Publicly Available Content Database; Research Library Prep (2678066617).

33 McGowan, *The Impossible David Lynch*, 131, 135.

34 McGowan, *The Impossible David Lynch*, 149.

35 McGowan, *The Impossible David Lynch*, 133.

36 Alex Frank, "Life, Liberty, and the Pursuit of Happiness: A Conversation with Lana Del Rey," *Pitchfork*, last modified July 19, 2017, accessed July 21, 2023.

37 I must concede I am not the first person to discuss Lynch's influence on Wallace. Dan Dixon presented a paper entitled "'David Lynch Is Interested in the Ear': The Shared Focus of David Lynch and David Foster Wallace" at Illinois State University's David Foster Wallace conference in 2015, in which he read "David Lynch Keeps His Head" as Wallace's "artistic manifesto." The popular online film magazine *Bright Wall/Dark Room* published an essay by Daniel Carlson on Wallace and Lynch in the fall of 2017, and Paolo Pitari published a sustained analysis of Lynch's influence on *Infinite Jest* in *Camera-Stylo* in 2017. While each piece has its merits, none captures the full scope of Wallace's engagement with Lynch. Dixon's presentation examines Wallace's essay on Lynch primarily as a site to better understand Wallace's views on artistic creation. Carlson uses *Infinite Jest* to discuss Lynch's cinema as "anticonfluential" but does not refer at all to Wallace's writing on Lynch. And Pitari's essay maps the plot of *Blue Velvet* onto *Infinite Jest*, going so far as to argue that Lynch is Paolo Pitari, David Lynch's Influence on David Foster Wallace's *Infinite Jest*." *Camera Stylo* 12 (2017): 156 and that "David Lynch Keeps His Head" should be considered part of the "essay-interview nexus," which he proposes renaming the "essay-interview-essay" nexus (156).

38 Wallace, "David Lynch Keeps His Head," 162.

39 Wallace, "David Lynch Keeps His Head," 200.

40 Wallace, "David Lynch Keeps His Head," 200, 201.

41 Wallace, "David Lynch Keeps His Head," 201.

42 Erica Sheen and Annette Davison, "Introduction: American Dreams, Nightmare Visions," in *The Cinema of David Lynch: American Dreams, Nightmare Visions*, reprinted ed. (London: Wallflower Press, 2005), 2; Rombes, "Blue Velvet Underground," 71.

43 Wallace, "David Lynch Keeps His Head" 149.

44 Pitari, "David Lynch's Influence," 156.

45 Adam Kelly, "David Foster Wallace: The Death of the Author and the Birth of a Discipline," *IJAS Online*, no. 2 (2010).

46 David Foster Wallace, "*E Unibus Pluram*: Television and US Fiction," in *A Supposedly Fun Thing I'll Never Do Again: Essays and Arguments* (New York, NY: Back Bay Books, 2008), 81.

47 Rombes, "Blue Velvet Underground," 75.

48 Wallace, "*E Unibus Pluram*," 81; "David Lynch Keeps His Head," 199, 198.

49 Hainge, "Weird or Loopy?," 149.

50 David Foster Wallace, "Octet," in *Brief Interviews with Hideous Men* (New York: Back Bay Books, 2000), 159, 160.

51 David Foster Wallace, "The Soul Is Not a Smithy," in *Oblivion: Stories* (New York: Back Bay Books, Little, Brown and Company, 2005), 113.

52 Wallace, "David Lynch Keeps His Head," 171, 167.

53 Wallace, "David Lynch Keeps His Head," 169; David Foster Wallace, "Good Old Neon," in *Oblivion: Stories* (New York: Back Bay Books, Little, Brown and Company, 2005), 180.

54 Nochimson, *The Passion of David Lynch*, 174.

55 McGowan, *The Impossible David Lynch*, 131.

56 Wallace, "David Lynch Keeps His Head," 211.

57 Rombes, "Blue Velvet Underground," 75.

58 Toles, "Auditioning Betty," 4.

59 Wallace, "Good Old Neon," 180.

60 Wallace, "Good Old Neon," 160, 145, 154.

61 McGowan, *The Impossible David Lynch*, 134.

62 Wallace, "Good Old Neon," 159.

63 Wallace, "Good Old Neon," 142.

64 Wallace, "Good Old Neon," 169.

65 Wallace, "Good Old Neon," 180, 181.

66 Wallace, "Good Old Neon," 180.

67 Nieland, *David Lynch*, 99.

68 Nochimson, *The Passion of David Lynch*, 202.

69 Nochimson, *The Passion of David Lynch*, 176.

70 Wallace, "Good Old Neon," 149; Nochimson "All I Need," 179.

71 Wallace, "Good Old Neon," 151.

72 Nochimson, *The Passion of David Lynch*, 4.

73 Nochimson, *The Passion of David Lynch*, 19.

74 Nochimson, *The Passion of David Lynch*, 9; emphasis original.

75 Wallace, "Good Old Neon," 179.

76 Lim, *David Lynch*, 176.

77 Richard A. Barney, "Worlds within Worlds within Worlds: *Inland Empire*," in *Inland Empire* (n.p.: Criterion Collection, 2023), 19, previously published in *David Lynch: Interviews*.

BIBLIOGRAPHY

Abebe, Nitsuh. "The Imagination of Lana Del Rey." *Pitchfork*. Last modified
    September 30, 2011. Accessed July 13, 2023. https://pitchfork.com/features/
    why-we-fight/8679-the-imagination-of-lana-del-rey/.
Alexander, John. *The Films of David Lynch*. Reprinted ed. London: Letts, 1995.
Allen, Graham. *Intertextuality*. 2nd ed. London: Routledge, 2011.
Alsop, Elizabeth. "'It's No Longer Your Film': Fictions of Authorship in Lynch's
    Mulholland Drive." *Journal of Film and Video* 71, no. 3 (2019): 50–64.
    Research Library Prep (2323121050).
Atkinson, David. "Magical Corpses: Ballads, Intertextuality, and the Discovery of
    Murder." *Journal of Folklore Research* 36, no. 1 (1999): 1–29. JSTOR.
Ayers, Sheli. "*Twin Peaks*, Weak Language, and the Resurrection of Affect." In *The
    Cinema of David Lynch: American Dreams, Nightmare Visions*, edited by Erica
    Sheen and Annette Davison, 93–106. London: Wallflower Press, 2004.
Bailey, Şteve. "Faithful or Foolish: The Emergence of the 'Ironic Cover Album' and
    Rock Culture." *Popular Music and Society* 26, no. 2 (2003): 141–59. https://doi.
    org/10.1080/0300776032000095486.
Ball, John Clement. "Max's Colonial Fantasy: Rereading Sendak's *Where the Wild
    Things Are*." *Ariel: A Review of International English Literature* 28, no. 1
    (1997): 167–79.
Ballas, Anthony. "'My Log Has a Message for You,' or Vibrant Matter and *Twin
    Peaks*: On Thing-Power and Subjectivity." In *Critical Essays on Twin Peaks: The
    Return*, edited by Antonio Sanna, 119–33. Cham: Palgrave Macmillan, 2019.
Barnard, Rita. "'When you wish upon a star': Fantasy, Experience, and Mass
    Culture in Nathanael West." *American Literature* 66, no. 2 (1994): 325–51.
    https://doi.org/10.2307/2927983.
Barney, Richard A. "Worlds within Worlds within Worlds: *Inland Empire*." In
    Inland Empire, 6–22. New York: Criterion Collection, 2023. Previously
    published in *David Lynch: Interviews*.
Barthes, Roland. "The Death of the Author," translated by Stephen Heath. In
    Image, Music, Text, 142–8. New York: Hill and Wang, 1977.
Barthes, Roland. "From Work to Text," translated by Stephen Heath. In *Image,
    Music, Text*, 155–64. New York: Hill and Wang, 1977.
Barthes, Roland. *S/Z: An Essay*. Translated by Richard Miller and Richard
    Howard. New York: Hill and Wang, 1974.
Beckman, Frida. "From Irony to Narrative Crisis: Reconsidering the *Femme Fatale*
    in the Films of David Lynch." *Cinema Journal* 52, no. 1 (2012): 25–44. JSTOR.
Berry, Betsy. "Forever, in My Dreams: Generic Conventions and the Subversive
    Imagination in *Blue Velvet*." *Literature/Film Quarterly* 16, no. 2 (1988): 82–90.
    Research Library Prep (226990228).

Blue Velvet. Directed by David Lynch. 1986. New York: The Criterion Collection, 2019. Blu-ray disc.

Boa, Elizabeth. "Creepy-crawlies: Gilman's 'The Yellow Wallpaper' and Kafka's *The Metamorphosis*." *Paragraph* 13, no. 1 (1990): 19–29. JSTOR.

Bonasera, Carmen. "Of Mirrors and Bell Jars: Heterotopia and Liminal Spaces as Reconfigurations of Female Identity in Sylvia Plath." *Humanities* 8, no. 1 (2019): 20. https://doi.org/10.3390/h8010020.

Britton, Luke Morgan. "Lana Del Rey Open to David Lynch Collaboration: 'I Would Love to Do Anything with Him.'" *NME*. Last modified December 11, 2015. Accessed July 13, 2023. https://www.nme.com/news/music/lana-del-rey-16-1203870.

Burn, Stephen J. "'Webs of Nerves Pulsing and Firing': *Infinite Jest* and the Science of Mind." In *A Companion to David Foster Wallace Studies*, edited by Marshall Boswell and Stephen Burn, 59–86. New York: Palgrave Macmillan, 2013.

Burt, Andrew T. "Is It the Wind in the Tall Trees or Just the Distant Buzz of Electricity?: Sound and Music as Portent in *Twin Peaks'* Season Three." In *Critical Essays on Twin Peaks*, edited by Antonio Sanna, 253–68. Cham: Palgrave Macmillan US, 2019.

Cantwell, Robert. "Smith's Memory Theater: The Folkways Anthology of American Folk Music." *New England Review* 13, no. 3/4 (1991): 364–97. JSTOR.

Cantwell, Robert. *When We Were Good: The Folk Revival*. Cambridge, MA: Harvard University Press, 1996.

Chion, Michel. *David Lynch*. 2nd ed. London: BFI, 2006.

Clayton, Jay, and Eric Rothstein. "Figures in the Corpus: Theories of Influence and Intertextuality." In *Influence and Intertextuality in Literary History*, 3–35. Madison, WI: University of Wisconsin Press, 1991.

Cohen, Daniel A. "The Beautiful Female Murder Victim: Literary Genres and Courtship Practices in the Origins of a Cultural Motif, 1590–1850." *Journal of Social History* 31, no. 2 (1997): 277–306. JSTOR.

Cohen, Sara. "Popular Music, Gender and Sexuality." In *The Cambridge Companion to Pop and Rock*, edited by Simon Frith, Will Straw, and John Street, 226–42. New York: Cambridge University Press, 2001.

Coogan, Ryan. "'Here's to the Pie That Saved Your Life, Dougie': The Weird Realism of *Twin Peaks*." In *Critical Essays on Twin Peaks: The Return*, edited by Antonio Sanna, 135–48. Cham: Palgrave Macmillan, 2019.

Cordle, Daniel. "Cultures of Terror: Nuclear Criticism during and since the Cold War." *Literature Compass* 3, no. 6 (2006): 1186–99.

Corrigan, Timothy. *A Cinema without Walls: Movies and Culture after Vietnam*. New Brunswick, NJ: Rutgers University Press, 1991.

Coughlin, Paul. "*Blue Velvet*: Postmodern Parody and the Subversion of Conservative Frameworks." *Literature/Film Quarterly* 31, no. 4 (2003): 304–11. JSTOR.

Cowart, David. *Don DeLillo: The Physics of Language*. Rev. ed. Athens, GA: University of Georgia Press, 2007.

Curren, Erik D. "Noir or Gothic: Visions of Apocalypse in the Depression-era L.A. Novel." *Southern California Quarterly* 78, no. 1 (1996): 11–18. https://doi.org/10.2307/41171792.

Daly, Kristen. "Cinema 3.0: The Interactive-Image." *Cinema Journal* 50, no. 1 (2010): 81–98. http://www.jstor.org/stable/40962838.

Dargis, Manohla. "The Trippy Dream Factory of David Lynch: [Review]." *New York Times* (New York), 2006. https://www.proquest.com/newspapers/trippy-dream-factory-david-lynch/docview/433477507/se-2?accountid=41521.

"David Lynch: David Lean Lecture." Video, 32:09. *YouTube*. Posted by BAFTA Guru, May 26, 2017. Accessed January 8, 2024. https://www.youtube.com/watch?v=SpomrL0qA-E.

"David Lynch in Competition for 4th Time: A Smooth Exterior but Wild at Heart." Research Library Prep. Last modified 2001. https://www.proquest.com/blogs-podcasts-websites/david-lynch-competition-4th-time-smooth-exterior/docview/2232301865/se-2?accountid=41521.

"David Lynch's Weather Report 12/2/21." Video, 01:28. *YouTube*. Posted by David Lynch, December 2, 2021. Accessed July 13, 2023. https://www.youtube.com/watch?v=6wVJv9Y53y0.

Davison, Annette. "'Up in Flames': Love, Control, and Collaboration in the Soundtrack to *Wild at Heart*." In *The Cinema of David Lynch: American Dreams, Nightmare Visions*, edited by Erica Sheen and Annette Davison, 119–35. London: Wallflower Press, 2004.

Delchamps, Vivian. "'A Slight Hysterical Tendency': Performing Diagnosis in Charlotte Perkins Gilman's 'The Yellow Wallpaper.'" In *Performing Hysteria: Images and Imaginations of Hysteria*, edited by Johanna Braun, 105–24. Leuven: Leuven University Press, 2020. https://doi.org/10.2307/j.ctv18dvt2d.9.

Denisoff, R. Serge. "'Teen Angel': Resistance, Rebellion and Death—Revisited." *Journal of Popular Culture* 16, no. 4 (1983): 116–22.

DiPaolo, Amanda. "Is It Future or Is It Past?: The Politics and Use of Nostalgia in *Twin Peaks*." In *The Politics of Twin Peaks*, edited by Amanda DiPaolo and Jamie Gillies, 35–52. Lanham: Lexington Books, 2019.

Dylan, Bob. "The *Playboy* Interview." By Nat Hentoff. Accessed May 10, 2022. https://www.interferenza.net/bcs/interw/66-jan.htm.

Eidizadeh, Hossein. "When You See Me Again It Won't Be Me: The Metamorphosis, Franz Kafka and David Lynch's Life-long Obsession." *Senses of Cinema*, no. 88 (2018). Accessed May 21, 2021. https://www.sensesofcinema.com/2018/feature-articles/when-you-see-me-again-it-wont-be-me-the-metamorphosis-franz-kafka-and-david-lynchs-life-long-obsession/.

Eraserhead. Directed by David Lynch. 1977. New York: The Criterion Collection, 2014. DVD.

Eyerman, Ron, and Scott Barretta. "From the 30s to the 60s: The Folk Music Revival in the United States." *Theory and Society* 25, no. 4 (1996): 501–43. http://www.jstor.org/stable/657909.

Fay, Jennifer. *Inhospitable World: Cinema in the Time of the Anthropocene*. New York: Oxford University Press, 2018.

Fisher, Mark. *The Weird and the Eerie*. London: Repeater Books, 2016.

Flinn, Caryl. "Sound, Woman, and the Bomb: Dismembering the 'Great Whatsit' in *Kiss Me Deadly*." *Screening the Past*. Last modified June 30, 2000. Accessed June 11, 2024. http://www.screeningthepast.com/issue-10-classics-re-runs/sound-woman-and-the-bomb-dismembering-the-great-whatsit-in%C2%A0kiss-me-deadly/.

Frank, Alex. "Life, Liberty, and the Pursuit of Happiness: A Conversation with Lana Del Rey." *Pitchfork*. Last modified July 19, 2017. Accessed July 21,

2023. https://pitchfork.com/features/interview/life-liberty-and-the-pursuit-of-happiness-a-conversation-with-lana-del-rey/.

Galloway, David D. "A Picaresque Apprenticeship: Nathanael West's *The Dream Life of Balso Snell* and *A Cool Million*." *Wisconsin Studies in Contemporary Literature* 5, no. 2 (1964): 110–26. https://doi.org/10.2307/1207326.

Garvey, Meaghan. "Lana Del Rey: *Lust for Life* Album Review." *Pitchfork*. Last modified July 25, 2017. Accessed July 13, 2023. https://pitchfork.com/reviews/albums/lana-del-rey-lust-for-life/.

Gilbert, Sandra M., and Susan Gubar. *The Madwoman in the Attic: The Woman Writer and the Nineteenth-century Literary Imagination*. 2nd ed. New Haven: Yale University Press, 2000.

Gilead, Sarah. "Magic Abjured: Closure in Children's Fantasy Fiction." *PMLA* 106, no. 2 (1991): 277–93. https://doi.org/10.2307/462663.

Gilman, Charlotte Perkins. "The Yellow Wallpaper." In *The Yellow Wall-paper, Herland, and Selected Writings*, 179–96. New York: Penguin Books, 2019.

Girard, Stéphane. "(Un)originality, Hypertextuality and Identity in Tiga's 'Sunglasses at Night.'" *Popular Music* 30, no. 1 (2011): 105–25. JSTOR.

Gruel, Todd B. "The Darkness within: 13 Films That Burrow into Our Psyches." *PopMatters*, 2018. https://www.proquest.com/magazines/darkness-within-13-films-that-burrow-into-our/docview/2126702212/se-2?accountid=41521.

Guan, Frank. "Where David Lynch and Lana Del Rey Meet." *Vulture*. Last modified July 25, 2017. Accessed July 13, 2023. https://www.vulture.com/2017/07/david-lynch-and-lana-del-rey-are-intertwined.html.

Gubar, Marah. "On Not Defining Children's Literature." *PMLA* 126, no. 1 (2011): 209–16. JSTOR.

Hainge, Greg. "Weird or Loopy? Specular Spaces, Feedback and Artifice in *Lost Highway*'s Aesthetics of Sensation." In *The Cinema of David Lynch: American Dreams, Nightmare Visions*, edited by Erica Sheen and Annette Davison, 136–50. London: Wallflower Press, 2004.

Halberstam, Jack. *Wild Things: The Disorder of Desire*. Durham: Duke University Press, 2020.

Hampton, Howard. "David Lynch's Secret History of the United States." *Film Comment* 29, no. 3 (1993): 38–49. JSTOR.

Haynes, Doug. "'Laughing at the Laugh': Unhappy Consciousness in Nathanael West's *The Dream Life of Balso Snell*." *The Modern Language Review* 102, no. 2 (2007): 341–62. https://doi.org/10.2307/20467282.

Hendershot, Cyndy. "Postmodern Allegory and David Lynch's *Wild at Heart*." *Critical Arts* 9, no. 1 (1995): 5–20. https://doi.org/10.1080/02560049585310031.

Herndl, Diane Price. "The Writing Cure: Charlotte Perkins Gilman, Anna O., and 'Hysterical' Writing." *NWSA Journal* 1, no. 1 (1988): 52–74. JSTOR.

Hiatt, Brian. "Lana Del Rey: Vamp of Constant Sorrow." *Rolling Stone*. Last modified July 31, 2014. Accessed July 13, 2023. https://www.rollingstone.com/music/music-news/lana-del-rey-vamp-of-constant-sorrow-74230/.

Hoberman, J. *Film after Film: (or, What Became of 21st Century Cinema?)*. New York: Verso, 2014.

Holden, Stephen. "Hollywood, a Funhouse of Fantasy: [Review]." *New York Times* (New York), 2001, late edition (East Coast) edition. https://www.

proquest.com/newspapers/hollywood-funhouse-fantasy/docview/431874226/se-2?accountid=41521.

Horn, Olivia. "Lana Del Rey: *Did You Know There's a Tunnel under Ocean Blvd* Album Review." *Pitchfork*. Last modified March 24, 2023. Accessed July 13, 2023. https://pitchfork.com/reviews/albums/lana-del-rey-did-you-know-that-theres-a-tunnel-under-ocean-blvd/.

Hornby, Nick. *High Fidelity*. New York: Riverhead Books, 1995.

Hume, Kiel. "Politicizing Lynch/Lynching Politics: Reification in *Blue Velvet* and *Wild at Heart*." *Quarterly Review of Film and Video* 27, no. 3 (2010): 219–28. https://doi.org/10.1080/10509200802350364.

Hunt, Alex. "Right and False Suns: Cormac McCarthy's *The Crossing* and the Advent of the Atomic Age." *Southwestern American Literature* 28, no. 2 (1998): 31–7.

Inglis, Ian. "A Brief Life: Broken Hearts and Sudden Deaths." *Popular Music and Society* 27, no. 4 (2004): 477–88. Research Library Prep (208069227).

Inland Empire. Directed by David Lynch. 2006. New York: The Criterion Collection, 2023. Blu-ray disc.

Jansen, Bas. "Tape Cassettes and Former Selves: How Mix Tapes Mediate Memories." In *Sound Souvenirs: Audio Technologies, Memory and Cultural Practices*, edited by Karin Bijsterveld and José Van Dijck, 43–54. Amsterdam: Amsterdam University Press, 2009. http://www.jstor.org/stable/j.ctt45kf7f.7.

Jerslev, Anne. "Beyond Boundaries: David Lynch's *Lost Highway*." In *The Cinema of David Lynch: American Dreams, Nightmare Visions*, edited by Erica Sheen and Annette Davison, 151–64. London: Wallflower Press, 2004.

Johnson, Jeff. "Pervert in the Pulpit: The Puritanical Impulse in the Films of David Lynch." *Journal of Film and Video* 55, no. 4 (2003): 3–14. JSTOR.

Johnston, Maura. "Review: Lana Del Rey Indulges in Nostalgia, Reverb on Fourth LP." *Rolling Stone*. Last modified July 25, 2017. Accessed July 13, 2023. https://www.rollingstone.com/music/music-album-reviews/review-lana-del-rey-indulges-in-nostalgia-reverb-on-fourth-lp-198155/.

Jones, Joshua. "'The Past Dictates the Future': Epistemic Ambivalence and the Compromised Ethics of Complicity in *Twin Peaks: The Return* and *Fire Walk with Me*." *NANO: New American Notes Online*, no. 15 (2020). Publicly Available Content Database; Research Library Prep (2356774067).

Joyce, Ashlee. "The Nuclear Anxiety of *Twin Peaks: The Return*." In *The Politics of Twin Peaks*, edited by Amanda DiPaolo and Jamie Gillies, 13–34. Lanham: Lexington Books, 2019.

Kaleta, Kenneth C. *David Lynch*. New York: Twayne, 1995.

Kappeler, Erin, and Tracy Ryan. "Editors' Introduction for NANO Special Issue 16: 'This Is What Makes Us Girls': Gender, Genre, and Popular Music." *NANO: New American Notes Online*, no. 16 (2022). https://www.proquest.com/scholarly-journals/editors-introduction-nano-special-issue-16-this/docview/2678066617/se-2?accountid=41521.

Kassabian, Anahid. *Hearing Film: Tracking Identifications in Contemporary Hollywood Film Music*. New York: Routledge, 2001.

Kehr, Dave. "The Plot's Thinning." *Chicago Tribune* (Chicago, IL), November 23, 1986. Accessed January 5, 2024. https://www.chicagotribune.com/news/ct-xpm-1986-11-23-8603280163-story.html.

Kelly, Adam. "David Foster Wallace: The Death of the Author and the Birth of a Discipline." *IJAS Online*, no. 2 (2010).

Klug, M. A. "Nathanael West: Prophet of Failure." *College Literature* 14, no. 1 (1987): 17–31. http://www.jstor.org/stable/25111719.

Kristeva, Julia. *Desire in Language: A Semiotic Approach to Literature and Art*. Edited and translated by Leon S. Roudiez. New York: Columbia University Press, 1980.

Lagayette, Pierre. "The Border Trilogy, *The Road*, and the Cold War." In *The Cambridge Companion to Cormac McCarthy*, Reprinted ed., edited by Steven Frye, 79–91. New York: Cambridge University Press, 2014.

Lee, Nathan. "David Lynch Made a Man out of Me." *The Village Voice* (New York), 2007, 60. https://www.proquest.com/newspapers/david-lynch-made-man-out-me/docview/232267941/se-2?accountid=41521.

Leitch, Thomas M. "Twelve Fallacies in Contemporary Adaptation Theory." *Criticism* 45, no. 2 (2003): 149–71. https://doi.org/10.1353/crt.2004.0001.

Lim, Dennis. *David Lynch: The Man from Another Place*. New York: Amazon Publishing, 2017.

Lim, Dennis. "David Lynch Returns: Expect Moody Conditions, with Surreal Gusts." *New York Times*. Last modified October 1, 2006. Accessed June 20, 2023. https://www.nytimes.com/2006/10/01/movies/01lim.html.

Lindroth, James. "Down the Yellow Brick Road: Two Dorothys and the Journey of Initiation in Dream and Nightmare." *Literature/Film Quarterly* 18, no. 3 (1990): 160–6. JSTOR.

Lost Highway. Directed by David Lynch. 1997. New York: The Criterion Collection, 2022. Blu-ray disc.

"*Lost Highway* Press Kit." *Lynchnet.com*. Accessed January 20, 2024. http://www.lynchnet.com/lh/lhpress.html.

Lovatt, Deborah. "A Terrible Beauty: The Nuclear Sublime in Philip Ridley's *The Reflecting Skin* (1991)." *European Journal of American Culture* 21, no. 3 (2002): 133–44. https://doi.org/10.1386/ejac.21.3.133.

Lowry, Elizabeth. "Extraterrestrial Intelligences in the Atomic Age: Exploring the Rhetorical Function of Aliens and the 'Alien' in the *Twin Peaks* Universe." In *Critical Essays on Twin Peaks: The Return*, edited by Antonio Sanna, 37–51. Cham: Palgrave Macmillan, 2019.

Lynch, David. "Harold Lloyd Masters Seminar." Los Angeles, CA: Lecture, American Film Institute, October 10, 2001.

Lynch, David, and Chris Rodley. *Lynch on Lynch*. London: Faber and Faber, 1997.

Lynch, David, and Kristine McKenna. *Room to Dream*. New York: Random House, 2018.

Lynch/Oz. Directed by Alexandre O. Philippe. Performed by Justin Benson, Aaron Moorhead, and Karyn Kusama. New York: Janus Films, 2022.

Mackenzie, Steven. "David Lynch: 'Home Is a Beautiful Word.'" *Big Issue*. Last modified July 8, 2019. Accessed January 5, 2024. https://www.bigissue.com/culture/film/david-lynch-wants-to-tell-us-why-home-is-a-beautiful-word/.

Mactaggart, Allister. *The Film Paintings of David Lynch: Challenging Film Theory*. Bristol: Intellect, 2010.

Makarushka, Irena. "Subverting Eden: Ambiguity of Evil and the American Dream in *Blue Velvet*." *Religion and American Culture: A Journal of Interpretation* 1, no. 1 (1991): 31–46. https://doi.org/10.2307/1123905.

Marcus, Greil. *Mystery Train: Images of America in Rock 'N' Roll Music.* 5th ed. New York: Plume, 2008.

Marcus, Greil. "New Songs in Old Skins." In *Bob Dylan: Writings 1968–2010*, 231–36. New York: Public Affairs, 2010.

Marcus, Greil. *The Old, Weird America: The World of Bob Dylan's Basement Tapes.* Updated edition. New York: Picador, 2011.

Markwardt, Chris. "David Lynch's Weather Report—Musical Musings." *Spotify.* Accessed January 20, 2024. https://open.spotify.com/playlist/0A28956ne2lgFcD IXEufGZ.

Marsh, Dave. "Barbara Allen." In *The Rose and the Briar: Death, Love and Liberty in the American Ballad*, edited by Sean Wilentz and Greil Marcus, 7–18. New York: W.W. Norton, 2005.

Martin, Richard. *The Architecture of David Lynch.* London: Bloomsbury Academic, 2020.

Mazullo, Mark. "Fans and Critics: Greil Marcus's *Mystery Train* as Rock 'N' Roll History." *The Musical Quarterly* 81, no. 2 (1997): 145–69. http://www.jstor.org/ stable/742456.

Mazullo, Mark. "Remembering Pop: David Lynch and the Sound of the '60s." *American Music* 23, no. 4 (2005): 493–513. https://doi.org/10.2307/4153071.

Mazullo, Mark. "Revisiting the Wreck: PJ Harvey's *Dry* and the Drowned Virgin-Whore." *Popular Music* 20, no. 3 (2001): 431–47. JSTOR.

McCarthy, Cormac. *The Crossing.* New York: Vintage International, 1995.

McCarthy, Cormac. *The Passenger.* New York: Alfred A. Knopf, 2022.

McCarthy, Donald. "How Mark Frost's *Twin Peaks* Books Clarify and Confound the Nature of Reality." In *Critical Essays on Twin Peaks: The Return*, edited by Antonio Sanna, 169–81. Cham: Palgrave Macmillan, 2019.

McGowan, Todd. "Accumulation and Enjoyment." *The Comparatist* 39 (2015): 101–15. http://www.jstor.org/stable/26254721.

McGowan, Todd. *The Impossible David Lynch.* New York: Columbia University Press, 2007.

Menchise, Donald. "Man and Quest as Evidence in the Novels of Nathanael West." *CLA Journal* 25, no. 1 (1981): 65–73. JSTOR.

Metz, Walter. "The Atomic Gambit of *Twin Peaks: The Return.*" *Film Criticism* 41, no. 3 (2017). https://doi.org/10.3998/fc.13761232.0041.324.

Miley, Mike. "David Lynch at the Crossroads: Deconstructing Rock, Reconstructing *Wild at Heart.*" *Music and the Moving Image* 7, no. 3 (2014): 41–60. https://doi.org/10.5406/musimoviimag.7.3.0041.

Miley, Mike. "'I Put a Spell on You': Affiliating (Mis)Identifications and Toxic Masculinity in David Lynch's *Lost Highway.*" *Music and the Moving Image* 13, no. 3 (2020): 36–48. https://doi.org/10.5406/musimoviimag.13.3.0036.

Miley, Mike. "'This Muddy *Both*ness': The Absorbed Adaptation of David Lynch by David Foster Wallace." *Literature/Film Quarterly* 48, no. 1 (2020). Accessed January 20, 2024. https://lfq.salisbury.edu/_issues/48_1/this_muddy_ bothness_the_absorbed_adaptation_of_david_lynch_by_david_foster_wallace. html.

Moist, Kevin M. "Collecting, Collage, and Alchemy: The Harry Smith *Anthology of American Folk Music* as Art and Cultural Intervention." *American Studies* 48, no. 4 (2007): 111–27. http://www.jstor.org/stable/40644108.

Morton, Timothy. *Hyperobjects: Philosophy and Ecology after the End of the World.* Minneapolis: University of Minnesota Press, 2013.

Moskowitz, Golan. *Wild Visionary: Maurice Sendak in Queer Jewish Context.* Stanford, CA: Stanford University Press, 2020.

Mulholland Drive. Directed by David Lynch. 2001. New York: The Criterion Collection, 2015. Blu-ray disc.

Murphy, Kathleen. "Dead Heat on a Merry-Go-Round." *Film Comment* 26, no. 6 (1990): 59–62. http://www.jstor.org/stable/43453539.

Nel, Philip. "Wild Things, Children and Art: The Life and Work of Maurice Sendak." *The Comics Journal*, no. 302 (2013): 12–27.

Nieland, Justus. *David Lynch.* Urbana: University of Illinois Press, 2012.

Nochimson, Martha P. "'All I Need Is the Girl': The Life and Death of Creativity in *Mulholland Drive.*" In *The Cinema of David Lynch: American Dreams, Nightmare Visions*, Reprinted ed., edited by Erica Sheen and Annette Davison, 165–81. London: Wallflower Press, 2004.

Nochimson, Martha P. *David Lynch Swerves: Uncertainty from Lost Highway to Inland Empire.* Austin: University of Texas Press, 2013.

Nochimson, Martha P. "Inland Empire." *Film Quarterly* 60, no. 4 (2007): 10–14. https://doi.org/10.1525/fq.2007.60.4.10.

Nochimson, Martha P. *The Passion of David Lynch: Wild at Heart in Hollywood.* Austin: University of Texas Press, 1997.

O'Connor, Tom. "The Pitfalls of Media 'Representations': David Lynch's *Lost Highway.*" *Journal of Film and Video* 57, no. 3 (2005): 14–30. JSTOR.

Okazaki, Brooke McCorkle. "Where Music Is Always in the Air: Voice and Nostalgia in *Twin Peaks.*" In *Music in Twin Peaks: Listen to the Sounds*, edited by Katherine M. Reed and Reba Wissner, 48–62. Milton: Routledge, 2021.

Orgeron, Devin. "Revising the Postmodern American Road Movie: David Lynch's *The Straight Story.*" *Journal of Film and Video* 54, no. 4 (2002): 31–46. http://www.jstor.org/stable/20688392.

O'Riordan, Louise. "The Popular Song Performs." In *CineMusic?: Constructing the Film Score*, edited by David Cooper, Christopher Fox, and Ian Sapiro, 85–96. Newcastle: Cambridge Scholars Publishing, 2008.

Paraskeva, Anthony. "Digital Modernism and the Unfinished Performance in David Lynch's *Inland Empire.*" *Film Criticism* 37, no. 1 (2012): 2–18. http://www.jstor.org/stable/24777846.

Parrish, Timothy. "History and the Problem of Evil in McCarthy's Western Novels." In *The Cambridge Companion to Cormac McCarthy*, Reprinted ed., edited by Steven Frye, 67–78. New York: Cambridge University Press, 2014.

Pitari, Paolo. "David Lynch's Influence on David Foster Wallace's *Infinite Jest.*" *Camera Stylo* 12 (2017): 153–65.

Plasketes, George. "Re-Flections on the Cover Age: A Collage of Continuous Coverage in Popular Music." *Popular Music and Society* 28, no. 2 (2005): 137–61. https://doi.org/10.1080/03007760500045204.

Plath, Sylvia. *The Bell Jar.* Bantam Windstone ed. Toronto: Bantam Books, 1981.

Plummer, Laura. "'I'm Not Laura Palmer': David Lynch's Fractured Fairy Tale." *Literature/Film Quarterly* 25, no. 4 (1997): 307–11. JSTOR.

Preston, Janet L. "Dantean Imagery in *Blue Velvet.*" *Literature/Film Quarterly* 18, no. 3 (1990): 167–72. JSTOR.

Reed, Katherine M. "'We Cannot Content Ourselves with Remaining Spectators': Musical Performance, Audience Interaction, and Nostalgia in the Films of David Lynch." *Music and the Moving Image* 9, no. 1 (2016): 3–22. https://doi.org/10.5406/musimoviimag.9.1.0003.

Reynolds, Kimberley. *Children's Literature: A Very Short Introduction*. Oxford: Oxford University Press, 2011.

Richards, Chris. "Lana Del Rey Suddenly Sounds like the Poet Laureate of Post-truth: Her New Album, *Lust for Life*, Proves That Dreaming Is Free, Even When Reality Is at Risk." Research Library Prep. Last modified 2017. https://www.proquest.com/blogs-podcasts-websites/lana-del-rey-suddenly-sounds-like-poet-laureate/docview/1923185861/se-2?accountid=41521.

Richardson, John. "*Laura* and *Twin Peaks*: Postmodern Parody and the Musical Reconstruction of the Absent *Femme Fatale*." In *The Cinema of David Lynch: American Dreams, Nightmare Visions*, edited by Erica Sheen and Annette Davison, 77–92. London: Wallflower Press, 2004.

Richardson, Mark. "Lana Del Rey: *Ultraviolence* Album Review." *Pitchfork*. Last modified June 16, 2014. Accessed July 13, 2023. https://pitchfork.com/reviews/albums/19449-lana-del-rey-ultraviolence/.

Rife, Katie. "*Lost Highway* Put David Lynch onto America's Car Stereos." *AV Club*. Last modified May 23, 2017. Accessed January 20, 2024. https://film.avclub.com/lost-highway-put-david-lynch-onto-america-s-car-stereos-1798262541.

Riffaterre, Michael. "Syllepsis." *Critical Inquiry* 6, no. 4 (1980): 625–38. http://www.jstor.org/stable/1343223.

Rings, Michael. "Doing It Their Way: Rock Covers, Genre, and Appreciation." *The Journal of Aesthetics and Art Criticism* 71, no. 1 (2013): 55–63. JSTOR.

Roberts, Mathew. "Bonfire of the Avant-Garde: Cultural Rage and Readerly Complicity in *The Day of the Locust*." *Modern Fiction Studies* 42, no. 1 (1996): 61–90. JSTOR.

Rodman, Ronald. "The Popular Song as Leitmotif in 1990s Film." In *Changing Tunes*, edited by Robynn Stilwell and Phil Powrie, 119–36. Florence: Taylor and Francis, 2005.

Rombes, Nicholas. "Blue Velvet Underground: David Lynch's Post-punk Poetics." In *The Cinema of David Lynch: American Dreams, Nightmare Visions*, edited by Erica Sheen and Annette Davison, 61–76. London: Wallflower Press, 2005.

Rosenbaum, Jonathan. "The Lynch-pin Fallacy." *JonathanRosenbaum.net*. Last modified January 29, 2022. Accessed January 27, 2024. https://jonathanrosenbaum.net/2022/01/out-to-lynch/.

Rosenbaum, Jonathan. "Two Forms of Adaptation: Housekeeping and Naked Lunch." In *Film Adaptation*, edited by James Naremore, 206–20. New Brunswick, NJ: Rutgers University Press, 2000.

Roy, William G. "Aesthetic Identity, Race, and American Folk Music." *Qualitative Sociology* 25, no. 3 (2002): 459–69.

Scheibel, Will. "A Fallen Star over *Mulholland Drive*: Representation of the Actress." *Film Criticism* 42, no. 1 (2018). http://dx.doi.org/10.3998/fc.13761232.0042.107.

Sendak, Maurice. *Where the Wild Things Are*. New York: HarperCollins Publishers, 1988.

Shaffer, Claire. "Lana Del Rey's *Chemtrails Over the Country Club* Is a Somber American Travelogue." *Rolling Stone*. Last modified March 22, 2021. Accessed July 13, 2023. https://www.rollingstone.com/music/music-album-reviews/lana-del-reys-chemtrails-over-the-country-club-1144980/.

Shaviro, Steven. "Southland Tales." *The Pinocchio Theory* (blog). Entry posted December 10, 2007. Accessed June 19, 2023. http://www.shaviro.com/Blog/?p=611.

Showalter, Elaine. "On Hysterical Narrative." *Narrative* 1, no. 1 (1993): 24–35. JSTOR.

Skinner, Katherine. "'Must Be Born Again': Resurrecting the *Anthology of American Folk Music*." *Popular Music* 25, no. 1 (2006): 57–75. JSTOR.

Smith, Christopher J. "Papa Legba and the Liminal Spaces of the Blues: Roots Music in Deep South Film." In *American Cinema and the Southern Imaginary*, edited by Deborah Barker and Kathryn B. McKee, 317–35. Athens, GA: University of Georgia Press, 2011.

Solis, Gabriel. "I Did It My Way: Rock and the Logic of Covers." *Popular Music and Society* 33, no. 3 (2010): 297–318.

Springer, John. "'This Is a Riot You're in': Hollywood and American Mass Culture in Nathanael West's *The Day of the Locust*." *Literature/Film Quarterly* 24, no. 4 (1996): 439–44. http://www.jstor.org/stable/43796758.

The Straight Story. Directed by David Lynch. 1999. Burbank: Walt Disney Pictures, 2000. DVD.

Strychacz, Thomas. "Making Sense of Hollywood: Mass Discourses and the Literary Order in Nathanael West's *The Day of the Locust*." *Western American Literature* 22, no. 2 (1987): 149–62. http://www.jstor.org/stable/43024023.

Taubin, Amy. "The Big Rupture." *Film Comment* 43, no. 1 (2007): 54–9. JSTOR.

Tavakoli, Mina. "Lana Del Rey: *Chemtrails Over the Country Club* Album Review." *Pitchfork*. Last modified March 19, 2021. Accessed July 13, 2023. https://pitchfork.com/reviews/albums/lana-del-rey-chemtrails-over-the-country-club/.

Taylor, Aaron. "Rough Beasts Slouch toward Bethlehem to Be Born: *Eraserhead* and the Grotesque Infant (Whose Hour Has Come Round at Last)." *Revue Canadienne d'Études Cinématographiques / Canadian Journal of Film Studies* 9, no. 2 (2000): 55–69. JSTOR.

Toles, George. "Auditioning Betty in *Mulholland Drive*." *Film Quarterly* 58, no. 1 (2004): 2–13. Research Library Prep (212275837).

Treichler, Paula A. "Escaping the Sentence: Diagnosis and Discourse in 'The Yellow Wallpaper.'" *Tulsa Studies in Women's Literature* 3, no. 1/2 (1984): 61–77. https://doi.org/10.2307/463825.

Twin Peaks. 1990. Los Angeles: Paramount Pictures Home Entertainment, 2007. DVD.

Twin Peaks: A Limited Event Series. Directed by David Lynch. 2017. Los Angeles: Paramount Pictures Home Entertainment, 2018. Blu-ray disc.

Twin Peaks: Fire Walk with Me. Directed by David Lynch. 1992. New York: The Criterion Collection, 2017. Blu-ray disc.

Tyree, J. M., and Ben Walters. *The Big Lebowski*. London: Palgrave Macmillan, 2007.

Veitch, Jonathan. "Reading Hollywood." *Salmagundi*, no. 126/127 (2000): 192–221. http://www.jstor.org/stable/40549236.

Wallace, David Foster. "David Lynch Keeps His Head." In *A Supposedly Fun Thing I'll Never Do Again: Essays and Arguments*, 146–212. New York: Back Bay Books, 2008.

Wallace, David Foster. "*E Unibus Pluram*: Television and US Fiction." In *A Supposedly Fun Thing I'll Never Do Again: Essays and Arguments*, 21–82. New York: Back Bay Books, 2008.

Wallace, David Foster. "Good Old Neon." In *Oblivion: Stories*, 141–81. New York: Back Bay Books, Little, Brown and Company, 2005.

Wallace, David Foster. "Octet." In *Brief Interviews with Hideous Men*, 131–60. New York: Back Bay Books, 2000.

Wallace, David Foster. "The Soul Is Not a Smithy." In *Oblivion: Stories*, 67–113. New York: Back Bay Books, Little, Brown and Company, 2005.

West, Nathanael. *A Cool Million: The Dream Life of Balso Snell: Two Novels*. New York: Farrar, Straus and Giroux, 2006.

West, Nathanael. *Miss Lonelyhearts and the Day of the Locust*. 35th ed. New York: New Directions, 2007.

Whitney, Jon. "Jon Whitney Interview—Part I." *Brainwashed*. Last modified May 5, 1997. Accessed January 20, 2024. http://www.brainwashed.com/coil/writings/jwint.html.

Wild at Heart. Directed by David Lynch. 1990. Los Angeles: MGM, 2004. DVD.

Williams, Raymond. *The Country and the City*. New York: Oxford University Press, 1973.

Wilmington, Michael. "Lynch's *Mulholland Drive* Takes Us to a Hair-raising Alternate World." *Chicago Tribune* (Chicago, IL), 2001, 1-7A.1. Research Library Prep (419472768).

Wilson, Eric. *The Strange World of David Lynch: Transcendental Irony from Eraserhead to Mulholland Dr.* New York: Continuum, 2007.

Wood, Jeff. "Hurricane Bob: Part 2." *3:AM Magazine*. Accessed February 10, 2021. http://www.3ammagazine.com/3am/hurricane-bob-part-2.

Wyrick, Deborah. "Dadaist Collage Structure and Nathanael West's *Dream Life of Balso Snell*." *Studies in the Novel* 11, no. 3 (1979): 349–59. JSTOR.

Zak, Albin J. "Writing Records." In *The Poetics of Rock: Cutting Tracks, Making Records*, 1–23. Berkeley: University of California Press, 2001. JSTOR.

Zoladz, Lindsay. "Pretty When You Cry." *Pitchfork*. Last modified June 19, 2014. Accessed July 13, 2023. https://pitchfork.com/features/ordinary-machines/9440-pretty-when-you-cry/.

INDEX

absorption 13; in David Foster Wallace's fiction 203, 209, 211, 213, 215; definition 196–7; in Lana Del Rey's music 200, 207

affiliating identifications: in *Blue Velvet* 10, 46, 47, 201; definition 4–5; in *Eraserhead* 10, 21, 44; in *Inland Empire* 13, 180, 195–9, 201, 218; in *Lost Highway* 146–7, 149, 152, 154, 158, 201; in *Mulholland Drive* 63, 201; in *The Straight Story* 164–5, 172–3; in *Twin Peaks* 127–8, 236n4; in *Wild at Heart* 11–12, 107–8

alchemy 166–8, 172, 177

Alsop, Elizabeth 6–7

Anthology of American Folk Music 13, 172–7; alchemy in 167, 172; description of 161–2, 240–1n3; similarities to characters in *Straight Story* 164, 169; transcendence in 171, 175–7

anthropocene/anthropocentrism 81, 85, 88–9

Arquette, Patricia 147, 148, 150, 153, 154, 158

artifice: in *Blue Velvet* 210–11; in David Foster Wallace 210–11, 212, 215; in *Inland Empire* 184–5; in Lana Del Rey 199, 205, 212; in *Mulholland Drive* 66–70, 74, 75, 79, 204; in *Wild at Heart* 121, 123

assimilating identifications 4–5, 164, 193

atomic bomb 11, 177, 231n45; in Cormac McCarthy and *Twin Peaks* (2017) 11, 81–99, 251n33; in *Eraserhead* 87; as hyperobject 83–4,

87–90, 93–5, 98, 231n46; impact on innocence 93–4, 98–9; impact on postwar era 95–6 (*see also* Trinity test)

auteur/auteurism 6–8, 184

authorship 6–8, 9, 146, 214–15; relationship to postmodernism 6, 8–9

Badalamenti, Angelo 68, 123, 145, 155, 157, 199, 239n34; score for *The Straight Story* 164, 171; score for *Twin Peaks* 125, 133; "Up in Flames" 111–12

Barthes, Roland 3–9

Basement Tapes, The 13, 161–2, 169, 171–3, 241n2; recording history of 167, 171–2, 176; time in 172–3, 176–7

Bell Jar, The 9, 20, 22, 23, 24–5, 26–7, 28–30

binaries challenge to/transcendence of 44, 53, 54; in children's literature 48; fantasy/reality 10, 47, 51, 218; Lynch's challenge of 3, 166, 218; patriarchal imposition of 10, 20–1; rational/irrational 10, 20–1, 29–30, 43–4

Blue Velvet 125, 168, 197; affiliating identifications in 10, 46, 47, 201; American iconography in 50, 52–3, 61–2, 128, 201–3, 226n27; artifice in 210–11; audience identification in 212–14; children's literature in 10, 45–62; ending 56–62, 216; genre in 125; influence on David Foster Wallace 197, 209–10, 247n37; innocence in 10, 46, 47, 49–50, 128,